IRISH SEA VEHICLE FERRIES
- THE FIRST EIGHTY YEARS

Nick Robins

PREFACE

The differences between the ***Princess Victoria*** which was commissioned by the London, Midland & Scottish Railway in 1939, complete with cattle and sheep pens below the vehicle deck, and the contemporary super ferries, such as Irish Ferries ***W B Yeats***, are spectacular. The story of this evolution in the Irish Sea trades is fascinating, with ferry operators struggling to maintain modern and efficient tonnage in order to gain the edge on their competitors.

Ships have always been designed to suit projected traffic volumes on specific routes. Economies of scale and fuel economy became increasingly important as time went on. Fast ferries were introduced to compete with the airlines, in a competition that was largely lost. The key drivers were the need for modern and efficient tonnage, reliability of schedules and, of course, safety, especially after the introduction of the SOLAS 90 regulations. The development of the roll-on roll-off concept for the Irish Sea services was also driven by a diverse range of external factors that included the Troubles, the Irish Peace Process and their impact on trade, state ownership and state subsidy of ferry companies, the global depression of the late 2000s, and latterly the impact of the Covid-19 Pandemic coupled with Great Britain leaving the European Union.

Much of this book was prepared during the Pandemic Lockdowns of 2020, an activity that brought welcome respite from the woes of our planet. While most of the photographs were taken by the author, more recent images include public domain stock and company press photos as travel to take original photographs has not been feasible. Images without credits, where the provenance is unknown, are from the author's own collection.

The text relies heavily on news reports recorded in diverse media with an emphasis on contemporary printed material such as newspapers and specialist journals. While some of the story is already documented piecemeal elsewhere (not always accurately), this full narrative of the evolution of the Irish Sea ferry industry includes a number of surprises. It has also been possible, with the benefit of hindsight, to analyse situations that arose within the Irish Sea Ferry industry set in the context of the larger environment that the industry occupied.

CONTENTS

1. Early days, the ***Princess Victoria*** tragedy 3
2. The car ferry era 13
3. The early 1970s and the Northern European influence 23
4. The first of the second-generation ferries 35
5. At the expense of the taxpayer 47
6. 1986-1990 – a period of stagnation...59
7. Of foreign flags, fast ferries and economic growth 72
8. The fast ferry fashion...86
9. The Millennium and into the 21st century 102
10. The contemporary era and a look back at how and why...116
References 130
Index of Vessels 131

Published by Mainline & Maritime Ltd, 3 Broadleaze, Upper Seagry, near Chippenham, SN15 5EY
Tel: 07770 748615   www.mainlineandmaritime.co.uk   orders@mainlineandmaritime.co.uk
Printed in the UK   ISBN 978-1-913797-07-2
© Mainline & Maritime Ltd, Author & Contributors 2022
All rights reserved. No part of this publication may be reproduced by any process
without the prior written permission of the publisher.

Front Cover (Upper): *Stena Adventurer* (2003) leaving Dublin off the Poolbeg Light.

Author

Front Cover (Lower): *Manx Maid* (1962) goes astern out of Douglas at the start of another crossing to Liverpool.

The late Laurie Schofield

Back Cover: *Seatruck Pace* (2009) loads trailers at Dublin Port on 27th October 2017.

Iain McCall

Title Page: The Isle of Man Steam Packet Company's 'Seacat' *Snaefell* sits at the Landing Stage at Liverpool on 12th May 2008, whilst a Norfolk Line vessel loads for Belfast on the other side of the river.

Iain McCall

CHAPTER 1
EARLY DAYS, THE *PRINCESS VICTORIA* TRAGEDY

An early example of a sea-going roll-on roll-off ferry: **Train Ferry No 1** *(1917) seen moored at the buoys off Parkeston Quay, Harwich, as* **Essex Ferry** *shortly before she was sold for demolition in 1957.*

The roll-on roll-off freight ferry was slow to emerge on the Irish Sea services despite the post-war pioneering efforts of the Atlantic Steam Navigation Company at Preston. The main reason for the retention of break-bulk cargo handling and a late entry into unit load traffic was the abject conservatism of the two main operators: British Railways and Coast Lines Limited.

Nevertheless, it had been the railways that alone ventured into the possibilities of wheeled freight traffic before World War Two when the passenger and vehicle ferry **Princess Victoria** was commissioned in 1939 by the London, Midland & Scottish Railway. She was the first railway-owned cross-channel ship to be equipped with oil engines, a pair of 7 cylinder engines built by Sulzer Brothers Limited at Winterthur in Switzerland, but her innovation went far beyond that. Loading ramps were constructed at both Stranraer and Larne for the ship to come astern and nudge her stern gate below the ramps which could then be lowered onto her vehicle deck.

Princess Victoria had accommodation for 65 cars on the garage deck and this extended almost to the bow of the ship with a headroom of just 3.7 metres. Passenger accommodation was situated on the promenade and upper decks. Primarily intended for passengers and their cars she also operated the daily milk run whereby a couple of milk-laden road tankers were reversed onto the open garage deck aft, and chained down for the morning departure to Stranraer. The empty tankers returned to Larne on the 1900 hours return sailing. She also had sheep and cattle pens below the vehicle deck which were in great demand for the sailings to Stranraer. But after only two months of commercial service the almost new **Princess Victoria** was requisitioned as a minelayer only to be lost at sea in 1940.

This modest beginning with freight vehicles was expanded during the Second World War for the carriage of military vehicles, men and equipment. At least one of the three Dover-based train ferries **Hampton Ferry**, **Shepperton Ferry** or **Twickenham Ferry** was usually available for much of the war. The ships were used as roll-on roll-off ferries rather than train ferries, and worked between the loading ramps at Stranraer and Larne.

The roll-on, roll-off concept was by no means new at the time the **Princess Victoria** was commissioned. The idea was first realised way back in 1850, when the train ferry **Leviathan** entered service between Granton and Burntisland on the Firth of Forth, to be joined a year later by sistership **John Napier**, named after the ships' designer and builder. A third vessel, the **Carrier**, was commissioned in 1858 to cross the Tay between Ferryport-on-Craig and Broughty Ferry. The three vessels each had twin rail tracks and could carry goods wagons with a maximum cargo deadweight of 140 tons, but no passengers. The wagons were shunted over a ramp and slipway on and off the ships which were double-ended. The two ferry crossings were important links for the Edinburgh, Perth and Dundee Railway, soon to be absorbed within the North British Railway. The train ferry concept was also widely adopted for river crossings in North America, as a cheaper option than a fixed bridge.

A pioneer sea-going train ferry, the **Drottning Victoria**, entered service just before the Great War. She was designed to carry a single passenger train comprising eight 22 metre long coaches, with four coaches shunted onto each of two tracks. The **Drottning Victoria** served in the Baltic between Sassnitz in Germany and Trelleborg in Sweden.

During the Great War, there followed three four-track train ferries as described in *The Evolution of the British Ferry*:

> The first British-flag sea-going train ferries were **Train Ferry No 1**, **Train Ferry No 2** and **Train Ferry No 3**, all built in 1917 by Armstrong Whitworth at Newcastle. The ships were 110 metres long by 18 metres broad with a capacity of 2755 tons gross. [They were] placed in service as Transports based at Richborough in Kent... The principal continental terminal was Dunkerque. The main deck was open aft, and two rail tracks ran forward over

Typical of the elderly break bulk steamers in service on the Irish Sea were the railways' steam turbine 'Slieve' class: **Slieve Bearnagh** *(1936) seen arriving at Heysham in August 1970 survived in service for a further two years.*

(Author)

the stern and divided into four tracks for almost the full length of the ships. The main deck was uncluttered as the funnels and exhausts were placed on either side of the ships. Loading was by means of a twin track drawbridge, lowered from the shore, and locked onto a pin at the stern of the ferry.

A fourth train ferry joined the trio in the spring of 1918. She was named simply **TF4**, and had been built in 1914 for the Canadian Government by Cammell Laird at Birkenhead, and named **Leonard**. She served between Quebec and Levis and was a substantial vessel of 3365 tons gross. Michael Pryce described her in a letter to the Editor of *Sea Breezes*, January 1982:

A strange-looking craft, she had a high framework of girders from bow to stern, with a gangway around the top, and the navigation bridge lay across the top of the girders. The girders supported a train deck, which could be raised or lowered by 18 feet, and had three parallel tracks for a total load of 550 tons. The **Leonard** became redundant with the opening of Quebec Bridge in December 1917, and was acquired by the British Government for use as a train ferry between Southampton and Cherbourg. On arrival in the UK her name was changed to **TF4**. The end of the war made her surplus to requirements, and she was sold to the Anglo-Saxon Petroleum Company Limited and converted into an oil tanker…

The train ferry concept probably delayed the move to carry commercial road vehicles by sea due to the complex and expensive terminal arrangements or the even more complex hoistable deck aboard ships such as the **Leonard**. Despite the modest size of post-Great War commercial vehicles, no attempt was made to develop the train ferry concept for the carriage of road vehicles. However, the train ferries frequently accommodated military road vehicles along with rail wagons and the **Hampton Ferry** was used for a time after the war as a road vehicle ferry at Stranraer. The reason why vehicle ferries were not pursued was simply that the capital cost of suitable ships and appropriate loading and unloading ramps at terminal ports was not justified by the amount of accompanied vehicle traffic then on offer.

Rail linkspans tended to be long so that the incline between ship and shore was enough to prevent longer rail units, such as passenger coaches, going aground at the top of the linkspan. When the passenger train service between Dover and Dunkerque was first visualised, the 8 metre tidal range at Dover meant that an extra-long linkspan would be required so that services could be independent of the tide. In the end it was decided to build a special dock in which the water level could be controlled by pumping to a fixed level to allow only a short ramp for passenger wagons to embark and disembark. Three ships were built for the service, the **Hampton Ferry**, **Shepperton Ferry** and **Twickenham Ferry**, the latter transferred to the French flag in 1938. The service started in 1937, although the ships had been completed before then but had to await the completion of the new dock at Dover. In the interim it was found that the three ferries were stiff in heavy seas with an uncomfortable jerky rolling motion. This was the result of the train deck, which was also the main or freeboard deck, effectively a 'tween deck carrying the entire cargo deadweight, that made the loaded metacentre much higher than that of a conventional cross-Channel passenger ferry. Permanent ballast was installed to successfully lower the metacentre and help mitigate the unpleasant motion of the ships.

After the Second World War, men were demobbed from the forces and returned home to find work. Britain was suffering food and materials shortages, but slowly the economy improved and the need for ration cards in shops lessened. As trade improved and ships were released from official duties, commercial traffic across the Irish Sea and elsewhere began to pick up. Trade between Great Britain and both the north and south of Ireland recovered slowly, with Irish cattle and dairy products heading towards ports in Great Britain with machinery, steel, and factored goods going to Belfast and consumer goods and materials to Dublin and other southern Irish ports. Everything arrived at the port by road or rail and was transferred to the hold of a ship by crane, with the process reversed at the end of the sea passage. There had to be better, cheaper and more efficient ways of handling goods, but new technologies were slow to develop, despite the benefits they provided for the shipper.

Initially, through the late-1940s and into the 1960s, there were two major cargo handling developments that were introduced into the Irish Sea trades. One was the introduction of former Landing Ships, Tank working as freight ferries between Great Britain and Northern Ireland and the second was the introduction of lift-on lift-off unit loads, unit loads being cargo put into large boxes, often at inland centres, and taken to a port for shipment. Both systems vied with traditional break-bulk cargo handling, a labour intensive and inefficient procedure that required multiple handling of goods and plentiful opportunities for damage and pilfering. Many elderly break-bulk steamers remained in service well into the 1970s, the railway owned 'Slieves' were just one set of these ships, while the Coast Lines group clung on to elderly motorships that were little better. Besides, stevedores and their unions were apprehensive about any new cargo-handling technique that might make the men fear for their livelihoods.

War has always been a provider of new technology. During the Great War the idea of small tank landing craft was conceived in the form of the X-Lighter. X-Lighters had a hull similar to a Thames lighter and were provided with a ramp that unfolded over the bow to enable vehicles to disembark onto a beach. This pioneer scheme was redeveloped in the Second World War as the larger Landing Craft, Tank and its various different classes, types and sizes and the even larger sea-going Landing Ship, Tank. The latter type of vessel was to become the pioneer roll-on roll-off freight ferry in peacetime, a development that would lead to a new and futuristic form of commercial transport that would ultimately revolutionise the short sea trades and also many of the long-haul deep-sea services.

One of the Type 3 Landing Ships, Tank inaugurated the first roll-on roll-off freight service to Ireland in 1948 with a service between Preston and Larne. The Atlantic Steam Navigation Company had already started a service from Tilbury to the Continent and was keen to progress into the Irish Sea. Rejected by both the Mersey Docks and Harbour Board and the Port of Belfast, the company was welcomed by the ports of Preston and Larne which both needed new trade and which offered to support the new enterprise.

The route was opened by the **Empire Cedric** (ex-**LST3534**) on 20 May 1948 with a cargo of just seven vehicles loaded through the bow doors. She had been altered to accommodate 48 persons, but less

*Chartered Landing Ship, Tank **Empire Gaelic** (1945) transferred from Tilbury to Preston in 1950 to open a new route direct to Belfast.*
(Atlantic Steam Navigation Company Limited)

than a third of this complement was berthed; sleeping berths were accessed from the open main deck - a long and sometimes wet and windy walk at night to the nearest sink or toilet! Vehicle loading through the bow door onto the tank deck at Larne was by means of a ramp installed by the army during the war, but at Preston Dock part of a Mulberry Harbour pontoon unit was acquired and a bridge installed to link it to the quayside adjacent to the cattle lairage. There was an internal ramp on board the ship to allow vehicle access to the upper deck which was also used for crane-loaded cargo in the form of unit loads. There were two derricks that served a hatch to the tank deck situated just before the bridge.

Business slowly built up and on 26 October 1948 the **Empire Cedric** was joined by **Empire Doric** (ex- **LST3041**) to increase the one ship twice weekly service to four sailings per week. On 6 January 1949 the **Empire Gaelic** (ex- **LST3507**) arrived from Tilbury to join the other two ships at Preston. **Empire Cedric** later inaugurated a new weekly service directly to Belfast on 15 January 1951, and in due course this was increased to twice weekly; the **Empire Doric** and **Empire Gaelic** maintaining four round trips to Larne. All three ships had passenger certificates and the Larne service was advertised to attract cars, drivers and passengers as well as freight traffic. From time to time the **Empire Celtic** (ex-**LST3512**) was drafted to Preston from her base at Tilbury as relief and to supplement existing services as inducement required.

An early attempt at rationalising cargo handling with unit loads was made by British Railways in 1949. A former Type 2 Landing Ship, Tank, the **Mowbray Road** (ex-**LST365**) was chartered from Seafreeze Industries Limited of Wakefield and deployed on a new cargo service between Barrow-in-Furness and Belfast, where she shared the linkspan with the Preston based former Type 3 LSTs. The **Mowbray Road**, named after a racehorse owned by the Chairman of Seafreeze Industries, had been used experimentally to freeze fish catches at sea, she was stripped of her refrigeration plant and chartered to British Railways for an initial period of twelve months. She carried standard unit load railway containers loaded onto wheeled flats and maintained a daily departure from each port. However, the full cargo

Empire Celtic (1945) served from Preston for part of 1949 and returned periodically thereafter. She is seen on the Tilbury to Hamburg service carrying military vehicles and equipment, a government contract without which that service would not have been viable.

deadweight could never be achieved even with both the tank deck and the upper deck fully loaded because of the deck space required by the flats.

Although a sensible development of the roll-on roll-off concept, allowing unit loads to be quickly and easily loaded and unloaded, there was insufficient inducement to retain the ship after the first twelve months and the service was terminated in 1950; the **Mowbray Road** was returned to her owners. No attempt was made to attract road transport, the railway commissioners preferring the containers to travel by rail on both sides of the Irish Sea. The unit load traffic that was available reverted to the Heysham and Belfast overnight cargo service. The **Mowbray Road** saw no further service under the Red Ensign and in 1952 was sold to the Indonesian Navy as **Adri I**.

A new **Princess Victoria**, of almost the same design as the prewar ship, was delivered for the Stranraer and Larne service in March 1947 by William Denny & Brothers, Dumbarton. Her Sulzer oil engines

Princess Victoria (1946) seen on trial on the Clyde, showing the stern vehicle access to the garage deck and the low freeboard provided by the protecting half gate.

(William Denny & Brothers, Dumbarton)

Hampton Ferry (1934) served between Stranraer and Larne with cars and passengers from 1950; she is seen at Dover in August 1965 working once again as a train ferry.

(Author)

were built under licence by Denny. She adopted a roster of 10 am outward from Stranraer with a return sailing at 7 pm. The new ship differed internally from her former namesake with a shorter garage deck that allowed for the first class lounge and 54 berths in cabins to be situated forward of the engine room casing on the same deck. *Princess Victoria* was licensed to carry 984 first class and 530 third class passengers and she had a crew complement of 51. Demand for milk tankers taking Irish milk into Scotland led to the vehicle deck being reinforced in the aft section where the lorries were carried; they returned empty.

The Dover train ferry *Hampton Ferry* returned to Stranraer in summer 1950 to enable cars to be carried on the morning departure from Larne with a return sailing from Stranraer in the afternoon. Working opposite the new *Princess Victoria*, cars were carried on all sailings until the *Hampton Ferry* returned to Dover in September and the passenger-only *Princess Margaret* took over the morning departures from Larne. This seasonal service was repeated in 1951 and 1952. It was principally for accompanied cars, but the ships also carried some commercial traffic.

By summer 1952, roll-on roll-off services comprised not less than five sailings between Preston and Larne, two or three a week between Preston and Belfast, and a twice daily sailing between Stranraer and Larne. The Preston-based services were essentially for commercial vehicles and the Stranraer route for private cars, while all the ships carried passengers and a mix of commercial and private vehicles. The Atlantic Steam Navigation Company's strap line, was 'Continental Line Transport Ferry Service, operates regular services between Tilbury and Hamburg and Preston/N Ireland. For the carriage of all types of vehicles and containers'.

Both the Preston and Stranraer routes were underwritten by the State. The railways had been nationalised in 1948 and the railway shipping divisions had become part of the British Transport Commission; any operational deficit was effectively picked up by the tax payer. Indeed, by the late 1950s, the British Transport Commission reported to Westminster that all of its Irish Sea services were operating at a loss. Atlantic Steam, meanwhile, enjoyed peppercorn charter fees with the Ministry of Transport for the former Landing Ships, Tank, the Ministry keen to see the ships operational and ready for state service should an emergency arise. Again, the tax payer was effectively subsidising the company's activities, and given such a powerful backer it was inevitable that these pioneer services would succeed.

For the moment, Atlantic Steam was not considered to be a threat to the established carriers on the Irish Sea as the company had neither capital nor assets it could use as collateral to promote its development. British Railways had no intention of developing car services at Heysham or Fishguard and Coast Lines were still building conventional cross-channel ferries to a 1920s Harland & Wolff design.

There did remain one significant obstacle preventing vehicle ferries from becoming properly established and that was the design of the ships themselves. The issue of free water on the vehicle or train deck of the stern-loading ferries had never been satisfactorily addressed, even to the point that conventional-sized, small scuppers were the only means of discharge back to the sea from the vehicle deck. Besides, safeguarding the stern entrance to the deck was by means of small folding gates that provided a low and vulnerable freeboard given a following sea. The train ferries did not even have the half-sized gate at the stern and these ships had an even lower effective freeboard. The other problem was that the vehicle deck on all ships, the Landing Ships, Tank included, was flat and without any camber to discharge free water towards the scuppers. These issues were to arise time and time again as vehicle ferries evolved and as vehicle ferries continued to be vulnerable to capsize, not only in British waters but in the Baltic and elsewhere.

The tragic loss of the new *Princess Victoria* on 31 January 1953, along with 133 men, women and children, very much underlined the shortcomings of contemporary vehicle and passenger ferry design. The *Glasgow Herald*, Monday 2 February 1953 carried the following eye witness account of the disaster:

The last minutes of the ship and the struggles of the survivors in mountainous seas were described by Mr James Carlin, manager of the Ayr Employment Exchange, whose wife, mother-in-law and sister-in-law are all missing... After the ship left Loch Ryan we felt there was something wrong... About 11 o'clock we heard

*The garage deck aboard the **Princess Victoria** (1946). Free water on the deck following damage to the stern doors caused a list to starboard, the scuppers not being large enough to discharge the water overboard and the vessel capsized with great loss of life.*
(William Denny & Brothers, Dumbarton)

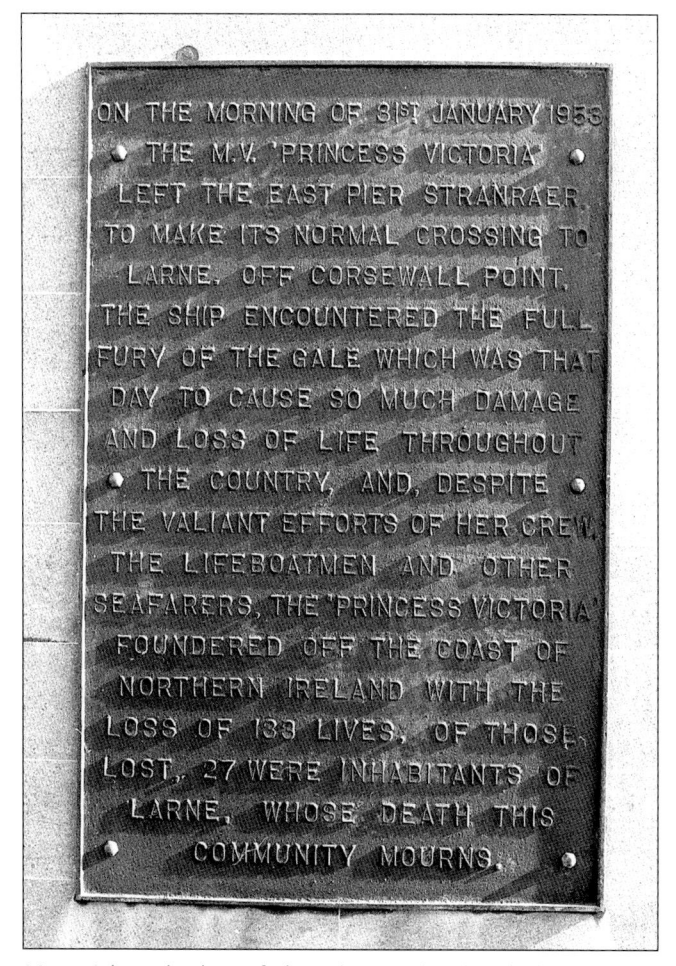

ON THE MORNING OF 31ST JANUARY 1953 THE M.V. 'PRINCESS VICTORIA' LEFT THE EAST PIER STRANRAER TO MAKE ITS NORMAL CROSSING TO LARNE. OFF CORSEWALL POINT, THE SHIP ENCOUNTERED THE FULL FURY OF THE GALE WHICH WAS THAT DAY TO CAUSE SO MUCH DAMAGE AND LOSS OF LIFE THROUGHOUT THE COUNTRY, AND, DESPITE THE VALIANT EFFORTS OF HER CREW, THE LIFEBOATMEN AND OTHER SEAFARERS, THE 'PRINCESS VICTORIA' FOUNDERED OFF THE COAST OF NORTHERN IRELAND WITH THE LOSS OF 133 LIVES. OF THOSE LOST, 27 WERE INHABITANTS OF LARNE, WHOSE DEATH THIS COMMUNITY MOURNS.

*Memorial to the loss of the **Princess Victoria** which is situated adjacent to the entrance to Larne Harbour.*
(Author)

over the loudspeaker system that everyone was to go to the upper deck and have their life jackets handy. We went out onto the boat deck... The ship's list seemed to get worse and we were told tugs and a destroyer were on their way.

About 1 o'clock the list was about 45° to starboard and everyone was told to get as high up on the boat deck as possible... The list on the ship soon became 50 or 60°. About 1.15 pm it was announced that we were to abandon ship, but that a destroyer would be alongside in 15 minutes.

I was still hanging onto the rail and could see my wife and her sister about 20 yards away. I could not get near them. I was trying to get towards them when the ship went over on its side. The syren was sounding for abandoning ship and the release of rafts and lifeboats. People were falling off the ship into the sea...

The **Princess Victoria** had drifted to the south and west and had capsized off Donaghadee. The master, Captain James Ferguson was unaware that the ship had travelled in an arc across the Irish Sea and kept giving his position incorrectly at points nearer his original course towards Larne. This delayed rescue craft which only arrived on the scene after the ship sank. There were 125 passengers and 52 crew aboard the ship when she sailed from Stranraer at 0745 hours on Saturday 31 January, but there were only 44 survivors, all of whom were men. The shipping forecast described rough seas and high winds but the reality was far more severe. It was reported that the ferocity of the storm encountered by the ship off Loch Ryan was unprecedented and it was believed that the stern gates were stove-in and the rudder lost before the ship had time to turn back for the shelter of Loch Ryan.

The subsequent enquiry heard a number of sobering criticisms of the ship's design. The tragedy, it was stated, was caused by free water entering the garage deck over the low stern half gates. It was known that the ship had a tendency to ship water over the stern with a following sea but that any free water on the garage deck had always, but slowly, discharged through the scuppers without affecting the stability of the ship. Sadly, this knowledge had not led the Marine Superintendent to request raising the stern gate or enlarging the scuppers.

Only a small volume of accumulated water was sufficient to capsize the **Princess Victoria**. It was reported that the size of the scuppers was far too small to allow the volumes of water that accumulated on the garage deck to discharge speedily overboard. As the depth and weight of water increased along the starboard side of the garage deck the list increased until the metacentric height fell below that of the centre of gravity. From then on, the ship was inherently unstable and was bound to capsize. It was also stated that there were no longitudinal or transverse barriers to inhibit free water flow on the vehicle deck, although it was also recognised that such safety features would greatly inhibit the serviceability of the deck for wheeled vehicle access. Lessons were learnt from the tragedy, but few recognised that it would take several decades before all these lessons would be applied to the overall safety and protection of vehicle ferries.

With almost immediate effect the Dover train ferries had watertight doors fitted at the end of the superstructure on the train deck. This increased the freeboard aft, a safety feature, had it been fitted, that would have prevented water entry onto the garage deck of the **Princess Victoria**. At the same time, much larger scuppers were fitted onto the new Dover car ferry **Lord Warden**, although she retained her half gate with no other protection to the vehicle deck.

Hampton Ferry returned to Stranraer to maintain the vehicle service. She was relieved periodically by **Shepperton Ferry**.

There were more lessons yet to be learnt about free water on the vehicle deck and some, in hindsight, were pretty obvious.

On 19 December 1982 the Larne and Cairnryan ferry **European Gateway** was serving temporarily on the Townsend Thoresen Felixstowe and Zeebrugge route when she left Felixstowe in gale force winds. As she approached the inbound Sealink ferry **Speedlink Vanguard** both masters decided to take evasive action which only increased the angle the **Speedlink Vanguard** struck the **European Gateway**. The breach caused by the impact allowed water to flood one of the ship's watertight compartments below the vehicle deck, and it was then realised that the manually operated doors in the adjacent watertight bulkheads could not be closed against the pressure of water; free water on the vehicle deck then caused **European Gateway** to list and roll rapidly onto her side when she stranded on a sand bank. Four crew members and two lorry drivers died in the incident. This accident led to power assisted doors in watertight bulkheads becoming mandatory in all vehicle ferries, the doors controlled either locally or remotely from the bridge.

Another disastrous wake-up call for the burgeoning roll-on roll-off industry occurred just 34 years after the loss of the **Princess Victoria**. On 6 March 1987 the Townsend Thoresen ferry **Herald of Free Enterprise** was serving as relief on the Dover and Zeebrugge service. On her evening departure from Zeebrugge she left the linkspan with her bow ballasted one metre below the normal mark, a requirement that was necessary to make her bow door compatible with the shore ramp. The bosun's assistant was asleep in his berth, having been on duty the previous eighteen hours, and missed the call to harbour stations. It was his job to shut the bow doors. The Chief Officer had seen somebody dressed in an orange suit near the door controls and assumed that the doors would be closed once clear of the ramp. He reported accordingly to the bridge and the ship set sail.

The **Herald of Free Enterprise** passed the harbour breakwaters at 1720 hours, having worked up to 15 knots, when the helmsman reported she was not responding. Water was being scooped up onto the main vehicle deck - it took just eight minutes before the ship rolled over on its side and grounded on a sand bank adjacent to the channel. The ship was two thirds submerged. There were 459 passengers on board, many enjoying a cheap day out sponsored by the newspaper *Daily Mail*, along with a crew of 80; 193 people lost their lives. This was a disaster that should not have happened and could have been prevented had a CCTV camera been installed to check the status of the door or a failsafe device been fitted to prevent the ship gaining significant forward headway while the bow doors were open.

The Inquiry also determined that the management of the owners was sloppy. Ships regularly sailed overloaded due to tally systems that provided the passenger figures to the master long after the ship had sailed while using a vehicle weight estimate table that was up to 15% light of reality. In addition, it was found that the draught marks

*The **Shepperton Ferry** (1934) served as relief at Stranraer in the 1950s; note the watertight doors installed after the **Princess Victoria** disaster to prevent ingress of water onto the train deck.*

(Author)

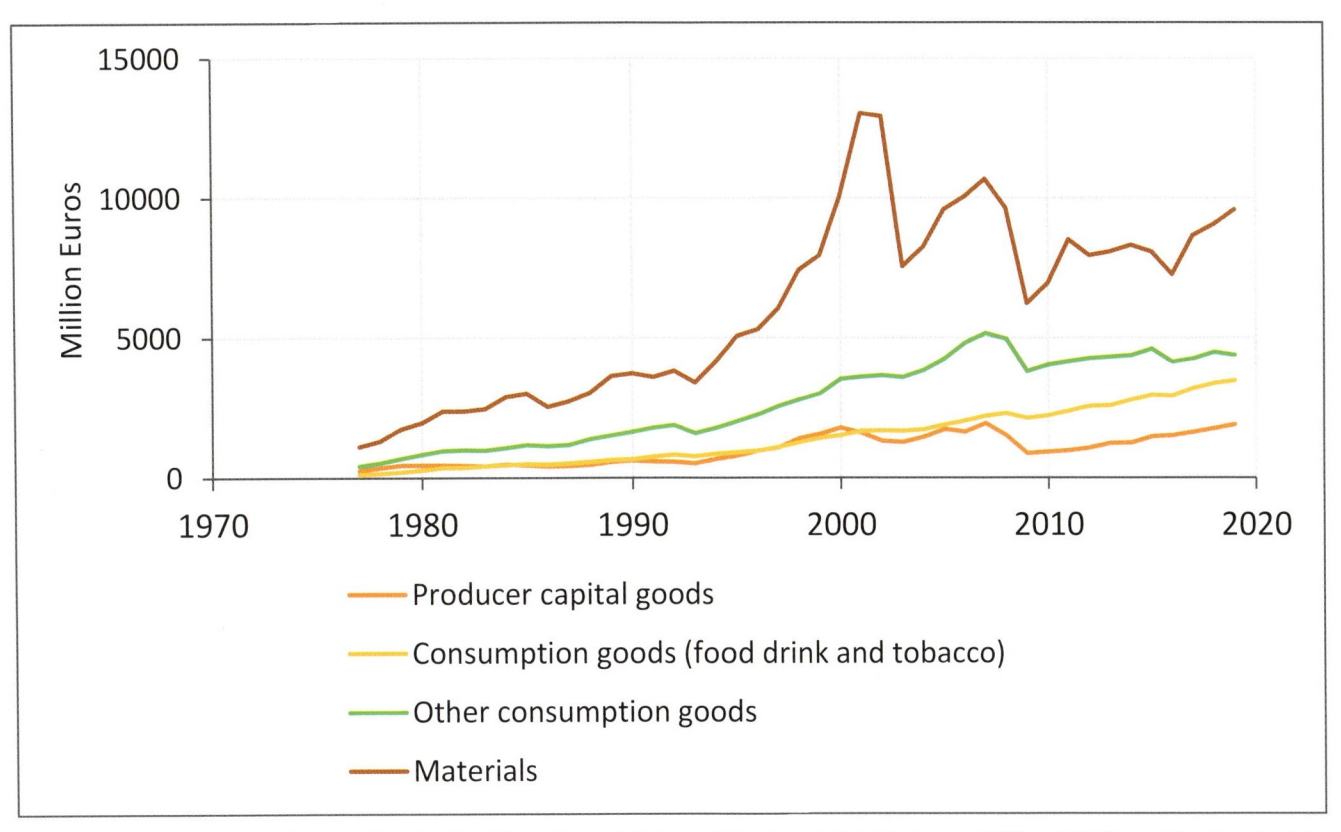

Figure 1 Annual imports to the Republic of Ireland from Great Britain and Northern Ireland between 1977 and 2019 – public domain data, Central Statistics Office.

(An Phríomh-Oifig Staidrimh)

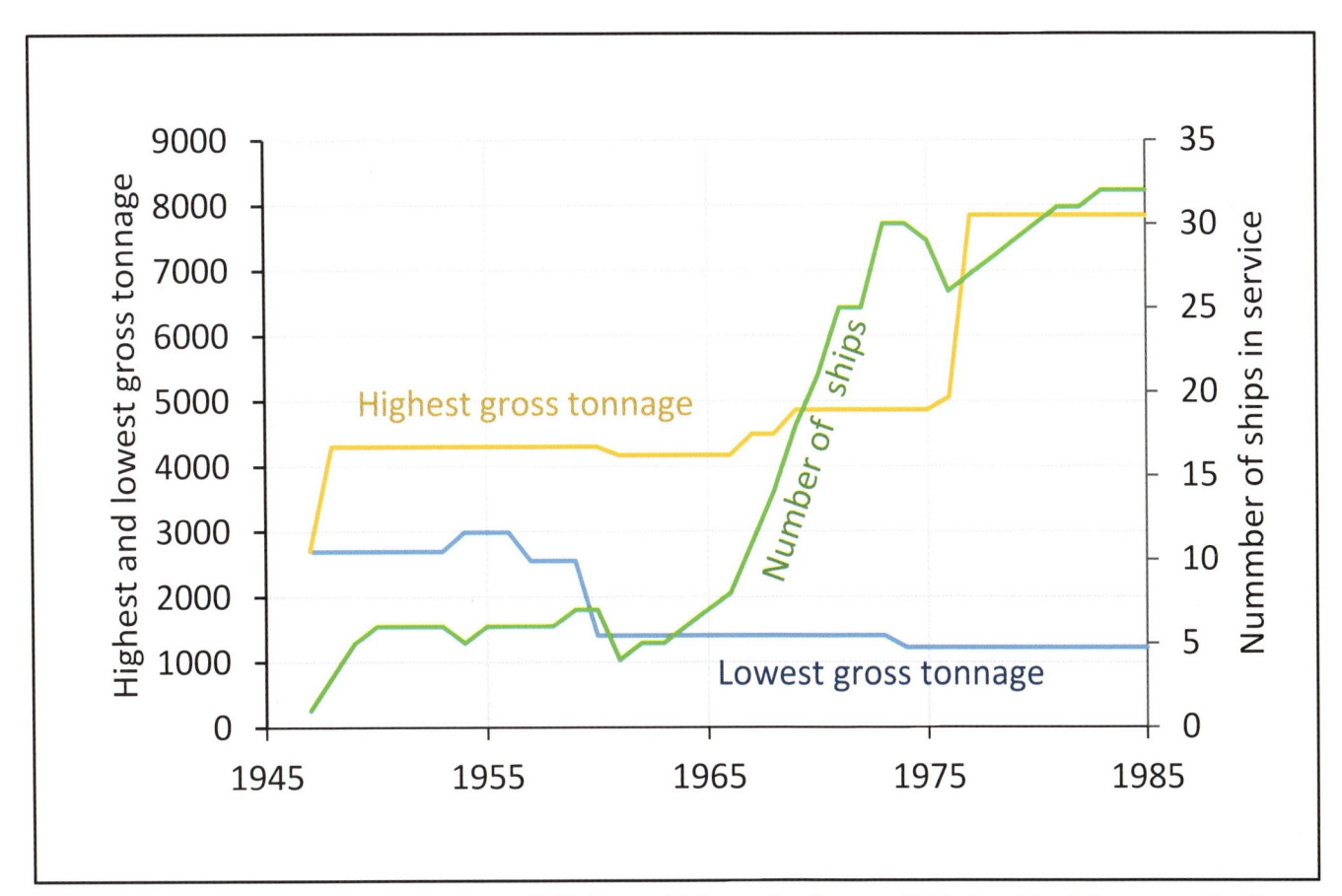

Figure 2 Illustrating the development of the roll-on roll-off ship on Irish Sea services between 1947, when Atlantic Steam started at Preston, and 1985, when the first second-generation vehicle and passenger ships were being introduced.

Herald of Free Enterprise (1979) seen on a routine and peaceful departure from Dover on 16 May 1981, just under six years before her catastrophic loss at Zeebrugge.

(Author)

Caledonian Princess (1961) was the successor to the Princess Victoria; note the watertight stern doors that sealed the ship to main deck level and obviated the need for scuppers on the vehicle deck.

(Author)

fore and aft could not be read from on board the ship and that figures had been regularly made up for entry to the log. The final indictment was that it took two hours to pump the water out of the forward ballast tanks to return the ship to level trim on leaving Zeebrugge. In the meantime, the vessel was at sea heading back to Dover with inadequate buoyancy towards the stern, wallowing at the bow and slow to answer the helm. This condition also would have serious implications for the permitted cargo deadweight given the reduced buoyancy of the ship. The same issues, of course, also applied to the two sister ships of the **Herald of Free Enterprise**.

The disaster had two outcomes: firstly, it was the end of the Townsend Thoresen company (Chapter 6) but more importantly it caused a complete redesign of the safety features aboard vehicle ferries right across the world. These requirements ultimately led to the installation of retractable transverse bulkheads to prevent longitudinal flow of water along the entire vehicle deck. However, free water on the vehicle deck remains a hazard to this day that has not yet been completely mitigated.

But some lessons had still not been learnt, and in 1994 the roll-on roll-off passenger ferry **Estonia** sank in severe weather in the Baltic with heavy loss of life. She had 22 hydraulically powered doors that could be controlled remotely from the bridge. When the ship foundered the bridge indicator showed all doors to be closed with 22 green lights showing on the indicator panel. At the subsequent inquiry it was suggested that the panel had been wrongly wired and that all the doors were open, a situation in which red warning lights should have indicated their true status. It was believed that a breach to one compartment caused flooding but it was never established whether all or some doors remained open and how this influenced the loss of the ship. A joint Swedish, Finnish and Estonian Commission of Enquiry concluded that the disaster was caused by poorly designed securing locks fitted to the bow visor which failed in the rough seas allowing free water to enter the main vehicle deck.

The advent of high speed ferries directed safety concerns in new and different directions. The loss of the Norwegian high speed ferry **Sleipner** on 26 November 1999, after hitting a rocky island 300 metres off course, and with the loss of 16 lives, was a serious setback for the high speed ferry industry. The accident was due to both the master and first officer concentrating on adjusting radar displays rather than focussing on navigation and so identifying the precise position of the vessel. This led to better structured watch keeping, and on tighter restrictions on small fast ferries putting to sea in adverse conditions.

Collectively, all these disasters have contributed greatly to the safety of modern roll-on roll-off vehicle ferries. All vessels serving on the Irish Sea comply with the evolving SOLAS regulations and with the requirements of the Flag State Regulatory Agency, in the case of the United Kingdom, the Maritime and Coastguard Agency (MCA) and previous to that the Board of Trade.

Although safety is the key driver, there have been a number of other constraints on the design and operation of vehicle ferries on the Irish Sea. A critical driver has always been the available trade on offer. Figure 1 shows the value of imports to the Republic of Ireland from the United Kingdom between 1977 and 2019 and reflects the growth in volume of traffic on offer to the Irish Sea trades, other than goods transhipped from Europe via the land-bridge across Great Britain. It shows the growth in four key categories: materials, producer capital goods for refabrication as consumer goods, food, drink and tobacco, other consumer goods, and materials for agriculture and other sectors. In the late 1980s there was a period of economic stagnation during which the value of goods imported to Ireland increased due to inflation but the volume of goods imported remained static. The chart shows the economic expansion that commenced in 1993 and, of course, the intense economic recession of the late 2000s after which trade only really picked up again from 2016.

Other drivers are diverse and include:
- the evolving Irish Peace Process and its positive impact on trade,
- state ownership and state subsidy of ferry companies,
- ferry company evolution,
- global depression of the late 2000s, and latterly the Covid-19 Pandemic and the impact of Great Britain leaving the European Union.

Issues regarding the design of the ships include:
- economies of scale,
- fuel economy,
- fast ferries preserving custom from the cheap airlines,
- over-capacity and competition,
- need for modern and efficient tonnage and of course the impact of the **Herald of Free Enterprise**, **European Gateway** and **Estonia** on ship design and on conversions of older ships to satisfy incoming regulations such as SOLAS.

All of these drivers were underpinned by technological advancement that allowed appropriate vessels to be designed and built. As costs increased, so the finance sector began to get involved with shipbuilding projects to offer a variety of packages to shipowners that ranged from loans and mortgages to direct ownership by banks and other institutions for charter, sometimes on a demise basis, to respective ship operators and managers.

The design of the ships went through a number of phases. The first was that of the first-generation car and passenger ferries through the late 1960s and into the 1970s. These were paralleled by the small first-generation freight vehicle ferries which were introduced to the

*The elegant Café Lafayette featured aboard the modern cruise ferry **W B Yeats** (2018).*

(Irish Ferries)

***Seatruck Pace** (2009) showing the clear upper vehicle deck and the fixed ramp to the lower vehicle deck, typical of modern second-generation freight ferries on the Irish Sea.*

(Seatruck Ferries)

Irish Sea in the early 1970s (Figure 2). Second-generation passenger ferries were introduced in the late 1970s and these started to be more general-purpose with vehicle decks with greater headroom that could accommodate freight vehicles; these are often classed as Ro-Pax ferries. By the mid-1980s there were 32 roll-on roll-off ferries in service in the Irish Sea the largest of which was the Holyhead and Dun Laoghaire ferry *St Columba*, albeit small by today's standards. The number of ferries in service has varied little since the mid-1980s although the available aggregate cargo deadweight has increased as new ships were built to larger dimensions.

Economies of scale led to the large cruise ferry of today, typically with over 3000 lane metres of freight vehicle stowage and additional low headroom decks for passenger's cars. Meanwhile the dedicated freight ferry had developed to provide uncluttered lower vehicle and upper main decks connected by a fixed ramp; these are sometimes classed as Ro-Ro ferries. Shore facilities had to keep up with developments at sea, with double deck ramps provided for ships that could load both upper and main decks simultaneously. And finally, the road network to and from ports had to be upgraded to suit the traffic that had been generated at the ports.

On reflection, the dark, wood panelled first class bar, with its fidded wooden tables and cosy alcoves, aboard the pioneer *Caledonian Princess* is a world apart from the open plan splendour of the present-day cruise ferry *W B Yeats* and her contemporaries. Besides, the banging of the ship's bottom as the she fell into the next trough coupled with the shudder as the propellers left the water, was a motion aboard the *Caledonian Princess* that has not been easy to forget, whereas the steady air-conditioned progression of the *W B Yeats* through equally rough seas is far less alarming.

The evolution of Irish Sea ferries over the last sixty years, since the *Caledonian Princess* was commissioned, encompasses technological development that could not have been envisaged back in 1961. Nevertheless, the key operators on the Irish Sea dragged their heels at the first instance and then had to work hard to catch up with technology that was led, for quite some time, by the Swedes and other North European countries whose innovative designs were targeted principally at the numerous Baltic services. But catch up they did, and today the ferry industry on the Irish Sea is recognised as a world leader with a safety record second to none.

The evolution of the key ferry companies is shown schematically in Figure 3. Clearly the railway shipping divisions within the British Railways Board progressed doggedly through the process of denationalisation ultimately into the ownership of Stena Line.

Equally, that of Coast Lines' Belfast Steamship Company and Burns & Laird Lines passed into the ownership of P&O, while the British & Irish Steam Packet Company and City of Cork Steam Packet Company led to Irish Ferries as a key part of the Irish Continental Group. A major success story has been that of Seatruck Ferries while others, including Merchant Ferries, Norse Irish Ferries and Belfast Freight Ferries disappeared through mergers and takeovers.

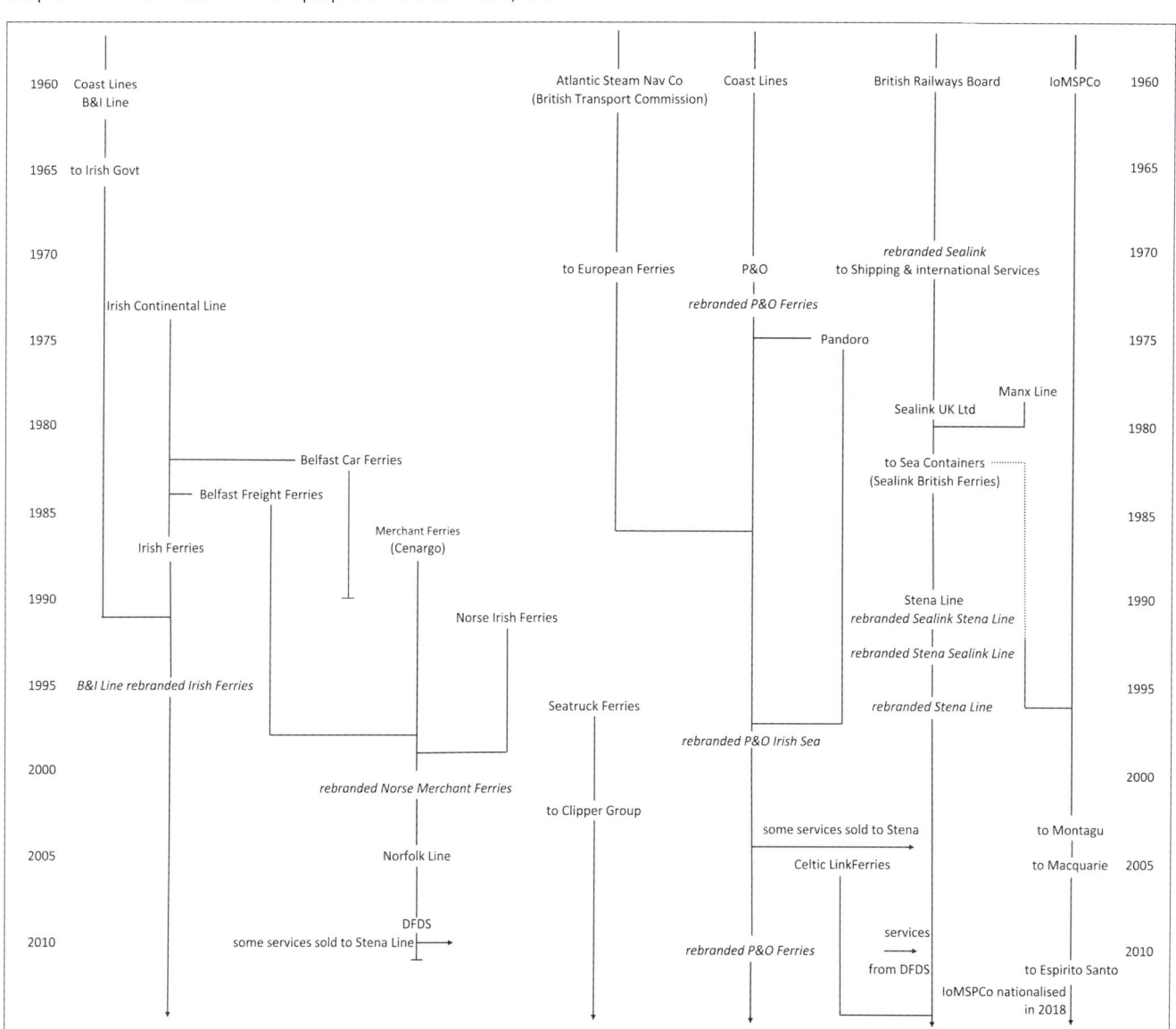

Figure 3 Schematic chart showing how the key operators on the Irish Sea evolved into the present day core of companies: Irish Ferries, Seatruck Ferries, P&O Ferries and Stena Line, showing also the Isle of Man Steam Packet Company.

CHAPTER 2
THE CAR FERRY ERA

Empire Nordic (1945) approaching the Preston Dock entrance on 18 August 1966 – note the gun platform forward and the cargo derricks serving a small hatch forward of the bridge.

(Author)

The Atlantic Steam Navigation Company's trade to Northern Ireland prospered despite the tidal nature of the port of Preston and the need for ships to follow behind the tidal bore when spring tides coincided with a north westerly wind. Ships arrived at the lock entrance to Preston Dock just before high tide and departed immediately afterwards on the ebb. A bow tug was required for safe passage along the half mile of constrained channel below the entrance lock and a tug was also needed while manoeuvring in the dock itself. Landing Ships, Tank were recruited from Tilbury to supplement the core services as inducement allowed.

Nevertheless, the new technology was still not seen as a threat to the existing shipping companies that were working on the Irish Sea because Atlantic Steam was still grossly undercapitalised. The directors of Coast Lines Limited were urged by their advisors to buy the company but they were unable to proceed, as also were British Railways, because of the binding constraints of the various Irish Sea conferences they were both members of. However, the threat that the new company now posed was at last recognised, although the existing operators' hands were tied, although it transpires in one case only very loosely.

The fortunes of the company were enhanced in April 1953 when the Atlantic Steam Navigation Company was acquired, in a swift and clandestine purchase, by the British Transport Commission (rather than British Railways). The majority ownership was subtly vested with the national haulier, British Road Services, in order to avoid compromising existing conference agreements signed by British Railways and the British Railways Board.

This move also brought an end to the British inhibition to allow UK commercial vehicles to venture to the Continent. With Government

Empire Nordic in position ready to pass into the lock entrance during the still water of high tide and with both lock gates open between river and dock – note the gun platforms aft on the boat deck.

(Author)

funding to support the company and the BTC doing its best to develop services that were complementary to the existing routes it maintained on the Irish Sea, two more Type 3 Landing Ships, Tank were brought into the fleet during 1955. These were the *Empire Cymric* formerly HMS *Attacker*, and the *Empire Nordic* ex-HMS *Charger*. They were converted by Harland & Wolff at Govan and fitted with 35 berths for drivers and passengers. Both ships served at Preston although the *Empire Cymric* also served at Tilbury.

During the Suez Crisis in the latter part of 1956, ten additional Landing Ships, Tank, that had been laid up in Reserve, were put back into service and entrusted to the management of the Atlantic Steam

Navigation Company. The total complement of seventeen ships, including the seven ships operating from Tilbury and Preston, were now managed on behalf of the Ministry of Transport.

The commercial services had to be closed so that most of the fleet could be sent to bases at Malta, Aden and Singapore. This meant that the commercial roll-on roll-off service between Preston and Northern Ireland was suspended between 17 August 1956 and 17 January 1957 when the **Empire Nordic** was again available to reopen the service to Larne. **Empire Cymric** and **Empire Cedric** came home shortly afterwards, while **Empire Gaelic** was back in service at Preston from 13 March after which a full service was operated. Chartered cargo ships had been used to maintain the unit load traffic and all road vehicles had been diverted to Stranraer where the **Hampton Ferry** was on duty.

Passage time in the LSTs could vary from the scheduled twelve hours at sea at 10½ knots plus the 2½ hours needed to negotiate the 14 mile long Ribble channel below Preston Dock, up to several days. Crossing the Ribble bar could not be accomplished in a strong north westerly wind and the ships had to lie in the lee of the Isle of Man to await more favourable conditions. Fog was also a problem which closed the port from time to time. In addition, the LSTs were naturally stiff and suffered a sharp and rapid frequency rolling motion which could only be moderated to prevent damage on the tank deck by sailing into the weather, sometimes adding many hours onto the passage time.

With this background, a brief was given to William Denny & Brothers at Dumbarton to prepare an outline design for two purpose-built ferries. Discussion with the builders commenced late in 1953 and continued through a prolonged design stage over the next two and half years until both builder and owner were satisfied that they had achieved the optimum design for the new ships. The dimensions of the ships were constrained by the 18 metre breadth between the lock gates at the entrance to Preston Dock; while the LSTs had a beam of just under 17 metres, the new ships were designed around a beam of 16 metres. The brief required that 70 trailers could be carried on the vehicle deck with stern access via a ramp and a water tight door sealing the vehicle deck from the sea.

As the owner was effectively the state and the bill for the ships was to be paid by the tax payer, the specification required extra strengthening of the vehicle deck for the carriage of heavy military equipment should the vessels be required to serve the state in an emergency. Headroom on the vehicle deck was to be enough to carry the tallest of vehicles; a double decker bus was applied as the standard. The ships also needed to carry unit load goods on the main deck aft and be equipped with a 20 ton electrically operated crane to handle the loads. In addition, high quality passenger accommodation was to be available for 17 first class passengers in five single and six twin berth cabins and in second class for a further 38 passengers and drivers in five twin berth cabins and seven 4 berth cabins. Light and airy public rooms, including separate dining saloons and lounges for each class, were to become the hallmark of the company.

A service speed of 14 knots was specified as was the requirement for Denny Brown stabilizers, more for the protection of the cargo than the comfort of passengers. The ships had twin screws and a pair of 10 cylinder Sulzer oil engines. The first of the pair, **Bardic Ferry**, was launched on 5 March 1957 and entered service between Preston and Larne on 2 September. For the next 13 months she was continually in service making three return trips each week to Larne. Sister ship **Ionic Ferry** was launched on 2 May 1958 and handed over to her owners on 4 October, taking her maiden voyage to Larne six days later.

Bardic Ferry then went for her guarantee overhaul and afterwards moved south to serve between Tilbury and Antwerp or Rotterdam. The **Ionic Ferry** worked alongside the LSTs on the Larne service while the **Empire Nordic** tended to maintain the direct service to Belfast supplemented by one of the other LSTs as inducement required. The **Empire Cedric**, **Empire Doric** and **Empire Gaelic** were disposed of in 1960, **Empire Doric** having been laid up in the Gare Loch since January 1957.

Ionic Ferry (1958) seen in the Ribble below Preston Dock on a routine arrival from Larne in September 1966.

(Author)

Bardic Ferry (1957) seen on the approach to Preston Dock in September 1968, the deck crane for handling unit loads having been removed in favour of the shear legs available at both Preston and Larne.

(Author)

The **Bardic Ferry** and **Ionic Ferry** were state-of-the-art. They were the first specially designed roll-on roll-off ferries for commercial vehicles and trailers as well as drivers. Not so some of the other ships commissioned for the Irish Sea at that time. The Isle of Man Steam Packet Company took delivery of the last of a sextet of passenger steamers based on a pre-war design, the **Manxman**, in 1955. Passengers' cars could be crane-loaded onto the main deck and stowed in the second class outside alleyways; the practice of mixing passengers with cars while at sea was eventually prohibited by the Board of Trade in the late 1960s. British Railways put three new steam turbine passenger and cargo ships on the Heysham and Belfast overnight service in 1956 and 1957. No special facilities were available for the carriage of passengers' cars which were crane-loaded onto the 'tween deck, an error realised in later years when a stern-loading garage was built into the **Duke of Rothesay** for 111 cars in 1967 and the **Duke of Argyll** and **Duke of Lancaster** for 105 cars each in 1970 (see Chapter 3). Coast Lines Limited was just as bad as the others and commissioned its 'mini-liner' **Scottish Coast** in 1958, a traditional passenger cross-channel vessel that was obsolescent even as she went down the slipway.

The British Railways Board ordered a composite roll-on roll-off cargo ship from Ailsa Shipbuilding Limited at Troon in 1959. This was the motor ship **Slieve Donard**, built specifically for service between Holyhead and Dublin and commencing service with a maiden voyage from Holyhead in January 1960. She was equipped to accommodate up to 150 trade cars loaded and unloaded onto the 'tween deck over a ramp and through the stern door, a facility little used in practice. On return, side-loading doors were used to embark and disembark up to 685 head of cattle that were accommodated in the lower holds. **Slieve Donard** also carried general cargo and small railway type containers could be stowed on deck fore and aft. She was an extremely versatile vessel for the trade then on offer and was the first Irish Sea cargo ship to carry wheeled vehicles. Her roll-on roll off facility was in demand in later years to supplement summer mail ship sailings at both Stranraer in 1964 and again at Fishguard in 1966. She also carried cars routinely in winter with passengers and drivers accommodated aboard the Holyhead and Dun Laoghaire mail ships, the passengers taken by road to meet their vehicles at the North Wall in Dublin.

At Stranraer the eventual replacement for the **Princess Victoria** finally arrived on duty in November 1961. The **Caledonian Princess** was the very last cross channel ferry to be built by William Denny & Brothers which ceased trading in 1963. The new ship had a number of innovative features including a Voith Schneider lateral thrust unit at the bow and Denny-Brown-AEG folding stabilisers. She was stern-loading with a single vehicle deck, with enough headroom for coaches at the after end with cars stowed forward beneath an accommodation deck. There was a comprehensive arrangement of exhaust fans and ducts to remove fumes from the vehicle deck during loading and unloading. Each year when the **Caledonian Princess** was dry docked it was found that her bottom had been polished clean down to the steel plates by the sand in suspension in the water in the shallow upper reaches of Loch Ryan! **Caledonian Princess** was fast enough to manage two round trips to Larne each day, with departures from Stranraer at 0700 hours and 14.30 hours. Her arrival allowed the **Hampton Ferry** to stand down and permanently return to Dover and **Princess Margaret** to lay up and await a buyer.

In 1961 two new ferries, **Doric Ferry** and **Cerdic Ferry**, were launched by Ailsa Shipbuilding Company Limited at Troon for the Atlantic Steam Navigation Company. They were based on the design of the earlier **Bardic Ferry** and **Ionic Ferry**, but the new ships were 7 metres longer than the earlier pair and had enlarged cargo space and deadweight. The new ships were designed for the Tilbury and

Continental services, and once the **Cerdic Ferry** had replaced the **Bardic Ferry** at Tilbury, the latter ship was able to return to Preston with a first voyage on 19 June 1961 and, thereafter, worked alongside her sister **Ionic Ferry** to provide an upgraded service to Larne. The **Empire Nordic** maintained the Belfast direct route. The **Doric Ferry** first came to Preston on 19 February 1962, for a four week period, as relief for the **Bardic Ferry** and then the **Ionic Ferry** which, one after the other, went away for overhaul.

In June 1960, a contract was awarded by the Isle of Man Steam Packet Company to Cammell Laird at Birkenhead for a new passenger ship to be broadly similar to the passenger only **Manxman** built at Birkenhead in 1955. The design included accommodation for 1400 passengers in two classes. The new ship would differ in that she would be equipped with a complex spiral of ramps so that up to 90 cars and light vans could be driven aboard from a quayside at any stage of the tide. This system was adopted because, at that time, there was no linkspan at Douglas, side-loading was preferred at Liverpool and the technique could also be carried out at the other ports used by the company during the summer season: Ardrossan, Heysham, Belfast and Dublin. Until then cars had been carried on the passenger ships but were craned on and off at Douglas although a portable ramp had been used at the Princes Stage at Liverpool.

Connery Chappell described the new ship:

> A spiral set of ramps at the stern links with the car deck so that the vehicles can be driven on and off from the appropriate level on departure or arrival. This patented system of ramps facilitates loading and unloading at any state of the tide at any of the company's ports. The decision to build a new generation of car-ferrying vessels was taken in 1959 and **Manx Maid** was launched in January 1962.

The **Manx Maid** was handed over to the Steam Packet company at Liverpool on 21 May 1962. She was immediately pressed into service, vehicles using a 5 metre long portable ramp to access the on-board spiral ramps at Princes Landing Stage and an 8 metre long shore ramp at Douglas. Like **Manxman** before her, the new ship was equipped with twin Pametrada steam turbine machinery which provided a service speed of 21 knots. Unlike previous steamers sailing to Douglas the **Manx Maid** was equipped with stabilisers in order to safeguard vehicles from damage. The success of the **Manx Maid** can be judged by a repeat order with Cammell Laird for an almost identical sister ship, **Ben-my-Chree**. The **Ben-my-Chree** took her maiden voyage from Liverpool on 12 May 1966.

The British Transport Commission was abolished by Act of Parliament in 1963 and the British Railways Board and the Transport Holding Company took over the shipping divisions. Growing demand for accompanied cars at Holyhead inspired the British Railways Board to order a steam turbine driven stern-loading car and passenger ferry for the service as a replacement for the passenger only **Princess Maud**. The new ship was given the name **Holyhead Ferry I** by John Bustard, formerly of the Atlantic Steam Navigation Company and grandson of its founder Frank Bustard. John had risen in the ranks to become manager of the Irish Sea Services and he thought up the name, 'Ferry' being added in keeping with the Atlantic Steam Navigation Company nomenclature and the suffix 'I' being given in anticipation of a succession of similar vessels at Holyhead.

The new ship was launched in February 1965 by Hawthorn Leslie (Shipbuilders) Limited at Hebburn. However, she was not ready in time to take the inaugural advertised sailing and **Normannia**, newly converted to car and passenger ferry, came up from the South Coast to start the service between Holyhead and Dun Laoghaire. **Holyhead Ferry I** took over ten days later on 20 July 1965, **Normannia** already having christened the new link spans at both ports. The car ferry service was suspended for the winter in October and **Holyhead Ferry I** was used as relief at Stranraer. Subsequent criticism of the soulless name **Holyhead Ferry I** led the British Railways Board to adopt the 'ancient kings' nomenclature commencing with the new Dover-based train ferry **Vortigern** in 1969.

*The Isle of Man Steam Packet Company's first car ferry, **Manx Maid** (1962), seen arriving from Douglas off Princes Landing Stage, Liverpool. Note the access ports to the spiral vehicle ramps located towards the stern.*

(Author)

***Normannia** (1952) was converted into a car and passenger ferry in 1964 for use at Dover but opened the new Holyhead and Dun Laoghaire car ferry service until the purpose-built **Holyhead Ferry I** was available.*
(Author)

***Holyhead Ferry I** (1965) working out of Dover in 1973 wearing the new Sealink livery.*
(Author)

***Dover** (1965) ran alongside the **Holyhead Ferry I** on the Holyhead service during the 1969 and 1970 summer seasons.*
(Author)

Ulster Prince (1966) on her early morning arrival at Liverpool from Belfast, seen at the Waterloo Dock entrance in July 1968.

(Author)

Lion (1967) at Ardrossan on 16 July 1969 on her afternoon departure for Belfast.

(Author)

Holyhead Ferry I was the first one class passenger ship in the railway fleet. She could accommodate 1000 passengers and offered 35 cabins ranging from two de-luxe state rooms to six 3 berth cabins. She could carry 125 cars on the main vehicle deck and a further 25 on the upper vehicle deck which was accessed via an internal ramp that could be raised out of the way. She offered the usual public rooms but there was no restaurant, instead passengers enjoyed a self-service cafeteria. A second ship to the same structural design was ordered from Swan Hunter, but her interior configuration differed to suit the Dover station. She too had an unimaginative title; a public competition to name the ship was overwhelmingly in favour of *Dover*. Both ships had hatches forward to load the mail and to remove cars in the event of the stern door failing to lift out of the way.

Holyhead Ferry I was popular with car drivers in the summer seasons and offered two sailings a day. From 1968 the *Holyhead Ferry I* assumed one of the mail ship's rosters and then maintained a year-round car ferry service. In 1969 and 1970 a two-ship summer roster had the *Dover* working alongside the *Holyhead Ferry I*. Inevitably, the *Holyhead Ferry I* was based at Dover in the early 1970s!

Coast Lines Limited finally realised that the roll-on roll-off era was here to stay. It sold the British & Irish Steam Packet Company and the City of Cork Steam Packet Company to the Irish Government in February 1965 for £3.6 million. The cash was earmarked to fund new car ferries for its Irish Sea passenger services. In the first instance, Coast Lines commissioned Cammell Laird to design two ships to a Coast Lines' brief for the overnight service between Liverpool and Belfast. The brief was ill-conceived and projections of how the traffic would develop over the life of the new ferries was grossly misjudged. They also delivered a brief for a ferry to run a daylight service between Ardrossan and Belfast, based on their experience with North Sea Ferries, of which Coast Lines was a partner, and the design of that company's drive-through ferry *Norwave*. Robins wrote of the Liverpool sisters in the history of Coast Lines:

> The directors made their last bad decision, they opted for a vehicle deck extending half the length of the ship, most of which had low headroom that excluded most commercial traffic and was accessed by a stern door. They then said we will carry unit loads in a hold forward of the machinery space. This was the outline specification that they took to Cammell Laird who then worked it up into a full design. Coast Lines was not alone in going for this design and Ellerman's Wilson Line ordered the bigger ferry *Spero* on the same lines as well; both companies learning the error of their ways in due course.

And of the Ardrossan ferry:

> By way of compensation a specification was later also drawn up for one more vehicle ferry to replace the Glasgow twins [*Royal Ulsterman* and *Royal Scotsman*] and to replace the Ardrossan to Belfast ferry, be it *Scottish Coast* or *Irish Coast*. This ferry was to operate between Ardrossan and Belfast on a daylight return schedule at a fast design speed of 20 to 21 knots. The specification also allowed for a drive-through garage deck, as had the *Norwave*, and headroom enough for all but the tallest of road vehicles. Northern Ireland Trailers agreed to use the new ship for unit loads stowed on trailers. The passenger accommodation was to be fitted out as a day boat with restaurants, cafes and lounges designed for passengers to spend their money in. This outline specification also went to Cammell Laird to work into shape, but at a later date.

The Liverpool and Belfast ferries were launched in 1966, the *Ulster Prince* by Harland & Wolff at Belfast on 13 October and the *Ulster Queen* at Birkenhead on 1 December. They were managed by Coast Lines' Belfast Steamship Company and could accommodate 120 accompanied cars and a handful of commercial vehicles placed towards the stern where there was a small area on the car deck with greater headroom. However, this was usually pre-booked for Royal Mail vehicles. Robins again:

> The *Ulster Prince* took her maiden voyage on 19 April and the *Ulster Queen* on 6 June, replacing the *Scottish Coast* and *Irish Coast* respectively. The service was stepped up from six nights a week to seven with the introduction of a Sunday night sailing. They were a compromise, with not enough headroom on the vehicle deck to stow commercial vehicles and a hold wastefully designed for unit loads. They were comfortable though, as far as passengers were concerned. They had accommodation for 288 first class passengers who enjoyed a restaurant, cafeteria, smoke room and a lounge with aircraft type seating for unberthed passengers. Second class offered berths for 140 passengers in two, three and four berth cabins.

The Ardrossan and Belfast ferry building for Coast Lines' Burns & Laird Lines Limited was much more suited to the traffic on offer. She was launched by Cammell Laird on 8 August 1967 and christened *Lion*. She was designed as a one class ship with accommodation for up to 1200 day passengers, 170 passengers' cars and about 40 commercial vehicles. The drive-through vehicle deck promoted rapid loading and discharge and included a retractable mezzanine deck for cars. The garage deck had a height of 4.4 metres. The *Lion* took her maiden voyage on 3 January 1968.

At almost the same time the British Railways Board commissioned a similar drive-through vessel, the *Antrim Princess*, for the Stranraer and Larne service. The *Caledonian Princess* had become increasingly popular with motorists and had been assisted by the *Slieve Donard* as a car carrier in summer 1964 and then by the Swedish car transporter *Lohengrin*, chartered from Wallenius Lines for summer 1965. In March 1966 the stern-loading *Stena Nordica* was chartered from Stena Line for an initial period of 18 months. This ship was almost brand new having only been delivered from her builders in France in June 1965. She offered accommodation for 1000 passengers and 120 cars and facilities included a restaurant with 126 covers and a cafeteria. She maintained a service speed of 17½ knots. *Stena Nordica* worked alongside *Caledonian Princess*, which managed 20 knots on service. The pair were later joined by the new *Antrim Princess*.

The order for the new ship was announced by the British Railways Board in March 1966. The *Antrim Princess* was a drive-through ship fitted with mezzanine decks for cars and enough height throughout the central lanes of the garage deck to accommodate tall commercial vehicles of up to 11 tons axle weights. She offered 346 lane metres of vehicle space up to a maximum cargo deadweight of 593 tons. *Antrim Princess* was equipped with two Crossley-Pielstick oil engines built by Ateliers & Chantiers de Nantes in France and these provided a service speed of 19½ knots. She could accommodate 1200 passengers with berths available for 70 persons and offered the usual public rooms and facilities in one class. She was delivered by Hawthorn Leslie in December 1967. However, the three-ship service did not last long and *Caledonian Princess* moved south in May 1969 to inaugurate a stern-loading roll-on roll-off service for passengers and cars between Fishguard and Rosslare. New linkspans had been installed at Fishguard at the inshore end of the quay and at Rosslare in the corner of the harbour near the dock entrance.

Car carrying between Fishguard and Rosslare had been developed by adapting the conventional ferry *St David* as a side-loading car and passenger ferry in 1964 with space for 66 cars. In May 1967 she was joined by the former Heysham passenger ferry *Duke of Rothesay*, now also converted as a side-loading car ferry. Commercial traffic had not been catered for. The arrival of the *Caledonian Princess* in 1969 displaced *St David* from the route.

Transport of new trade cars across the Irish Sea had always been lucrative although as yet there were no purpose-built ships being

Stena Nordica (1965) was chartered to the British Railways Board for use at Stranraer between 1966 and 1969 – she adopted the twin arrow device on a red funnel with a black top in 1967.

(Stena Line)

Antrim Princess (1967) leaving Stranraer in 1984 with the bow visor in evidence.

(Bernard McCall)

St David (1947) wearing the funnel colours of the Fishguard & Rosslare Railways and Harbours Company. The new car doors are below the small while post on top of the bulwarks.

(Author)

used for the available traffic. Coast Lines Limited recognised the importance of the trade when it converted its redundant break-bulk cargo ship **Lancashire Coast** into a car and cattle carrier. The History of Coast Lines reports:

> The **Lancashire Coast** was converted by Harland & Wolff into a car and cattle carrier in 1969. Her masts and cargo handling derricks were removed, the three original hatches were plated over and two new hatches were created on both the upper and main decks. Cargo doors were fitted on the side of the ship's side shelter deck plating and by means of a shore ramp, cars could be driven on and off the ship and cattle walked on and off on the hoof. Cars for stowing in the lower hold could be shore craned-on and -off through the two newly fitted hatches. On completion she took up service between Liverpool and Belfast.

Lancashire Coast remained in the trade for the next decade, latterly under various owners after Coast Lines had been taken over by the P&O group. Cars were loaded at Liverpool and cattle took their place at Belfast. How the Northern Irish car salesmen dealt with the smell of cattle pervading from the otherwise pristine vehicles in their showrooms remains a secret to this day!

The **Empire Nordic** soldiered on until her last sailing on 30 December 1966 when she was declared to be unworthy of further investment in order to pass her annual survey. She was laid up at Barrow pending sale and was sold in January 1968. Her place was taken by a converted American LST, the **Pima County** built in 1945 at Ambridge, Pennsylvania, by the American Bridge Company. She was adapted for commercial service at Middlesbrough, given the name **Baltic Ferry** and configured to carry 45 trailers on the tank deck and to carry containers on the upper deck. She served between Preston and Belfast, but she had no passenger accommodation and could not carry drivers. This arrangement derived from the traffic which at that time was mainly unaccompanied trailers.

In 1968 the Atlantic Steam Navigation Company continental services transferred from Tilbury to Felixstowe and a new ship, **Europic Ferry**, replaced the **Doric Ferry** while sister ship **Cerdic Ferry** remained based at Tilbury. The **Doric Ferry** moved north to run the Preston to Belfast service in November 1968 reinstating passenger facilities on that route, and the **Baltic Ferry** was withdrawn and laid up at Barrow. With a dedicated Belfast passenger ship the service was increased from weekly to three times a week, and a new terminal was opened at Belfast in December specifically for use by the **Doric Ferry**. The **Baltic Ferry** was chartered to British Rail who put her in service between Stranraer and Larne from June 1970. She was finally sold in 1972 and scrapped the following year.

Winter refits were covered by the **Cerdic Ferry** at Preston in January 1966. In January 1967 the chartered Norwegian ferry **Viking I** was used for a few weeks on the Preston and Belfast service. **Viking I** was one of the drive-through ships owned by Thoresen Car Ferries and based at Southampton; on the Irish Sea she was used only as a stern-loading ferry.

Thus far, the prize for the most innovative design must clearly be awarded to the British Transport Commission and Atlantic Steam Navigation Company for the **Bardic Ferry** and **Ionic Ferry**. This pair of commercial vehicle and private car carriers was ahead of its time, the ships built to a design that was repeated with two near sisters and later two more larger vessels which were adapted for higher operating speeds. The novelty award inevitably must go to the Isle of Man Steam Packet Company for its side-loading car ferries **Manx Maid** and **Ben-my-Chree**, ships built around a traditional passenger only design that stemmed from before the Second World War. First Prize, however, goes jointly to Coast Lines for the **Lion**, and to the British Railways Board for the **Antrim Princess**; at last, it was recognised that the drive-through concept was acceptable for passenger carrying ferries and that a mix of commercial and private vehicles could readily be accommodated with the use of retractable mezzanine decks.

Duke of Rothesay (1956) leaving Fishguard Harbour on 23 June 1969. The side-loading car door is just below the group of three seagulls.
(Author)

Coast Line's *Lancashire Coast* (1953) was converted in 1969 into a side-loading cattle and trade car carrier - cattle to Liverpool, cars to Belfast.
(World Ship Society Photo Library)

The American Landing Ship, Tank *Pima County* (1945) lying at Albert Edward Dock, North Shields, on arrival from Philadelphia, preparatory to conversion to commercial use for the Atlantic Steam Navigation Company.
(Press Photo, Shields Gazette)

Doric Ferry (1961) moved from Tilbury to Preston in 1968 displacing **Baltic Ferry** and reinstating the passenger service between Preston and Belfast.

(Author)

Atlantic Steam Navigation Company's **Baltic Ferry** (1945) at Stranraer on 26 August 1970, on charter from Preston to support the burgeoning commercial traffic on the route to Stranraer and Larne.

(Author)

CHAPTER 3
THE EARLY 1970s AND THE NORTHERN EUROPEAN INFLUENCE

Munster (1968), the smallest of the 'ships with witches hats' seen leaving Liverpool.

(The late Laurie Schofield)

Coast Lines' (Burns & Laird Lines) **Lion** and the British Railways Board's **Antrim Princess** had introduced the mixing of private cars with commercial freight vehicles on passenger ferries on the Irish Sea. The success of these ships in attracting both accompanied private cars and commercial traffic to the Ardrossan and Stranraer services was a huge fillip to all operators on the Irish Sea as it paved the way for the next stage of development of the roll-on roll-off technology between Great Britain and both the north and south of Ireland.

The undoubted leaders in the design and development of the roll-on roll-off ferry during the 1970s were the Swedes. One shipping company in particular, Stena A/B of Gothenburg, owner of the chartered **Stena Nordica** at Stranraer, was responsible for a number of extremely successful classes of commercial vehicle ferry as well as larger passenger and vehicle units. The company worked in collaboration with German and other north European shipbuilders to produce a succession of cleverly designed, functional and flexible ships, some of them finding their way into service on the Irish Sea. German and Dutch shipyards were well suited to constructing the new designs as these yards had been newly laid out and retooled when they were rebuilt after the war. The European yards used modern techniques with widespread use of prefabrication to assist in construction to a predetermined schedule. By comparison, most British yards were cramped with little if any space for prefabrication and were poorly equipped for jobs such as machine welding.

When the Irish Government acquired the British & Irish Steam Packet Company in 1965 it was conscious that major fleet upgrades would be required. This had not deterred the Government from the purchase, besides, talks over the deal had been ongoing over the preceding thirty years. The Irish Government was determined that the company's ships should raise the Irish Tricolor, be manned by Irish crews and become ambassadors for the Republic of Ireland. The replacement passenger ships were indeed ambassadors. They were known as the 'ships with witches hats' because of the distinctive configuration of funnel and main mast, and the new Swedish-designed **Munster**, **Leinster**, and **Innisfallen** were indeed of landmark design. The three ships replaced conventional passenger ferries with the same names that had all been built in the late 1940s.

In spring 1967 the Irish Government signed a contract with Werft Nobiskrug at Rendsburg in Germany for a ship of the same design as **Kronprins Carl Gustav**, completed in 1966 for Lion Ferry A/B (Bonnerforetagen-Wallensius) of Halmstad, Sweden. The keel was laid in September with delivery scheduled for May 1968. In December 1967 orders were confirmed for two additional near sisters, one to be built at Rendsburg and the other at the Verolme Cork Dockyard at Rushbrooke near Cobh. The total cost of the three ships amounted to GB £7.5 million.

The first ship was named **Munster** at her launch in Germany on 25 January 1968. As promised, she was delivered on time ready for her maiden voyage from Liverpool to Dublin on the evening of 15 May. Her vehicle deck included one lane with a headroom of 3.9 metres. Malcolm MacRonald wrote in *The Irish Boats*:

> She had capacity for 1,000 passengers, including 238 berths in 41 two-berth and 39 four-berth cabins and 332 'pullman sleep seats'. There was space for 210 cars on two decks, the higher of which was hinged to make extra room for tall vehicles. The public rooms were located on two decks. The promenade deck, immediately above the car decks, had a cafeteria at its forward end, and a childrens' playroom, an entrance area with a shop and a purser's office, a bar and a verandah lounge at its after end. The cafeteria and the verandah lounge extended the full width of the ship; the other rooms were to port only, with the galley and catering accommodation to starboard. The boat deck had a restaurant and cocktail bar at its forward end and a pullman lounge and open deck space aft.

At Liverpool the **Munster** could not negotiate the winding passage from Waterloo to Princes Dock. Instead, she used a temporary berth and linkspan installed at Carriers Dock and moved to a permanent site at Trafalgar Dock, accessed via the Waterloo Dock entrance, in

Innisfallen (1969) arriving at the Swansea Car Ferry Terminal on 22 June 1969 having commenced on the new service on 2 May.
(Author)

Leinster (1969) arriving at Liverpool on 11 July 1969 after entering service the previous month.
(Author)

1970. At Dublin she berthed at the new Ferryport at the seaward end of the dock estate on the north bank of the Liffey. Initially the **Munster** maintained three return sailings every two days requiring all of her service speed of 22 knots to maintain the schedule which allowed only one hour for turn-around at each port.

The old **Leinster**, now renamed **Leinster I** to release her name for one of the new ships, maintained her existing schedule of one sailing per night between the old terminals. The new consort for the **Munster** was launched at Rushbrooke on 19 November 1968 and predictably christened **Leinster**, while the third ship destined for a new route between Cork and Swansea was christened **Innisfallen** at her launch at Rendsburg on 7 December 1968. The **Innisfallen** was first to be delivered taking her maiden voyage from Liverpool to Dublin on 14 April 1969 allowing the **Munster** to undergo her guarantee overhaul. Two weeks later the new ship sailed for Cork, taking her maiden voyage to Swansea on 2 May where she berthed at a new linkspan in the River Tawe adjacent to the dock entrance. The three ships were broadly the same, the main differences being that **Innisfallen** had a marginally faster service speed than the Dublin ships in order to maintain a nine hour crossing between Swansea and Cork, and that **Innisfallen** and **Leinster** were some 9 metres longer than the first ship, the **Munster**, and had a greater cargo deadweight including accommodation for 1200 passengers. **Innisfallen** and **Leinster** also offered a Sky Bar on the uppermost deck above and abaft the bridge; this was stripped out in both ships ready for the 1971 season and replaced by rows of seats. The new services were marketed as the B+I Motorway and the ships quickly established a reputation for good service and punctuality, not only acclaimed by car drivers and passengers but also by a growing number of commercial hauliers.

In 1970 the remaining Heysham passenger ships, **Duke of Argyll** and **Duke of Lancaster**, were converted into stern-loading car ferries with garages that could accommodate up to 105 cars. Work included moving the steering gear to a lower deck, and relocating some of the crew quarters. The vehicle deck could accommodate two coaches reversed on board and stowed along the centre line aft. At the same time, the passenger accommodation was modified as one class, although it reverted back to separate classes in 1973. The sisters maintained their normal overnight service to Belfast in winter but operated additional daylight sailings in the summer months. They had been built by Harland & Wolff Limited at Belfast whereas the building of the third quasi-sister, **Duke of Rothesay**, was sublet to William Denny & Brothers at Dumbarton. There were differences in their construction, the Denny-built ship had been constructed with a lighter scantling than her two sisters and conversion of her to anything but a side-loading car ferry would not have been easy.

Unfortunately, conversion of the **Duke of Argyll** and **Duke of Lancaster** to suit tourist passengers and their cars coincided with a deterioration in the political situation in Northern Ireland. The start of the Battle of the Bogside and the deployment of British troops in Northern Ireland during August 1969 heralded the renewal of the Troubles. As a consequence, tourist traffic decreased rapidly. In an attempt to increase passenger carrying and recoup some of the costs of converting the two Dukes it was proposed that the daylight sailings in 1971 would call at Douglas. However, the lack of a linkspan at that port meant that only passengers could embark and disembark and the idea was not pursued (much to the delight of the Isle of Man Steam Packet Company).

Thus, in 1970 at the start of the new decade there were drive-through passenger, car and commercial vehicle ferries operating between Ardrossan and Larne, Liverpool and Dublin and Swansea and Cork. There were passenger, car and commercial vehicle stern-loading ferries working between Preston and Larne and Preston and Belfast, Holyhead and Dun Laoghaire and between Stranraer and Larne. There was a stern-loading passenger and car ferry service between Heysham and Belfast, Liverpool and Belfast, and between Fishguard and Rosslare, the latter supported by a make-do side-loading ferry, and various side-loading services to and from the Isle of Man. As yet there were no dedicated commercial vehicle ferries other than the bow-loading, converted Landing Ship, Tank **Baltic Ferry**, which was working between Stranraer and Larne in 1970. Apart from the services between Liverpool and Belfast, Ardrossan and Larne and routes to and from the Isle of Man, all the other services were state-owned and state-operated either by the British Government or the Irish Government.

Significantly there were no new ships on order during 1970 for use in the Irish Sea. The Irish Government was talking about a repeat order of the **Innisfallen** to work between Rosslare and a port in France with occasional sailings to Spain, although this idea was later dropped. Despite there being no confirmed plans for new tonnage it seems that change, improvement and flexibility were already recognised as the key to all future operations.

The *Belfast Telegraph*, 11 March 1970, reported a plan to introduce a new ferry service between Campbeltown in Argyll and Red Bay near Glenariff in County Antrim using Western Ferries **Sound of Islay**. Western Ferries had introduced its innovative stern-loading ferry **Sound of Islay** on a new service to Islay in 1968. She had been replaced early in 1970 by a larger drive-through ship, **Sound of Jura**, and the **Sound of Islay** was intended to go to a new service on the Clyde between McInroy's Point near Gourock and Hunter's Quay near Dunoon. When authorisation for that service was delayed, the **Sound of Islay** was allocated for the new Irish ferry service. Fares were less than the Burns & Laird Belfast and Glasgow route and the new route was targeted at Irish tourists travelling to the Western Highlands of Scotland. The service started on 7 May 1970 with a departure from Campbeltown at 0900 hours returning from Red Bay at 1300, with a double round trip at weekends. The crossing took 3½ hours. The inauguration of the service coincided with a drivers'

*The newly converted stern-loading car ferry **Duke of Argyll** (1956) arriving at Heysham, as always stern first, during low tide on 15 August 1970.*

(Author)

***Duke of Lancaster** (1955) approaching her berth at Heysham in September 1973 with the Sealink banner proudly on display. Heysham Power Station is under construction south of the harbour.*

(Author)

strike at the Cookstown Cement Works; pickets prevented export to Scotland via Larne but there was no such obstruction at Red Bay! The service was suspended at the beginning of September when *Sound of Islay* had to deputise on the Islay run with *Sound of Jura* needing damage repairs.

The *Sound of Islay* was built in 1968 by Ferguson Brothers (Port Glasgow) Limited to a Norwegian design. She could accommodate 20 cars and up to 75 passengers, the passenger lounge was basic but comfortable. At the end of the first season on the Irish service the *Sound of Islay* was advertised principally for cargo shipments. Although the timber industry supported the initiative, the winter service did not pay its way and the ship was soon withdrawn until the spring. Nevertheless, the seasonal service was maintained until September 1973 when the *Sound of Islay* was put up for charter along the west coast of Scotland. In 1976 the larger *Sound of Jura* was sold and *Sound of Islay* was retrenched to the Islay route, a service which finally closed in 1981 when the *Sound of Islay* was also sold. Various other possible routes were considered for the *Sound of Islay* from time to time but none were pursued.

In 1969 the regional management of the British Railways Board's shipping divisions were merged into the Shipping & International Services Division. This was an important step as it pooled the diverse resources and the overall manpower which could now be managed directly from offices at Liverpool Street in London. In November 1969, the new brand name 'Sealink' was announced for all the ships and for marketing purposes. The significance of this, particularly in the context of the Irish Sea routes, was that ships could be more readily transferred, even borrowed, from what were previously separate divisions. This had already happened to a limited extent when the *Hampton Ferry* was deployed at Stranraer in the early 1950s and the *Dover* assisted at Holyhead in 1969 and again in 1970.

An early initiative in privatising some of the state-owned shipping services was made in 1971 by the Transport Holding Company, into whose auspices the Atlantic Steam Navigation Company had been placed in the 1960s. Atlantic Steam had been identified as a viable unit that could survive in the private sector. Some imaginative bookwork managed to obscure asset depreciation making the unit even more attractive to prospective buyers, while interested parties were allowed full access to the company records, its apparent financial status and an assessment of future prospects. They were also invited to inspect the ships and services. In the event, the company and its two subsidiary holding companies were bought, in November 1971, by European Ferries Group, owners of the Townsend Thoresen Ferries, the product of a merger between Townsend Brothers Ferries, Limited and Otto Thoresen Shipping Company (Thoresen Car Ferries) that took place in 1968. Little outward change to Atlantic Steam was apparent under the new owners.

During the 1960s part of the wartime military port at Cairnryan in Galloway had been bought by the Atlantic Steam Navigation Company from Shipbreaking (Queenborough) Limited with the consent of the Transport Holding Company. The Transport Holding Company and the British Railways Board were conscious of the breadth limitations of ships using the Port of Preston and of the draft limitations of ships based at Stranraer. Although the quay frontage at Cairnryan was in disrepair, the sale included an area of reclaimed land enclosed by three quays, with deep water berths beneath the south and west walls and shallower water beneath the north wall. The purchase price was £60,000 for a site that was a likely candidate as a ferry terminal but was also considered to offer potential as a container handling facility. European Ferries were quick to realise the importance of this asset and decided that operations at Preston would be better relocated at Cairnryan. Work was put in hand to renovate the deep-water berths on the south and west side of the site and to prepare for the installation of a modern linkspan on the south quay.

Ionic Ferry closed the Preston and Larne service in March 1973 and received modifications, including two extra lifeboats, to increase her passenger certificate to 219 persons. Mobile buildings were erected as a passenger terminal adjacent to the main road at Cairnryan and the new port was inaugurated on 10 July 1973 when *Ionic Ferry* sailed for Larne at 1230 hours with a repeat sailing at 1930 hours. The shorter passage time and the time saved in not having to negotiate the River Ribble up to Preston at times which were dependent on the tides, allowed a much shortened passage time and a regular sailing

*Western Ferries **Sound of Islay** (1968) leaving Campbeltown for Red Bay on Saturday 22 August 1970.*

(Author)

Ailsa Princess (1971) seen arriving at Stranraer on Monday 24 May 1976.
(Author)

Dalriada (1971) seen alongside at Stranraer after the adoption of the Sealink branding in 1973. Note the Swedish flag flying from the mainmast.

Dragon (1967) off Itchen Quays, Southampton on her normal service to Le Havre 31 May 1970.
(Author)

schedule. This was attractive to shippers as the shorter passage at sea more than compensated for the increased road journey, and passenger and vehicle fares were pitched just under the Sealink fares from Stranraer. The **Bardic Ferry** and **Doric Ferry**, however, still maintained the Preston and Belfast service as before.

In July 1971 two new ships started on the Stranraer and Larne service. The first was the **Ailsa Princess** (see chapter 2) which replaced the **Caledonian Princess**, allowing her to return to Fishguard, and the second was a brand new freight ferry chartered from the Swedish Stena Line A/B. This ship was launched as the **Stena Trailer** but was renamed **Dalriada** before she was completed and then painted in full British Railways Board colours, registered in Gothenburg, but with a crew provided by British Transport Ship Management (Scotland) Limited. The **Dalriada** offered 540 lane metres of vehicle space on three decks and replaced the **Baltic Ferry** which was returned to the Atlantic Steam Navigation company. The new ships worked alongside the **Antrim Princess** to provide a three-ship service. The **Ailsa Princess** offered 326 lane metres of garage space up to a maximum cargo deadweight of 600 tons and could accommodate up to 1200 passengers.

For part of the summer season from 1968 until 1971, Southampton based Normandy Ferries ran a passenger and vehicle service between Le Havre and Rosslare with the ferries **Leopard** and **Dragon**. Normandy Ferries was jointly owned by P&O and the French company SAGA, and was P&O's first venture into ferry services. The agent at Rosslare was Government owned Irish Shipping Limited. With nothing scheduled for 1972, Irish Shipping set about creating a new company to continue the service throughout the year to Le Havre. In the event, Irish Shipping put up half the costs of acquiring a new ferry and Lion Ferry A/B of Sweden and Fernley & Eger of Denmark subscribed the remainder. Lion Ferry had on order a suitable drive-through passenger ship under construction at Schichau Unterweser of Bremerhaven in Germany and the contract was transferred to the new company and the ship completed with the name **Saint Patrick**. The service to Le Havre commenced in summer 1973 once the **Saint Patrick** had arrived at Rosslare from her builders. The significance of this development was twofold. Firstly, it diverted traffic from the Irish Sea services by providing a direct link to France and secondly, the new company, trading as Irish Continental Line, would later become an important player on the Irish Sea itself.

During the summer season the **Saint Patrick** left either port on alternate days at 5 pm, and arrived at her destination at 1 pm the next day. This required a service speed of 21 knots. She commenced the service on 2 June. Paul Clegg wrote in *Sea Breezes*, August 1973:

> There are drive-through facilities for 200 cars/30 by 12 metre commercial vehicles (or, of course, a combination of both). Most of the 158 cabins (550 berths) have their own toilets and shower facilities, and all accommodation is air conditioned. There are the usual lounge bars, duty free shop and cafeteria and restaurant, the last two having a combined seating capacity for 560 persons. Total passenger capacity is 1,000.

A freight roll-on roll-off service was commenced between Liverpool and Belfast in February 1971 by the Belfast Steamship Company, part of the Coast Lines group of companies. A second service was started later in the year jointly with British Rail running between Heysham and Belfast. Shortly afterwards the Coast Lines group was bought by P&O.

The Directors of the Belfast Steamship Company were conscious of the inadequacies of the **Ulster Prince** and **Ulster Queen** on the Liverpool and Belfast route and needed to recoup the freight traffic that was diverting to other companies. The Belfast Steamship Company chartered the almost brand-new freight ferry **Donautal** from J S Reinecke of Hamburg and placed her in service between Belfast Donegal Quay and South Nelson Dock at Liverpool, starting on 3 March 1971. She used the Burns and Laird linkspan at Belfast and had to move when the **Lion** came in to berth. The **Donautal** could accommodate up to 30 commercial vehicles and provided berths for 12 drivers. The main deck was arranged for unit loads but dockers

*Donautal (1974), registered at Lübeck, seen arriving at Heysham with the oil jetty beyond her, while she was on charter to the Belfast Steamship Company. The Belfast company bought her in 1974 and renamed her **Ulster Sportsman**.*

refused to handle the ship and she only ever carried wheeled traffic. Nevertheless, her success can be judged by Belfast Steamship buying the vessel in 1974 and giving her the name **Ulster Sportsman**. Under the auspices of P&O, she later adopted the names **Dorset** (for charter to Truckline Ferries at Poole) and from 1978 she was named **St Magnus** when she served on P&O Ferries Orkney and Shetland routes.

The **Saaletal**, sister to the **Donautal**, was also taken on charter in 1971 and placed on the new service between Heysham and Belfast. The **Saaletal** started on the Ardrossan and Belfast route in June 1971 before moving to Heysham in October to join the service that was run jointly with British Rail. In October 1973 a fire aboard **Lion** on the Ardrossan and Belfast route had the **Donautal** deputising for a short period carrying commercial vehicles and drivers only. The vehicle ferry **Sailormark** was chartered from Heier to cover for the **Donautal** at Heysham.

Sister to the **Sailormark**, the **Nanomark**, was chartered by B&I to run between Dublin, Swansea and Le Havre in November 1973. These ships were completed in 1972 for the charter market and were similar to the **Donautal** only smaller. Paul Clegg reported in Sea Breezes, February 1973:

> Figures released last November show that the B & I Line has increased its share of the car traffic between the UK and Eire, to 51% of the total although the troubles in Ulster have led to a general decline in traffic in 1972 by some 37% compared with 1971.

In 1973 the **ASD Meteor** was taken on charter by the Belfast Steamship Company (P&O Ferries) for the joint service with British Rail from Heysham. She had been built as the **Holmia** in 1971 for the Finnish company Silja Line, being renamed **ASD Meteor** two years later. Early in 1975 she was bought outright by the Belfast Steamship Company and in February was chartered for two years to British Rail with the new name **Penda**. Her consort then was the **Ulster Sportsman** but throughout March the **Ulster Sportsman** was at Ardrossan on relief for the **Lion** and the second ship at Heysham was the chartered commercial vehicle ferry **Roro Cimbria**. Sister ship **Roro Dania** was chartered for use at Stranraer while the **Ailsa Princess** was overhauled in April; the Dover based **Maid of Kent** came north to maintain the passenger schedule with cars carried aboard the **Roro Dania**.

In June 1980 the **Penda** was sold to P&O Ferries and given the name **nf Jaguar**. Shortly afterwards she was chartered to the Isle of Man Steam Packet Company which later purchased the ship and named her **Peveril**.

A new service commenced on March 1973 between Barry in South Wales and Dublin. Marketed as Seaspeed Ferries (Seaspeed Ferry Company) in association with Morland Navigation of London, it employed the car transporter **Seaspeed Ferry**, registered in Famagusta. The service was primarily for the transport of trade cars for the Ford Motor Company but it was also available to light commercial freight vehicles, although there were limitations on the height and width of freight vehicles. Seaspeed had purchased the vessel from Elder Dempster Limited of Liverpool, for whom she had been managed by the Mountwood Shipping Company Limited along with three other car carriers. Elder Dempster had given her the name **Clearway** and shortly after renamed her **Speedway**. She had been employed on the trade car traffic from the Continent to and from Southampton. The vessel had been built in 1968 as the **Sealord Challenger** and had been bought by Elder Dempster the following year.

A second quasi-sister, the stern-loading **Seaspeed Trailer**, was purchased in mid-September and shortly afterwards transferred to a new route between Barry and Waterford, once the new linkspan at Waterford had been completed. The **Seaspeed Trailer** was registered in Famagusta under the ownership of Seaspeed Trailerships Limited. She too came from Elder Dempster Limited for whom she had traded as the **Skyway**. Also completed in 1968 the **Seaspeed Trailer** was originally ordered as the **Mandeville** for Norwegian owners.

*Elder Dempster's car carrier **Skyway** (1968) seen here off Test Quays at Southampton in April 1970, was bought by Seaspeed Ferries Limited in 1973 and renamed **Seaspeed Trailer**.*

(Author)

Caledonian Princess (1961) in full Sealink livery approaching Holyhead off the breakwater on 5 September 1974.
(Author)

Free Enterprise III (1966) partnered the *Ionic Ferry* on the Cairnryan and Larne service during the summer months in 1974.
(Author)

Free Enterprise I (1962) seen in the original Townsend Thoresen livery, was sent up from Dover to work from Cairnryan between May and October 1975 alongside *Bardic Ferry*.
(Author)

In 1974 the **Seaspeed Trailer** was replaced by a larger ship, **Seaspeed Challenger**, which had been built as the Italian stern-loading ferry **Monica Rusotti** in 1973. The new ship was registered in Piraeus and also focussed on the trade car traffic for the Ford Motor Company as well as freight vehicles of all sizes and shapes when it inaugurated a new service from Barry to Dublin. The Waterford terminal was then changed to Cork where better facilities for onward transport were available. Paul Clegg wrote in *Sea Breezes*, January 1975:

> From the South Wales port of Barry, Seaspeed Ferries introduced the first of two larger replacement vessels at the end of October [1974]. Named **Seaspeed Challenger**, she has a deadweight of 3,300 tons, a speed of over 21 knots, and can carry up to 75 trailers and 140 cars. Accommodation in cabins is provided for 100 drivers, and she replaced the **Seaspeed Trailer** on the services to Cork and Dublin...

In 1973 the Fishguard and Rosslare route was reduced to just one passenger ship, the **Caledonian Princess**. Extra car space had been constructed in the form of a half mezzanine type deck increasing her capacity from 103 cars to 131. In July the commercial vehicle carrier **Neckartal**, owned by J S Reinecke, was chartered, initially for 18 weeks, to develop the commercial traffic with one round trip a day. However, she could not use the linkspan at Rosslare one hour either side of low tide as her garage deck offered too little freeboard. As a consequence, she was transferred to Stranraer at the end of November. That year the **Caledonian Princess** deputised at Heysham while the two Dukes were overhauled. As the Sealink ships emerged from overhaul in 1973 they retained the same monastral blue-grey hull and red funnel with twin arrow device as before but now had the banner SEALINK emblazoned along their sides in white, an experiment tried in 1972 on the Folkestone based ships. The **Neckartal** was replaced in 1974 by the **Stena Carrier** which adopted the name **Ulidia** ready to work alongside the **Dalriada** at Stranraer. The **Ulidia** offered 500 lane metres garage space and could accommodate 36 passengers.

The **Isartal** (a sister to **Saaletal** and **Neckartal**) was chartered from J S Reinecke by Atlantic Steam for some months towards the end of 1973 and in February 1974 was used at Preston to relieve the Preston and Belfast ships. The **Doric Ferry** made her last trip from Preston to Belfast on 11 May 1974 and the **Bardic Ferry** closed the service on 28 June when Preston ceased to be a ferry port.

On 1 July 1974 the Cairnryan and Larne service received the **Free Enterprise III** from Dover to work alongside the **Ionic Ferry**. The registered owner of the **Free Enterprise III** was the Stanhope Steamship Company Limited, which was then a shell company under Townsend Thoresen ownership. She offered vastly superior accommodation to any ship previously employed on the route with much larger passenger accommodation and better facilities than the **Ionic Ferry**. She was intended to develop the tourist traffic as well as the commercial vehicle service. Her schedule offered three departures from both ports, lying overnight at Larne. She stood down for the winter in October, and the **Bardic Ferry**, like her sister with enhanced passenger accommodation, then joined the **Ionic Ferry** to provide four sailings a day. Despite heavy bookings during holiday periods the **Free Enterprise III** had made an overall loss on the route.

The port of Larne was acquired by European Ferries during 1973 in order to ensure suitable berthing slots for its vessels at that port, while a second linkspan was constructed at Cairnryan. In 1975 the Cairnryan and Larne service was operated by **Bardic Ferry** and **Ionic Ferry** and over the summer period, starting on 22 May 1975, also by the **Free Enterprise I** on transfer from Dover. Smaller than **Free Enterprise III**, and with little space for commercial traffic, she too lost money on the route despite her popularity during the summer holidays.

The **Isartal**, which briefly carried the name **Antwerpen**, was bought by the P&O subsidiary Rollonoff Shipping Company Limited of London in 1974 and chartered in April to the British Transport Commission. She was renamed **Preseli** and put in service between Fishguard and Rosslare. In November her owners became P&O Ferries although outwardly there was no change. **Preseli** deputised at Stranraer that autumn, but she otherwise served on the Fishguard station until the charter ended in April 1977.

The Heysham and Belfast service operated by the **Duke of Argyll** and **Duke of Lancaster** was closed on 6 April 1975. The **Duke of Lancaster** took over the Fishguard route from **Caledonian Princess** in May, and was replaced on 18 July by the **Avalon**, formerly at Harwich, and newly converted at a cost of £1.7 million into a stern-loading car ferry with capacity for 198 cars. The **Caledonian Princess** then left the Irish Sea for duties at Weymouth. By way of compensation, the **Holyhead Ferry I** inaugurated a new all-year-round commercial vehicle service between Holyhead and Dun Laoghaire while a new ship was ordered for the route for delivery in 1977. In the meantime, either **Holyhead Ferry I** or **Dover** was stationed at Holyhead.

The **Avalon** had a deep draft which caused problems at Rosslare and in January 1976 she was switched to Holyhead. Nevertheless, her arrival in the Irish Sea coupled with the closure of the Heysham-Belfast passenger service in April released both the **Duke of Rothesay** and **Duke of Argyll** which were sold in the autumn, the former scrapped at Faslane, the latter for service under the Greek flag.

As from 7 July 1975 the joint P&O Ferries and British Rail service between Heysham and Belfast was terminated. The **Ulster Sportsman** was withdrawn leaving the **Penda** in charge of a reduced schedule. The **Ulster Sportsman** was chartered to Seaspeed Ferries at Barry as a replacement for the **Seaspeed Challenger**. The **Ulster Sportsman** carried a converted car road transporter which was discharged at both Dublin and Cork and used to drive new Ford cars from the upper deck directly onto the quayside.

The **Seaspeed Challenger** had been transferred to a new Felixstowe to the Mediterranean service. The inaugural sailing from Felixstowe was on 18 July and was managed by Seaspeed Ferries International of Piraeus and Monrovia, later trading as Fred Olsen Seaspeed Ferries.

The Barry and Cork/Dublin services closed in September 1975, the Ford Motor Company contract then awarded elsewhere, and the original ship, the **Seaspeed Ferry**, was sold to the Carlton Steamship Company of Newcastle. The **Ulster Sportsman** was returned to Belfast Steamship Company and renamed **Dorset** for a charter to Truckline Ferries at Poole which had just been awarded a contract to import new Citroen cars from Cherbourg.

In July 1974, P&O announced an intention to start a new commercial vehicle and trailer service between Fleetwood and Larne commencing in February 1975 under the title Pandoro Limited. Stena Line A/B had speculatively ordered two stern-loading vehicle carriers from J J Sietas KG Schiffswerft GmbH in Hamburg. P&O bought them on the stocks and directed their completion as the sisters **Bison** and **Buffalo**. The intention was that the ships would be managed by the Belfast Steamship Company. The vehicle decks were arranged with a fixed ramp to access the main deck, with a 32 ton lift from the central vehicle deck to the lower deck. A joint arrangement with the B&I Line was announced the following January whereby a second route would be inaugurated between Fleetwood and Dublin.

The **Bison** started at Liverpool in January 1975 carrying cars to Belfast but transferred to the Fleetwood and Larne route once the Fleetwood terminal was ready at the end of February. The other ship, the **Buffalo** was placed under the ownership of WL Ferries Limited (WL standing for Wyre and Liffey), which was owned jointly by P&O subsidiary Pandoro (P AND O Roll On/off) and B&I. She started on the Dublin service in early April using the B&I terminal at Dublin. This began a long and productive partnership between the **Buffalo** and

Bison, both ships later to have extensive passenger accommodation added and hulls lengthened plus other modifications to suit the evolving needs of the Irish Sea trades. As built, they had 1190 lane metres of stowage, but this had been increased to 1674 lane metres in the case of the ***Bison*** by 1995 and to 1608 lane metres aboard the ***Buffalo*** from 1998.

Trade Unions were powerful bodies in the 1970s and were held in respect by shipowners and shippers alike. A strike of Scottish lorry drivers during the late summer 1974 had little effect on the ferries but that of the Northern Irish drivers, which followed, brought all vehicle services between Scotland and the port of Larne to a standstill. Although an unofficial strike, aggressive picketing made loading and unloading untenable. The Larne and Cairnryan sailings were suspended on 31 October 1974, the ***Lion*** stopped running between Ardrossan and Larne on 4 November and the Sealink service between Stranraer and Larne was suspended the following day. The ***Lion*** had only just transferred her Northern Irish terminal from Belfast to Larne. Overnight services between Belfast and Heysham and Belfast and Liverpool were unaffected, just as the old schedule of the ***Lion*** would also have continued without hindrance.

On 12 September 1974, a new commercial vehicle ferry was launched at the Verolme Cork Dockyard and christened ***Dundalk***. She was actually owned by Allied Irish Banks Limited and leased to B&I. The ***Dundalk*** was designed principally for service between Liverpool and Dublin. However, before she was delivered British & Irish had committed itself to a joint service with the new Pandoro freight route between Dublin and Fleetwood and the new ship was effectively redundant. In October 1974 she was advertised for sale for £3.5 million as lying at Verolme yard in Cork. There were no takers. Fortunately, she was able to take up a charter to Citroen cars on delivery to B&I in January 1975, working on a service between St Nazaire and Vigo. Thereafter, the ***Dundalk*** drifted from one charter to the next with occasional service for her owners in the Irish Sea.

On 27 September 1975, ***Lion*** closed the Ardrossan and Larne service. The route had suffered at the hands of European Ferries at Cairnryan and the ship was badly needed elsewhere in the P&O network. ***Lion*** was refitted for service on the English Channel without change of name.

The period 1971 to 1975 had been one of dynamic growth for the roll-on roll-off services between Great Britain and the island of Ireland. Drive-through vessels were established and dedicated commercial vehicle ferries had come into service, albeit chartered from a diverse range of shipowners. One significant change was tenure, a ship could be brought into the Irish Sea for any period between a few weeks or months to a few years. None were expected to last for the 20 or 30 years of service on one route that the conventional ships before them had enjoyed.

The first class service offered in the 1960s was withdrawn as one class ships came on stream. This was most notable in the case of the Atlantic Steam Navigation ships which had offered a very high standard in first class between Preston and Larne and Preston and Belfast. Once transferred to Cairnryan the ships catered for greater numbers of passengers in one class, no longer offering a silver service restaurant or allowing car drivers to leave their vehicles on the quayside so that a driver in white coat and gloves could load them aboard before the ship sailed.

During all the exciting developments of the early 1970s the Isle of Man Steam Packet Company still resisted the idea of stern-loading vehicle ferries and ordered two more, by now rather quaint, spiral-ramp-access car and passenger ferries. There had been a warning shot across the company's bows in 1969 when a new company, Norwest Hovercraft Limited, ran the chartered stern-loading roll-on roll-off passenger ferry ***Stella Marina*** between Fleetwood and Douglas for passengers only in the summer season. The company had been set up the previous year to run an experimental side wall Denny D2 class hovercraft, which had been designed and built by Denny Hovercraft Limited, a subsidiary of William Denny & Brothers of Dumbarton. Hovercraft ***002*** was advertised at Fleetwood with the name ***Denny Enterprise***. The plan was to run a passenger service from Fleetwood with a view to opening a route to Douglas – it was not a success as John Hobbs reported in *Sea Breezes*, August 1979:

> What Denny did was to form in 1968 a subsidiary, Norwest Hovercraft Ltd, and plan a service between Fleetwood and Barrow. After being made ready at Poole, ***002*** travelled under her own power to Fleetwood... The first passenger runs between the two north west ports were made on August 19, but only on that day because it was decided that a more profitable and less vulnerable operation would be 30 minute runs out and back from Fleetwood. A trans-Mersey route was mooted for the following year but came to nothing and ***003*** was operated out of Fleetwood for a time in 1969...

The shipping interests came about as a supporting venture to bring much needed income to the company and this side of the business was championed by motorcycle ace Geoff Duke. At the end of the 1969 summer season operating ***Stella Marina*** to Douglas, the company asked the Isle of Man Harbour Board if a linkspan could be built on the north side of King Edward Pier so that they could better utilise their ship next summer. Happily, for the Steam Packet company, the proposed charter of a bigger roll-on roll-off ship for use the following year fell through and construction of the linkspan was not pursued. The company went into liquidation at the end of the 1970 season.

In August 1969 the Board of the Steam Packet company outlined their proposed new car ferry. She was to be similar to the earlier steam turbine ferries, ***Manx Maid*** and ***Ben-my-Chree***, the only radical change being that oil engines were preferred over steam.

The first new ship was built by Ailsa Shipbuilding Company at Troon and christened ***Mona's Queen***, at her launch on 21 December 1971, and was delivered in time for the next summer season although engineering work delayed her arrival at Douglas until after the TT Races. A repeat order led to the delivery of the ***Lady of Mann*** in June 1976.

Development of roll-on roll-off traffic on the Irish Sea in the early 1970s took place during increased unease and tension in both the north and south of Ireland. By mid-1972 there were 200 British soldiers in Northern Ireland for every 1000 head of population. This tension was accompanied by terrorist attacks on civilian targets. However, in 1973 the Sunningdale Agreement laid the way for the establishment of the Northern Ireland Assembly. Unsurprisingly, tourist traffic was almost at a standstill, and economic expansion was stagnating.

The severity of the situation in Ireland was brought home to seafarers on Irish Sea services with the death of Captain Curry in May 1973. Captain Curry of the unit load ship ***Orwell Fisher*** was shot dead in a terrorist attack in Tomb Street, near Donegall Quay, Belfast. The ship, owned by James Fisher, was on charter to Atlantic Steam Navigation Company and served between Belfast or Larne and Preston; Captain Curry had been appointed master of ***Orwell Fisher*** in March 1972 and was highly regarded.

Avalon (1963) approaching Parkeston Quay on 30 August 1974, ready to embark passengers for her final voyage to Hoek van Holland before being withdrawn and converted into a car ferry for the Fishguard and Rosslare service.
(Author)

Buffalo (1975) as built and in the original livery of black hull and blue funnel with a black top.
(Author)

Bison (1975), lengthened in 1988 and as modified in summer 1995 with an additional uppermost third vehicle deck and stability sponsons. She was photographed arriving at Larne on 16 May 1996.
(Author)

33

*Steamship **Ben-my-Chree** (1966) leaving Liverpool off Princes Landing Stage on 11 July 1969.*

(Author)

*Motor vessel **Mona's Queen** (1972) off Princes Landing Stage on 21 September 1973 and clearly of the same pedigree as the steamships.*

(Author)

CHAPTER 4
THE FIRST OF THE SECOND-GENERATION FERRIES

*The last conventional Irish Sea passenger mail ship **Hibernia** (1948), seen arriving from Dun Laoghaire off the Holyhead Breakwater, 5 September 1974.*

(Author)

By the mid-1970s the British Railways Board was accused of deliberately running down those services that were least profitable with a view to closing them. This was encapsulated in a short paper issued by the Merchant Navy and Airline Officers' Association entitled *British Rail Shipping – is there something wrong?*. At that time the Belfast and Heysham service had just been closed while the newly converted stern-loading ships on the service, **Duke of Argyll** and **Duke of Lancaster**, had been found to be largely unsuitable for the traffic on offer. Unit load services on the route had also been reduced. Shortly afterwards the *Irish Times* accused British Rail of 'running down the Fishguard and Waterford cargo service' to make it unprofitable as an excuse to close this crane-on, crane-off service altogether. Could it be that this decline was to optimise the sale price of the Sealink organisation which would inevitably be offered to the private sector at some time in the future?

Both Sealink (Shipping and International Services Division) and B&I were bound by Government red tape. Commitment by Sealink of expenditure greater than £0.5 million required ministerial approval, the lead time for which was at least nine months. Equivalent approval in the private sector amounted to just one or two weeks. Although new ships were yet to be commissioned, reliance on chartered vessels became increasingly important to Sealink. For the moment B&I was financially underpinned by the Irish Government and foresaw no problems with money. In June 1976 they announced that extensive discussions with the Irish Government had allowed them to order a new ship from the Cork Verolme Shipyard at a cost of £11.5 million. The new ship was destined for the Dublin and Liverpool route and would displace either **Munster** or **Leinster** to the Cork service.

The announcement that the **Holyhead Ferry I** was to be rebuilt as a drive-through vehicle ferry with additional space for commercial vehicles did little to instil confidence in the Sealink brand. At an estimated cost of £1.8 million the conversion would provide an additional ship (to be renamed **Earl Leofric**) for the Dover Strait services, albeit an expensive oil-fuelled steam turbine unit. Her sister **Dover** was undergoing a major refit to suit the Fishguard and Rosslare service. Nevertheless, work had been put in hand to widen the harbour at Holyhead ready for the new ship building in Denmark. She was launched at Aalborg on 17 July and christened **St Columba**.

But for the moment business was good, and even the unsuitable Belfast Steamship Company vessels, **Ulster Queen** and **Ulster Prince**, enjoyed a good year in 1975 with traffic up by 30%. The company lost its identity the following winter when it was rebranded as a component of P&O Ferries. The ships received blue funnels and the hulls were defaced with their new owner's name.

The conventional passenger ferry **Hibernia** followed her sister **Cambria** into retirement with a final arrival at Holyhead from Dun Laoghaire on 5 October 1975. There was considerable outcry from regular travellers who had enjoyed the overnight sleeping berths offered by the conventional ships with disembarkation at their leisure. The **Hibernia** was sold to Greek owners for further service. The **Cambria** and **Hibernia** had maintained the Holyhead and Dun Laoghaire service following the introduction of the car ferry **Holyhead Ferry I** (or **Dover**). However, the car ferries were found to be difficult to berth in high winds and on many occasions the mail ships sailed as normal while the car ferry was delayed or did not sail at all.

In March the **Avalon** hit the harbour wall at Holyhead and had to be withdrawn for three weeks. Meantime, the **Maid of Kent** was brought to Fishguard to allow the **Dover** to stand in for the **Avalon**. The **Maid of Kent** was relieved by **Duke of Lancaster** at the beginning of April until **Avalon** finally returned to Fishguard on 25 June 1976.

*The Dover- and latterly Weymouth-based **Maid of Kent** (1959) was an increasingly familiar sight on the Irish Sea standing in for vessels on a variety of routes but mainly at Fishguard.*

(Author)

***Free Enterprise IV** (1969) seen leaving Cairnryan on 24 May 1976, four days after her inaugural sailing on the Cairnryan and Larne service.*

(Author)

The big news on the Scottish front was the announcement that the *Free Enterprise IV* would serve on the Cairnryan and Larne link from 20 May onwards. This intended transfer from Dover took heed of the loss-making seasons of the previous two years when first *Free Enterprise III* and then in 1975 the smaller *Free Enterprise I* were used on the route. However, neither ship offered much commercial vehicle space whereas the *Free Enterprise IV* provided much needed accommodation for any conceivable mix of commercial and private vehicles that might be required. This was a bold move on the part of European Ferries, but a move which later proved to have established the Cairnryan-Larne link as the premier commercial and passenger vehicle service to Northern Ireland.

The arrival of the *Free Enterprise IV* allowed the *Doric Ferry* to withdraw to Harland & Wolff at Belfast for the enlargement of her passenger facilities for 120 passengers and drivers. An additional pair of lifeboats were added in compliance with the requirements of the enlarged passenger certificate. When *Doric Ferry* returned to Cairnryan the *Cerdic Ferry* went back to the Felixstowe routes. Meanwhile, the *Bardic Ferry* and *Ionic Ferry* were sold in April for further service under the Italian flag. As their faster consorts had grown in size and capacity these two smaller ships had become outmoded, their job of pioneering the modern roll-on roll-off traffic in the Irish Sea completed. The *Cerdic Ferry* returned to Larne in mid-September to work alongside *Doric Ferry*, while *Free Enterprise IV* was being refitted at Belfast before she returned to Dover. *Free Enterprise IV* came back to the Larne service in March the following year, 1977.

At Stranraer both the *Ulidia* and *Dalriada* were working the freight service out of Stranraer, and sister *Anderida* was working until the end of June between Heysham and Belfast. The *Anderida* had previously been employed at Dover as a train ferry but she also offered 560 lane metres of road vehicle capacity up to a maximum cargo deadweight of 760 tons. The pioneer stern-loader *Slieve Donard* was sold in June; a versatile ship that was used to bring cattle to Wales and send new cars to Ireland for much of her career, as well as support the passenger mail ships in a car-carrying mode during summer periods. P&O chartered the German freight ferry *Roro Anglia* as a replacement for the *Lion* for service from Ardrossan - once again to Belfast and not Larne. However, the National Union of Seamen were investigating the legitimacy of a ship flying the German flag with a German crew being allowed to work between Great Britain and Northern Ireland.

The *Penda* suffered a serious engine room fire on passage from Belfast to Heysham on 19 October 1976. Her 18 crew fought the blaze for an hour before bringing it under control. She was able to proceed on one engine to Heysham to discharge before going to the engineering section at Holyhead for repairs. The former LMS dry dock and engineering unit was still active and dealt with a number of the ships in the fleet over the year, for example the *Earl Godwin* from Weymouth was dry docked in November and the *Anderida* had work done to her bow later the same month. The *Penda* was replaced at Heysham by *Anderida* from 26 October until the return of *Penda* from Holyhead on 20 November.

The new Pandoro services between Fleetwood and Larne and the joint service with B&I to Dublin had made significant inroads. Fleetwood was convenient for the motorway system which allowed ready access to the Midlands and the south of England as well as the industrial north-west of England. The services quickly became popular with the unaccompanied trailer traffic; a road tractor unit dropped its trailer in the dispatch compound and collected an inbound trailer from the arrivals compound for inland delivery. At the appropriate time the outward trailer would be collected by a port tractor and pushed trailer first aboard ship ready for it to be quickly towed off at the destination. Throughout the latter half of 1976 sailings achieved over 80% capacity.

Early in 1977 Pandoro was empowered by P&O to order two new ships which were intended for the Fleetwood and Dublin service. The ships were ordered from Mitsui Zosen at Tamano in Japan with delivery scheduled for mid-1979, and the design centred on three vehicle decks with capacity for a total of 125 trailers. In order to develop the service and ensure that the services were not over-booked the *Stena Trailer* was chartered from Stena Line A/B and offered a scheduled departure from Larne at 1100 hours with the *Bison* leaving at 2300 hours for Fleetwood. The *Stena Trailer* was replaced later in the year by the chartered and brand new *Jaguar*.

Anderida (1972) started on Fishguard-Rosslare freight sailings in May 1977 as a replacement for the chartered Preseli.

(Author)

*The **Jaguar** (1977) was chartered by Pandoro from Stena Line in April 1977, fresh from her builders where she was launched as **Stena Timer**. She is seen on the approach to Fleetwood.*

(Bernard McCall)

The **Jaguar** was launched at the end of January as **Stena Timer**, but delivered to her charterers as **Jaguar**. She adopted the company's blue funnel although she retained her owner's white hull. She was of the same pedigree as **Bison** and **Buffalo** and offered exactly the same cargo capacity as these ships except she had no berths available for drivers.

The story at Fishguard was quite different with Sealink/British Rail reportedly losing £365,000 on the service to Rosslare during 1976. Reduced services were announced, including the replacement of the cargo only **Preseli** by **Anderida** during April, with a schedule of only one round trip rather than two per day. The **Preseli** was returned to her owners, now P&O Ferries, and was put in service between Ardrossan and Larne as a replacement for the chartered **Roro Anglia**. **Preseli** was renamed **Pointer** later in the year.

British Rail's new ship for the Holyhead and Dun Laoghaire service, **St Columba**, arrived at Holyhead on 6 April 1977, berthing at the new outer harbour at Salt Island. Her arrival into service in early May was marred by the Irish Minister of Local Government announcing a cap on the number of lorries passing through Dun Laoghaire of just 100,000 per year and forbidding the transport of cattle on lorries being loaded at Dun Laoghaire. **St Columba** commenced her twice daily return trips on 2 May making the crossing in 3½ hours with ease; her passenger certificate was increased at the end of May to 1600 persons. However, passenger access at Holyhead was often via a steeply inclined gangway, not an easy entrance to the ship for the elderly and infirm. She was supported by **Duke of Lancaster** which did one round trip a day, two at peak holiday times. **Earl Siward** (ex-**Dover**) deputised on the route during October.

The **St Columba** was a drive-through ship with space for up to 335 cars or 36 standard 12 metre long commercial vehicles. There were no berths available for passengers but ample covered seating was available for everybody except at peak times when seats were at a premium. She offered self-service cafeterias and a waiter served restaurant as well as two bars (aptly named Lansdowne and Cardiff Arms), a discothèque, shops and television lounges. As the political unrest in Ireland had subdued the ship attracted tourists wishing to travel with their own cars. At times during that first summer **St Columba** was fully booked with little space left for commercial vehicles.

British Rail placed an order with Harland & Wolff at Belfast for a new ship to operate on the Stranraer and Larne service. The existing vessels on the service had lost a lot of traffic to the Townsend Thoresen ships that were working from Cairnryan, and a new vessel for Stranraer was intended to recoup some of these losses. The design differed from that of the **St Columba** and focussed on vehicle decks that could be loaded and unloaded simultaneously to accommodate 60 standard length lorries or 300 private cars. Delivery was anticipated in time for the 1979 summer season. Considerable dredging work was put in place at Stranraer to allow access for the ship and construction of a new twin level linkspan was also started at Larne.

Following pressure from the Irish Government, the Irish Continental Line bought out the Swedish Lion Ferry A/B share of the company with Coras Iompar Eireann retaining 20% of the ownership on behalf of the Irish Government. The **Saint Patrick** continued to operate alone between Rosslare and Le Havre but the company stated that a second or larger ship would be desirable in due course. The **Saint Patrick** was unable to cope with the peak summer demand and some intending passengers were regularly directed to alternative routes.

In January 1978, Irish Continental Line announced that it had signed a contract to purchase the **Stena Scandinavica** from Stena A/B. She had been built in 1973 by Titovo Brodogradiliste at Kraljevica in Yugoslavia. The ship could accommodate 250 cars plus commercial vehicles, and up to 1500 passengers with 857 berths. The purchase deal was completed on 21 February 1978 although the ship remained on her Gothenburg and Kiel route on charter from her new owners with the new name **Saint Killian** and the port of Wexford on her stern. Later repainted with the new Irish Continental Line colours and

St Columba (1977) departing Holyhead stern first – a large ship in a small channel.

(Author)

a green funnel and large white shamrock, she left for Rosslare on 9 April. Her first duty was to relieve the **Saint Patrick** which returned from overhaul also adorned with the new funnel colours. Thereafter, the two ships maintained a summer schedule that provided five round trips to Le Havre and two to Cherbourg.

The B&I Cork and Swansea service suffered declining patronage during 1977. This reflected the upgraded Sealink service between Fishguard and Rosslare and the long passage time required on the Cork service. The outcome was an announcement by B&I that they intended to move from Swansea to Pembroke Dock as the Welsh terminal in summer 1978. A new terminal was built at Pembroke Dock in the spring of 1978 at a cost of £4 million while new terminal facilities at Cork were being constructed at Ringaskiddy. The **Stena Germanica** was chartered to cover the winter overhaul period.

An unusual charter cover for overhauls was that for the **Ailsa Princess** and **Antrim Princess** when the rival European Ferries ship **Cerdic Ferry** appeared at Stranraer for five weeks. **Cerdic Ferry** had her company name painted out on her orange hull and the funnel painted red for the duration.

A new ship, **Darnia**, was commissioned for the Sealink Stranraer and Larne service. The **Darnia** was one of three identical ships ordered by Stena Line A/B from Osterreiche Schiffswerften AG, Linz-Korneuburg in Austria. She was launched as **Stena Topper**, and towed down the Danube to be fitted out in Romania. The ship was then bought by James Fisher & Sons Limited of Barrow for charter to Sealink for the Stranraer and Larne service. Her Stena Line livery was promptly replaced by Sealink colours and the ship renamed **Darnia**. Initially she only had accommodation for 18 drivers but had an impressive 915 lane metres of garage space. The passenger certificate was increased to 75 and stabilizers were added before she entered into service; passenger accommodation increased again to 412 persons in the early 1980s.

The new double-deck linkspan at Larne was commissioned in April ready for the **Darnia** to use. Delays in modifying the ship for service meant that she did not start at Stranraer until 10 August 1978. That same day, the **Dalriada** left for Holyhead to replace the chartered **Transbaltica**, the freight ship taking the commercial traffic to allow the passenger vehicle ferries **St Columba** and **Duke of Lancaster** to concentrate on tourist traffic. Both **Duke of Lancaster** and **Dalriada** stood down on 9 November.

British Rail announced that the Fishguard service would be increased to three ships for summer 1978 with **Anderida** and **Avalon** supplemented between 13 July and 3 September by the venerable car ferry **Lord Warden** from the Dover Strait. **Lord Warden** was scheduled to provide an overnight return to Rosslare departing Fishguard at 2200 hours and a day return to Dun Laoghaire departing Fishguard at 0800. Passage time on the Dun Laoghaire service was 5½ hours. For service on the Irish Sea her half gate across the stern was raised to the poop deck and her passenger certificate reduced to 600. The ship offered few creature comforts particularly on the night service as she was essentially a day boat. **Lord Warden** is remembered on the Irish Sea for her anachronistic character, small capacity and especially for the dried-out croissants kept for too long under an infra-red heater in the cafeteria display cabinet.

A newly formed company registered in Douglas, Isle of Man, the Manx Line, announced the purchase of the **Monte Castillo** for £5 million from the Spanish Aznar Line in February 1978. The new company was promoted by motor cycle champion Geoff Duke. He had also been responsible for the Norwest Hovercraft initiative to run a roll-on roll-off ferry to Douglas in the early 1970s (see Chapter 3). The objective of the new company was to operate the stern-loading ferry on a new service between Heysham and Douglas in direct competition with the Isle of Man Steam Packet Company and its unique side-loading car ferries. The new company would offer a service that not only included cars and passengers but would also offer space for commercial vehicles. The Steam Packet company had dragged its heels for so long on the issue of commercial traffic that the Isle of Man Harbour Board had openly canvassed for a new service. Work was immediately put in hand to build a new approach road to the Victoria Pier where a new linkspan was also being constructed.

*1976 brochure for the Irish Continental Line's Rosslare and Le Havre service featuring the **Saint Patrick** (1973).*

(Author's Collection)

The Harbour Board were nervous about the ship coming into harbour stern first and insisted that she be converted to drive-through with a new bow door. This work was undertaken at Leith while the ship was repainted in the new company livery and renamed **Manx Viking**, with Douglas as her port of registry. In addition, the refrigeration plant used to chill the lower hold, previously used to import fresh produce to England, was stripped out, and five additional bulkheads fitted in this cargo space. She retained her 450 ton fuel oil bunker which had allowed over three weeks at sea. She offered accommodation for 1000 passengers and 250 cars or a mix with commercial vehicles. The scheduled start date was 1 June 1978 – but this was not to be. Rescheduled for 1 July, an onboard fire made this impossible too and the service finally started on 26 August.

The start of the new service was not auspicious as on 8 September the port engine failed. Repairs allowed a cargo only service to resume from 18 September but she was again withdrawn for further attention five days later. In October **Manx Viking** resumed cargo sailings but on one engine and on 23 October she started the nine round trips a week, cargo only winter schedule. Within days it was announced that James Fisher & Sons Limited and British Rail had taken over the company which would continue to trade under its own name. James Fisher took a 40% share and British Rail a 60% share. Storms sank the linkspan at Douglas in December but, undeterred, the **Manx Viking** was sent to Belfast to have her accommodation enlarged for 840 persons and she was ready to start again once the linkspan was reinstated. The full cargo and passenger service recommenced the following summer with the first voyage taken on 26 August 1979.

Darnia (1977) seen arriving at Stranraer Pier in May 1984, the twin arrow logo removed from her funnel in readiness for the new Sealink British Ferries logo.

(Author)

Pandoro took the Stena Line ship **Union Melbourne** on charter in November 1978 for the service to Larne. She replaced the chartered **Jaguar**. The attraction of the new ship was that although she was a sister to **Bison** and **Buffalo** she had been lengthened on completion by 17 metres to increase her freight capacity to 110 standard trailers. Her name reflected her first charter which was to the Union Steamship Company of New Zealand. Pandoro had now also developed a substantial road haulage fleet offering door to door transport of trailers.

Once again, the **Cerdic Ferry**, **Doric Ferry** and **Free Enterprise IV** maintained the Cairnryan and Larne link. However, **Cerdic Ferry** left for Felixstowe in July 1979.

It was announced that the net profit of the B&I Line in 1978 was up by a staggering 83% over the previous year at £1.35 million. This scale of expansion was not to last. Brittany Ferries had started a weekly service from Cork to Roscoff and B&I dearly wanted something similar. However, this was not to be realised.

Launched on 20 June at Cork, the new B&I ferry **Connacht** entered service on 7 February 1979 with a maiden departure from Cork to Swansea. Like **St Columba**, the **Connacht** was truly a second-generation multi-purpose ferry offering much greater capacity than her earlier consorts with accommodation for 1500 persons and up to 350 cars or 40 standard commercial vehicles. Cabin accommodation was provided above and below the vehicle decks with passenger accommodation spread over five decks. Her Welsh terminal switched to Pembroke Dock from 22 May 1979 and, thereafter, she maintained a departure from Cork at 0930 hours and from Pembroke Dock at 2200 hours. With the arrival of **Connacht** in service B&I announced that they had placed an order for a sister ship from the Cork Verolme Shipyard for delivery in 1981 at a cost of £20 million.

Lord Warden (1952) was brought to Fishguard from Dover in July 1978 to operate extra overnight sailings to Rosslare and a new daylight service to Dun Laoghaire.

(Author)

Connacht had displaced the **Innisfallen** which moved to Liverpool to relieve the **Munster** and **Leinster**. A three ship summer service was anticipated between Liverpool and Dublin but traffic did not come up to expectations and the **Munster** was withdrawn, later chartered to Brittany Ferries, and after lay up in Dublin was reactivated as relief ship in October to stand in for the **Innisfallen**.

As from 1 January 1979 the Sealink brand was enhanced to Sealink UK Limited, a company which from then on owned or leased nearly all the former British Rail/Sealink ships. This company was a wholly owned subsidiary of the British Railways Board and was intended to take the shipping division forward to privatisation sometime in the early 1980s. There was no obvious reason why Government should retain these assets any longer and the belief was that they would be better resourced and developed in the private sector.

A new ship for the Fishguard and Rosslare service was ordered from Harland & Wolff at Belfast in October 1978 as a sister to the vessel

*The stern-loading vehicle and passenger ferry **Manx Viking** (1976), seen arriving at Heysham on the second day of her new service between Heysham and Douglas for the newly formed Manx Line.*

(Author)

*The second-generation B&I vehicle and passenger ferry **Connacht** (1978) seen arriving at Holyhead on 17 July 1984 with the owner's name and route details painted on her hull.*

(Author)

***Stena Normandica** (1974) was chartered in March 1979 from Stena Line A/B to serve between Fishguard and Rosslare as a replacement for **Avalon** until the new build was available. She is seen at Fishguard.*

(Bernard McCall)

already on order for use at Stranraer (**Galloway Princess**). In the meantime Stena Line's **Stena Normandica** was taken on an initial 19 month charter to replace the **Avalon** at Fishguard. This allowed the **Avalon** to move to Holyhead and the **Anderida** to return to Dover. The design of the **Stena Normandica** and her three sisters was innovative as described by Rickard Sahlsten and his co-authors in their history of the Stena Line:

> Articulated lorries and trailers could be loaded onto two fixed loading decks – the upper via a 19 metre ramp – which provided the capacity for as many as 44 by 18 metre articulated lorries or 63 by 12 metre trailers. For passenger traffic, there was space for as many as 480 private cars on a total of four decks, two of which were platforms which could be raised and lowered.
>
> These ships were also built as semi-catamarans as the below water section aft was shaped like a catamaran hull. This meant improved propeller efficiency and stability but also gave a higher block coefficient which gave a greater load capacity.

The **Stena Normandica** was welcomed at Fishguard when she arrived on 2 March 1979. Her arrival certainly helped to put the Fishguard and Rosslare route back on the map; both passenger and freight numbers had increased by mid-summer and prospects at last began to look up for the route. However, for the first few weeks in service she only provided the freight capacity while passengers were carried aboard the old **Lord Warden**.

Both **Avalon** and **Anderida** went to Holyhead to provide relief for **St Columba** while the latter ship was undergoing her annual overhaul. However, **Anderida** had suffered an engine room fire in February and was still under repair and so the former Pandoro ship **Jaguar**, again renamed **Stena Timer**, took her place until **Anderida** was available later in the month. **Stena Timer** had also stood in for the **Darnia** at Stranraer in January while the latter was off service for engine repairs. The former Heysham steamer **Duke of Lancaster** was sold, sadly to end her days rotting in a concrete berth in North Wales.

*The new freight ferry **Ibex** (1979) led the way for the second-generation of freight ferries on the Irish Sea – she is seen leaving Fleetwood on 8 April 1980.*

(Author)

During the early summer, the **Stena Normandica** broke down and was taken off service. The **Lord Warden** was on duty between 13 July and 2 September and then stood down to lay up awaiting sale. The small roll-on roll-off freighter **Ilkka** was chartered to help, her owners were Tejo Leasing Limited of London, a company operating mainly overseas charters.

The new Stranraer ship was launched on 24 May at Belfast. There was neither ceremony nor naming of the vessel but as she took to the water it was announced that her name was to be **Galloway Princess**. The cost of her construction had been underwritten by Midland Montagu Leasing. It would be nearly a year before the ship was ready to enter service. In the meantime, the **Stena Timer** resumed at Stranraer in April after finishing at Holyhead. **Stena Timer** was back at Holyhead in the Autumn supporting **Maid of Kent** while **St Columba** was off duty with failed gears.

The two new ferries for Pandoro were built at a cost of £1.5 million. The first of them, named **Ibex**, was delivered in May 1979. The **Ibex** had been launched by her Japanese builders, Mitsui Zosen, the previous December. The new ship was found difficult to handle at Fleetwood and went to Belfast to have modifications made to her propellers. She returned on duty in September, initially working between Fleetwood and Larne to allow the **Union Melbourne** to relieve the **Elk** on the P&O Ferrymasters cargo service from the Tees to Gothenburg, after which the **Ibex** transferred to the Dublin and Fleetwood route.

The sister to the **Ibex** was launched on 20 April 1979 and named **Puma**. On completion she was renamed **Tipperary** and registered at Dublin, having been sold by P&O Ferries to Ensign Tankers (Leasing) Limited and chartered to B&I Line. She commenced on the Fleetwood and Dublin service in late October 1979, in full B&I livery, working alongside her sister **Ibex**. The commissioning of **Tipperary** in

*The **Tipperary** (1979) in full B&I livery, departing Fleetwood for Dublin on the high tide on 25 October 1980.*

(Author)

43

Ulster Queen (1967) off the Waterloo Dock Entrance at Liverpool on 31 July 1976 preparing to enter the lock then to move up to the Princes Dock to discharge passengers and cars.

(Author)

turn allowed the B&I vessel **Dundalk** to be sold, her charter work and short service on the Irish Sea now over with the Dublin and Liverpool service transferred to Fleetwood.

John Lucas reported on the **Ibex** and her sister in *Sea Breezes*, January 1980 – these second-generation dedicated freight ferries were hugely impressive:

> The ships have a cargo deadweight of 2,801 tonnes and are 150 metres long by 20.7 metres wide. Up to 125 12 metre trailers can be accommodated on the tank top deck, main deck and upper deck, all extending under the accommodation deckhouse forward. Trailers are loaded over a 12 metre wide stern ramp onto the main deck with access to the upper deck via a fixed internal ramp and to the tank top deck via a 40 tonne capacity cargo lift. Facilities are provided for refrigerated trailers, and heavy unit loads up to 18 tonnes can be carried. The accommodation provides for 29 crew members and 12 drivers.
>
> Propulsion is by means of two Mitsui medium speed oil engines, each producing 9,000 bhp and each coupled to a controllable pitch propeller to give a service speed of 19 knots. This speed enables each ship to complete the sea crossing [between Fleetwood and Dublin] in seven hours with five hours in port for loading and unloading. Twin bow thrusters and Kawasaki stabilizers are fitted.

P&O had preliminary designs drawn up for replacements of the Liverpool and Belfast car ferries **Ulster Queen** and **Ulster Prince**. Harland & Wolff were responsible for the details against a brief from P&O that would embrace the cruise-ferry concept with the carriage of private and commercial vehicles. The ships were to be compatible with the requirements of Fleetwood as a possible alternative terminal to Liverpool and would likely serve both Belfast and another Irish port, possibly Greenore. When P&O went to the banks to obtain funding for the project they were firmly told to set their own affairs in financial order first, the infamous takeover of Bovis Homes in 1974 having reduced financial confidence in the group which still had a cumbersome and complex company structure that clouded its own profit and loss balance sheets.

Instead of new passenger and vehicle ferries, P&O opted for a freight ferry service between Liverpool and Larne. It argued that impending European Union Guidelines would restrict driver hours making the longer overnight service more attractive. Robert Sinclair wrote in his book on the Belfast Steamship Company:

> Accordingly, P&O set to work at North West Alexandra Dock, Liverpool, where a ramp and marshalling space for 250 trailers were provided. Pandoro schedules were recast… From 15 October 1979, nightly ro-ro sailings commenced from Liverpool to Larne with a return daylight service each day. From Fleetwood there were daylight services with return sailings each night.
>
> So successful were the new schedules that P&O invested £4 million in their Larne operations. The **Union Melbourne** was purchased and sent to the Tyne Ship Repair Group for alterations to her accommodation. She returned to service in November and was renamed **Puma**. The **Bison** followed her to the Tyne for lengthening and accommodation changes. As a result, both vessels could now cater for 40 drivers in 20 two berth cabins with private toilet and shower.

The arrival of the **Puma** on the Fleetwood and Larne service working alongside **Bison** allowed the larger **Ibex** to be chartered to North Sea Ferries as the **Norsea**, later renamed **Norsky**. **Ibex** was replaced on the Fleetwood and Dublin service by the **Buffalo**.

During 1979 B&I had accrued a net loss of £1.1 million, so it came as no surprise when B&I announced in February 1980 that they had agreed to sell the **Innisfallen**. She was handed over to Torship Company SA (Corsica Ferries), Panama, at the end of the month.

Puma (1975) seen arriving at Fleetwood in May 1990 in corporate P&O colours and with a new accommodation block aft.

(Author)

The stern-loading **Espresso Olbia** then had to be chartered for relief during the spring overhaul period.

In the second half of May a new service between Rosslare and Pembroke Dock had been advertised and this was inaugurated by **Viking III** chartered from European Ferries fleet at Southampton. She had just completed a charter to the Manx Line while **Manx Viking** was refitted. **Viking III** was later replaced at Pembroke Dock by the chartered **Stena Nordica**, sister to the **Stena Normandica** on Sealink's Fishguard and Rosslare route and which had earlier stood in for her sister at Fishguard while she was away for refit. Towards the end of the year the **Leinster** took over from the **Connacht** on the Pembroke Dock and Cork service and was renamed **Innisfallen** to release her name for the new ferry building at the Verolme yard.

Up until 1979 B&I had shown progressive growth in profit for a number of years but events then conspired against the company. There was firstly a significant downturn in tourist traffic due both to the attraction of southern European destinations and the ongoing political problems in Ireland; secondly fuel costs were increasing at a rate far above inflation and inflation in the United Kingdom was at an all time high; and thirdly the company suffered badly at the hands of the labour unions on both sides of the Irish Sea.

By way of contrast to B&I, Sealink UK Limited made a net profit of £13.5 million in its first year of trading. Sealink UK Limited enjoyed growth on the North Sea and English Channel routes which outweighed the marginal increases on the Irish Sea services, the latter caused by political unrest in Ireland and stagnation of the Irish economy.

At Heysham the chartered **Dalriada** and **Penda** were replaced in January 1980 with the **Ilkka** and **Anu**, the **Ilkka** having already served between Fishguard and Rosslare. The ships were renamed **Lagan Bridge** and **Lune Bridge** respectively and painted in British Rail/Sealink livery, although the **Lune Bridge** retained her owner's grey hull her sister was repainted with the word 'Sealink' on the corporate monastral blue hull. The **Lagan Bridge** was now owned by Parang Shipping Company of London, and the **Lune Bridge** by Latila Shipping Limited of London, but like their earlier registered owner Tejo Leasing, both companies were component parts of the Javelin Shipping Company Limited of London.

The **Dalriada** returned to Stena Line A/B as **Stena Trader** (she was originally named **Stena Trailer**). The **Penda** was renamed **nf Jaguar** and started work at the end of May on a Southampton and Le Havre freight service, for her owners P&O Ferries, before retiring to lay up at Liverpool in October.

The **Lagan Bridge** and **Lune Bridge** provided an overnight service at Heysham. They served during some weekends between Holyhead and Dublin and were both also used at times to support the Manx Line Heysham and Douglas service. Useful though the ships were, their core service between Heysham and Belfast was consistently running at a loss and this continued throughout 1980. The route was closed in mid-December with an anticipated loss of £1 million during the year; the two ships were returned to their respective owners.

While the ships had supported the Manx Line during the year it was announced in October that Sealink had increased its holding in the company by a further 20% to 80%, with James Fisher & Sons retaining the remainder. Thereafter the company was marketed as Manx Line/Sealink.

At Stranraer, the new **Galloway Princess** finally entered service on 1 May 1980. Quite different from anything seen before she had a blunt square superstructure topped by two athwartships funnels. Before her arrival the **Penda** had supported the route and later the chartered **Stena Timer**. The **Galloway Princess** could accommodate 1000 passengers and 300 cars or 62 standard freight vehicles.

*The chartered **Lune Bridge** (1972) along with sister **Lagan Bridge** worked between Heysham and Belfast during 1980.*

***Galloway Princess** (1979) arriving Stranraer Pier on 1 May 1984 when the twin arrow device had been removed from the funnels.*
(Author)

At Holyhead, the **St Columba** was again away for repairs. **Ailsa Princess** deputised with supplementary cargo services provided by **Lagan Bridge** and the Harwich train ferry **Cambridge Ferry**. The **Avalon** finished her last season of work on the Irish Sea in September and was put on the For Sale list, later scrapped in India. On 25 September the new **St David**, a larger quasi-sister to **Galloway Princess**, was launched at Belfast destined for the Fishguard and Rosslare service. This ship was funded by Barclays Mercantile Industrial Finance. In the meantime, two similar ships to **St David** were nearing completion for the Dover Strait, named **St Christopher** and **St Anselm**.

At Cairnryan, the **European Gateway** arrived from the English Channel on 17 March 1980 to relieve first the **Free Enterprise IV** and then the **Doric Ferry** before returning south again in June. The **European Gateway** was registered under the ownership of Monarch Steamship Company Limited, (Raeburn & Verel) of Glasgow, now a shell company owned by European Ferries.

The big news of the year was the announcement made by the Transport Minister on 14 July 1980 regarding the denationalisation of British Rail's shipping and hotels sections. It was hoped that this could take place by 1983 at the latest. Sir Peter Parker, chairman of British Rail acknowledged that the shipping division and other subsidiaries had been seriously under-resourced in recent years:

> The introduction of private capital should increase the scope and unlock the great potential of the subsidiary businesses. Investment has been limited because of the thin spread of resources and subsidiaries have been starved.

The 1970s had been a period of steady but slow growth impeded by the political difficulties prevailing in Ireland. These problems all but destroyed the tourist traffic in the second half of the 1970s and put a serious strain on the finances of the major passenger operators. The first of the second-generation vehicle and passenger ferries were commissioned, bigger obviously, to enjoy economies of scale, but also fuel conscious in times of rising costs, so not necessarily any faster than their predecessors.

The long-delayed **St Columba** was well received by the travelling public at Holyhead despite being dogged by mechanical failures in her first year of operation. B&I's **Connacht** was commissioned at a time of financial difficulties that meant one of her older running mates had to be sold and replaced by chartered tonnage. During the decade, ships were chartered in from a variety of sources from far and wide. One notable player in the charter market was Stena Line A/B of Gothenburg, a company that would, in due course, become a prominent operator on the Irish Sea as the ultimate successor to Sealink.

So far there has only been one totally new operator, Manx Line, and that company seemed set to disappear into the Sealink empire. The long-standing, even traditional, operators were British Railways, later British Rail and which then adopted the Sealink brand and became Sealink UK Limited in 1979; Coast Lines (Belfast Steamship Company, Burns & Laird Lines which was taken over by P&O and Coast Lines (British & Irish Steam Packet Company) which was purchased by Coras Iompair Eireann for the Irish Government as B&I Line. With Sealink UK Limited being prepared for sale to the commercial sector at the end of the 1970s only the B&I Line would then remain state owned.

CHAPTER 5
AT THE EXPENSE OF THE TAXPAYER

St Christopher (1981) took her maiden voyage from Holyhead in March and only took up duty in her intended role between Dover and Calais the following month; she is seen at Dover on 16 May 1981.

(Author)

The Troubles had become firmly entrenched in the north of Ireland. Activity escalated with the IRA bombing military ceremonies in London in 1982. On 12 October 1984 it upped its sights when it attempted to assassinate the British Prime Minister, Margaret Thatcher, during the Conservative Party annual conference which that year was held at Brighton. These activities offered few favours for Northern Irish industry which had long been plagued by sectarianism; demand on the Irish Sea ferries remained largely stagnant.

During the early 1980s Sealink UK Limited began to lose significant amounts of money. As it was a nationalised company underwritten by the state, travellers not only paid the tariff to board ship but also subsidised the shipowner through their taxes. Profits were made on the Dover Strait, the Harwich services more or less broke even, but the Channel Islands service and all the Irish Sea operations ran at a loss. The Irish Sea services had been badly hit by the political issues that were worsening in Ireland, and the consequent strain that this imposed on the economy of both Northern Ireland and the Republic. Tourist traffic to Ireland was declining year by year, exacerbated by the ease that a family could now take their car across the Channel to sunshine destinations far and wide. Given this background, Len Merryweather was appointed Chairman of Sealink UK Limited in 1982, with the simple remit that he was to aid the sale of the company to the commercial sector.

The same story of financial losses had impacted the state-owned B&I Line. Diminishing returns were suffered on all routes at no obvious fault of the management or their marketing strategy, and in 1981 B&I returned a net loss of £7.5 million with bigger losses to follow in subsequent years.

Despite the poor returns on all the Irish Sea services there were two new ships on order – the highlight of 1981 was the arrival of the *St David* for Sealink and the *Leinster* for the B&I Line. But before they arrived there was yet another maiden voyage on the Irish Sea, that of the *St Christopher*, which took place from Holyhead to Dun Laoghaire on 17 March. The *St Columba* had malfunctioned yet again and a stand-in was urgently required at Holyhead. As it happened the *St Christopher* was ready to sail from her builders at Belfast to take up her regular station at Dover. She was the third of a quartet of ships built by Harland & Wolff for Sealink, the first was the *Galloway Princess* and the last was the *St David*. Once the *St Columba* was back on duty the *St Christopher* moved to Fishguard to relieve the *Stena Normandica*, and finally arrived at Dover in March where she joined her sister (the second of the quartet) *St Anselm*.

The new *St David* had been intended for Fishguard but was reallocated to Holyhead to work with the *St Columba*. The *St David* was advertised to start at Holyhead on 22 June 1981, but the ship was still being fitted out ready for service at the builder's yard in Belfast. The steamer *Earl Leofric*, formerly the *Holyhead Ferry I*, was drafted in as she was already at Holyhead for refit; the *Earl Leofric* now boasted a total of twelve lifeboats despite it having been demonstrated repeatedly that rafts were the preferred option for evacuation if free water had accessed the main vehicle deck. On 9 July, *Earl Leofric* was replaced by the *Prinsessan Desiree*, hastily chartered from Rederi A/B Goteburg-Fredrickshavn-Linjen, Gothenburg. Built in 1971, the *Prinsessan Desiree* was not really a match for the *St Columba* although she was fit for over 20 knots, but she was available, having just completed a short charter to the B&I Line to cover that company's annual refit period.

On 10 August 1981, the morning sailing from Holyhead was taken by the *St David* which had arrived at the port earlier in the week. Of the four Harland & Wolff ships the *St David* was by far the most passenger friendly. Her dining saloon was forward with views over the bow of the ship, she had a small cinema with seating for nearly 60, and a duty free walk-through shop. For entry to Holyhead she was given a stern bridge

Earl Leofric (1965), one-time *Holyhead Ferry I*, and now with an impressive array of lifeboats, was back on her old patch when she stood in for the *St Columba* in March 1981.

(Fotoflite)

St David (1981) was intended for the Fishguard and Rosslare service but was reallocated to Holyhead before she was completed – note the docking bridge aft.

(Author)

European Gateway (1975) on a morning arrival at Larne 31 March 1981. She had been lengthened by 15.7 metres.

(Author)

Doric Ferry (1961) seen arriving at Cairnryan on 24 May 1976 was finally sold along with her sister Cerdic Ferry in July 1981 to Compania Armadora du Sudamerica, Piraeus.

(Author)

and she had internal ramps to access the upper vehicle deck as neither Holyhead nor Dun Laoghaire yet had double-deck loading access. As a consequence, the **St David**, and for that matter the **Galloway Princess**, offered 744 lane metres of garage space, whereas the **St Christopher** and **St Anselm**, which were equipped with vehicle lifts, had slightly more space at 780 lane metres. All four ships could accommodate 1000 passengers.

Of the arrival of the new B&I Line ferry **Leinster**, Malcolm MacRonald wrote:

> **Leinster**'s entry to Liverpool-Dublin was scheduled for June 1981, but her delivery was about one month behind schedule. She entered service with an overnight crossing from Liverpool on 3 July. **Leinster** had cost £23.5 million, £3.5 million more than the figure originally expected and £7 million more than **Connacht**'s cost only two years previously. She was virtually identical to **Connacht** but there were a few internal alterations based on experience with **Connacht**. Her passenger and vehicle capacities were identical to her sister's.

The two ships each maintained one return trip between Liverpool and Dublin at weekends, with an 8¾ hour passage overnight but only 7 hours by day. For the remainder of the week there was only the overnight service, the ships laying over in port during the day, one at the Trafalgar Dock terminal at Liverpool, the other at the B&I Ferryport at Dublin.

Munster maintained the Pembroke Dock and Rosslare service. To reduce losses on the service her schedule was reduced in October from eleven to just four round trips per week, with the ship laying over at Rosslare from Sunday morning until Wednesday evening. This was not a sustainable situation and the service was terminated on 22 November with the **Munster** laid up and put up for sale. Meanwhile **Innisfallen**, ex-**Leinster**, continued on the Pembroke Dock and Cork service, with Irish Continental Lines **Saint Patrick** covering her refit period.

The **Manx Viking** retuned from her spring overhaul on 17 April 1981 in full Sealink livery. In the meantime, she had been covered by **Antrim Princess**, **Earl Godwin** (from Weymouth) and finally by Townsend Thoresen's **Viking Victory**. P&O's **nf Jaguar** was chartered by the Steam Packet company in May to offer a freight service between Hornby Dock, Liverpool and Douglas, starting on 19 June with a return sailing each 24 hours.

At Cairnryan the **European Gateway** returned to work alongside the **Free Enterprise IV**. During the winter the ship had been lengthened by 15.7 metres with enhanced garage space and a passenger certificate for 326 persons. Loadings declined in the second half of the year due to recession exacerbated by the Irish troubles. Although it was announced that the **Free Enterprise IV** would be withdrawn from the route in the autumn, this did not happen and the two ship service was maintained throughout the winter period. Both **Cerdic Ferry** and **Doric Ferry**, which had been laid up at Barrow, were sold.

The Liverpool and Belfast ships **Ulster Queen** and **Ulster Prince**, operated by P&O Ferries, were withdrawn. They were of an unfortunate pre-first-generation vehicle and passenger design that did not allow for more than four commercial vehicles and they also had an underused hold serviced by a single hatch. Their end was heralded by a strike over manning levels late in December 1980 followed by an announcement on New Year's Eve that the service had been closed due to the economic recession. There was a brief reprieve and the service resumed on 8 January 1981, but neither staff nor travelling public were convinced by P&O's conviction to make the service pay. The service finally closed on 12 November. Almost immediately interest in the route was announced by Oceanbrook Developments, a company that was 25% owned by Irish Shipping Limited and 75% owned by Allied Irish Banks. Oceanbrook identified the Irish Continental Line's **Saint Patrick** as a contender for the new service.

Oceanbrook Developments' proposal was confirmed early in 1982 when Irish Continental Line announced that they had agreed to purchase the **Aurella** from the Viking Line of Mariehamn, Âland

Saint Colum I (1973) passing towards Langton Dock on departure from Liverpool to Belfast on 15 May 1982, just two weeks after the service commenced.

(Author)

Saint Patrick II (1973) making an early morning arrival at Le Havre in July 1985.

(Bernard McCall)

Darnia (1977), seen leaving Stranraer complete with her extended passenger accommodation on the bridge deck.

(Bernard McCall)

Ailsa Princess was renamed **Earl Harold** (1971) in April 1985 for use on the Channel Island services but returned to Stranraer and Larne duties in the autumn. She is pictured leaving Fishguard during a relief spell on the Rosslare service.

(Bernard McCall)

Islands, to free up the **Saint Patrick**. Purchase of the new ship was financed by the capital allocated by its owners to Oceanbrook Developments. In due course, the **Aurella** was refitted and renamed **Saint Patrick II**, while the **Saint Patrick** was renamed **Saint Colum I** and registered at Belfast under the ownership of Belfast Car Ferries Limited, a company wholly owned by Irish Continental Line. The third change was that the **Saint Killian**, which had been lengthened over the winter for the Continental services, returned to duty with the new name **Saint Killian II**.

Saint Colum I started her new service on 1 May 1982 with a departure from Donegal Quay, Belfast to Langton Dock, Liverpool. The return trip was delayed by stormy weather and the ship arrived back in Belfast 2½ hours late. Some work remained to be completed with 30 of the new cabins yet to be fitted out and the shop and cafeteria still occupied by workmen. Nevertheless, everybody wished the new venture a success. Engine trouble caused the service to be suspended for a week at the end of June but otherwise the new route quickly built up trade. In early November the **Saint Colum I**, with her red funnel, rather than green, and white shamrock, stood down for repairs and was replaced by Irish Continental Line's **Saint Patrick II**, sporting the original green funnel and white shamrock.

With Belfast Car Ferries now up and running as the first really successful new company to enter the Irish Sea trades, it was inevitable that other new proposals would project their own prospects for success. Two other new services were put forward in the summer and autumn of 1982. First was Seabridge Marine of Oban which announced an interest in reopening the Heysham and Belfast freight service, closed eighteen months previously by Sealink. In due course the company stated that it had inspected Brittany Ferries' **Penn-ar-Bed** which it considered to be suitable for the route. A slight economic upturn had begun since Sealink pulled out of Heysham, but whether this was sufficient to support even a one-ship service was yet to be tested. The second proposal was an interest voiced by a concern calling itself Bristol Commercial Ferries which was keen to start a freight service between Avonmouth and Rosslare with three return voyages per week.

Most operators were well aware of the difficulties in setting up new ferry links which would compete with existing well-established services. They also knew of the benefits of door-to-door services on both sides of the Irish Sea and the attraction of in-house haulage and trailer hire. That the established operators were all losing money on the Irish Sea at that time must have warned them that the economic environment was not appropriate for new services. In the event, neither proposal came to fruition.

B&I Line was still looking to reduce its losses. In 1982 it proposed to better utilise its Liverpool and Dublin vessels, the **Connacht** and **Leinster**, by putting them on a daytime return from Dublin to Holyhead. The idea was treated with disdain by Sealink staff at Holyhead and the first two sailings by **Connacht**, on 5 and 7 March for berthing trials and an inaugural advertised sailing, found the harbour blocked by a fleet of small boats. The same happened to **Leinster** on 9 March.

The situation deteriorated when the **St David** arrived at Dun Laoghaire to find the **Munster** lying just off the harbour mouth, but on the following day the **Munster** allowed **St David** to dock as there was an urgent medical case on board. Sealink suspended further sailings until talks led to an agreement that allowed both the Sealink and the new B&I services to recommence in mid-March. In the meantime, the **St David** had been for refit and the **St Columba** was deputising at Fishguard for the **Stena Normandica** which was also on refit.

The twin service at Holyhead soon led to consumer confidence and traffic built up throughout the summer. **St Columba** was then converted to one class with consequent reduction in seagoing staff, with **Ailsa Princess** standing in while she was away. The bad news at Holyhead was the announcement that the dry dock and engineering works were to close – newer ships having become too large for the dock and specialist engineering equipment too expensive to maintain for the work on offer.

Ailsa Princess become spare ship at Stranraer in 1982. **Darnia** received enhanced passenger accommodation in the spring to make

*The last conventional passenger ferry on the Irish Sea: the **Manxman** (1955) on her final departure from Fleetwood on Sunday 15 August 1982.*
(Author)

Gaelic Ferry *(1963), in full Townsend Thoresen livery, deputised for the **Free Enterprise IV** and **European Gateway** at Cairnryan prior to Easter 1982.*
(Author)

Europic Ferry *(1967) arriving at Cairnryan on Wednesday 2 May 1984.*
(Author)

*The Isle of Man Steam Packet Company's **Peveril** (1971) was formerly the **nf Jaguar** and before that the **Penda** operating for Sealink between Heysham and Belfast.*

(Author)

her compatible with the **Galloway Princess** and **Antrim Princess**. This allowed **Ailsa Princess** to be released for Weymouth and Channel Island duties. The wisdom of this was challenged when first Brittany Ferries **Breizh Izel** and then the SNCF Dieppe-based ferry **Villandry** were chartered in to cover for absences. Nevertheless, the **Ailsa Princess** was renamed **Earl Harold** and moved south for the summer, returning to Stranraer duties in the autumn.

At Heysham, the Sealink-owned **Manx Viking** finally settled to her duties. The new Isle of Man Steam Packet Company freight ferry service to Douglas from Liverpool with **nf Jaguar** continued to attract good loadings despite being stern-loading as her bow door was incompatible with the linkspan at Douglas. However, the operation of the four side-loading ferries, albeit largely on a seasonal basis, but including the two fuel-inefficient turbine steamers **Ben-my-Chree** and **Manx Maid**, and the passenger only turbine steamer **Manxman**, brought the overall balance sheet for the Manx company in 1981 to a loss of £0.6 million, down by over £1 million on 1980. The four side-loading ferries and the **Manxman** maintained a diverse schedule of sailings in the short summer season with services between Douglas and Dublin, Belfast, Llandudno, Fleetwood and Ardrossan, as well as the core all year-round service to Liverpool. The **Manxman** was sold at the end of the season.

Cairnryan continued to offer both the **Free Enterprise IV** and the **European Gateway** on the service to Larne; this despite Townsend Thoresen threatening to withdraw the **Free Enterprise IV** early in the year. The **Gaelic Ferry** had deputised for both ships until Easter.

The year 1982 was also the 25th anniversary of the commissioning of the **Bardic Ferry** and shortly afterwards that of her sister ship **Ionic Ferry**. This iconic pair of ships set the trend for the future as general-purpose ferries suitable for both commercial vehicles and private cars, and their drivers and passengers. Accommodation was in two classes with car drivers and passengers enjoying first class, segregated from the commercial drivers in second class, a policy the ferry companies have retained to this day, although ships are now one class with a special suite for the commercial drivers.

The first-generation ferries that followed were passenger and car carriers led by the **Caledonian Princess**. These ships were a valuable transition towards the second-generation ships which eventually led to the modern-day general-purpose ships. The first-generation ferries reflected a desire to keep passengers and cargo separate with ships designed for passengers and their cars and perhaps a handful of commercial vehicles.

At first sight the only difference between the second-generation ferries of the early 1980s and the **Bardic Ferry** and **Ionic Ferry** was one of scale, certainly economies of scale meant an ever-increasing size of ships with ever greater lane metreage on the vehicle decks, drive-through loading and unloading, plus larger passenger certificates. Speed had also become important ensuring that passage times were kept to a minimum with quick port turnarounds to maximise the use of the ship – a ship is only earning money when it is at sea. This was not the case in the 1950s when extended lay overs in port allowed the crew to rest between voyages and for unloading and loading to be carried out at leisure.

By the 1980s ships were charged with at least two duty masters and the officers and men rotated on a shift system to allow vessels to be kept in service 24 hours a day. The downside is that understanding of routine and procedures between officers and crews can vary with each crew change as new faces appeared on the call to 'Harbour Stations' at regular intervals.

The ships themselves have evolved although the overall design still centres around the garage space. Engines had been reconfigured by the early 1980s so that they fitted neatly below the main vehicle deck without engine casing emerging above that level. Propeller design had improved to provide greater thrust at low speeds to enable rapid acceleration on leaving harbour, and, of course, the provision of powerful bow thrust units coupled with bow rudders for going astern enhanced manoeuvrability in confined waters.

*The **Stena Sailer**, one-time B&I Line's **Dundalk**, was taken on charter in March 1984 for the new Belfast Freight Ferries service between Heysham and Belfast.*

However, the nature of a ship that had a vehicle deck with no watertight bulkheads, situated at a low level above the sea, meant that roll-on roll-off ferries needed to adhere to a complex set of load restrictions for a given set of operational conditions. Most had two cargo deadweights and passenger certificates, one, the C1 capacity was that allowed for the breach of a single watertight compartment below the vehicle deck, and C2 was for the breach of two adjacent compartments.

Strict load line limits were set and curves available for various different trims of the ship and how they would affect buoyancy. It was imperative that the master knew his cargo deadweight before he sailed, which includes the passengers, and that he knew that neither his load marks nor his passenger certificate had been contravened.

The most interesting aspect of ferry development, particularly on the Irish Sea, was that the general-purpose ferry had become the ideal configuration. Freight-only ferries were highly successful, not least those operated by Pandoro in the trailer market, but even these offered space for private individuals and their cars. However, the need to run freight-only ships alongside passenger ships was an expensive luxury that Sealink had enjoyed with the cargo ships **Preseli**, **Penda**, **Dalriada** and **Ulidia**, while the Isle of Man Steam Packet Company did the same thing with the **nf Jaguar**. Clearly the economics of one large general-purpose ship configured to best suit the trade on offer is the superior model, and this was the direction in which the Irish Sea ferry industry was progressing.

Appropriate configuration meant repeated upgrades for ships including lengthening and partial rebuilding. The **European Gateway**, for example, was lengthened to increase her capacity before she took up duty at Cairnryan in 1982, having operated briefly in her original form the previous year when she was found to be too small for the traffic on offer.

The **European Gateway** moved south on relief duties in the winter to operate between Felixstowe and Rotterdam. On 19 December 1982 she left her berth at Felixstowe at 2230 hours with 70 crew and passengers and 48 lorries on board. Twenty minutes into the voyage she collided with Sealink's freight ferry **Speedlink Vanguard** and within ten minutes the **European Gateway** was lying on her side in shallow water adjacent to the deep water approach to the River Stour. Again, the lifeboats could not be used due to the speed of the sinking and six lives were lost during the evacuation to life rafts; the ship had heeled over to 45° within three minutes of the collision.

The accident again demonstrated the vulnerability of roll-on roll-off ships to collision damage. The need for improved protocols in navigating in confined waters was underlined and the subsequent inquiry also reported that the operation of manually operated watertight doors beneath the main vehicle deck was impossible in such circumstances and that all similar ships should be equipped with bridge and locally controlled mechanically or hydraulically operated doors (see Chapter 1).

The **Gaelic Ferry** moved to Cairnryan in the New year and with **Europic Ferry** also on duty the two ships allowed the **Free Enterprise IV** to stand down for refit. The **Europic Ferry**, fresh from the Falkland Islands War, stood down on the return of the **Free Enterprise IV** in May.

The Isle of Man Steam Packet Company continued to buck the trend for general-purpose ferries when it had chartered **nf Jaguar** from P&O from June 1981. James Fisher bought the **nf Jaguar** from P&O for £1.2 million in December 1982 and demise chartered it to the Isle of Man company with the Manx name **Peveril** and Douglas as the port of registry. She was relieved on the Liverpool and Douglas route by **Stena Sailer** (formerly the B&I Line freight ferry **Dundalk**) in April.

*The **Lady of Mann** (1976) arriving at Heysham in April 1985 with her owner's name on her side, lest anyone should ever forget!*
(Author)

*The 'new' **Mona's Isle** (1966) leaving Heysham for Govan on 15 April 1985 for further modifications before she eventually entered service.*
(Author)

***Manx Viking** (1976) at Douglas.*
(Iain McCall Collection)

55

The closure of the B&I Pembroke Dock and Cork service took place on 2 February 1983; it had accrued a loss of £1.7 million in 1982. At the request of the Irish Government the *Fennia* was chartered from Silja Line to resume the service in mid-June for the summer period until mid-September. Meanwhile, the *Innisfallen* was used to maintain two return trips a day between Pembroke Dock and Rosslare. Two separate companies then proposed to take up the displaced traffic should the Cork service really close, with Bristol Commercial Ferries still champing at the bit and a new company called Welsh Irish Ferries Limited planning a route from Barry. The latter actually commenced on 31 March with the small stern-loading freight ferry *Ugland Trailer* sailing from Barry. In a bid to attract private car traffic the company offered car drivers and passengers a Dan Air flight from Cardiff to Cork to meet their cars at the other end. The National Union of Seamen was unimpressed by the Norwegian-flagged and crewed vessel working three sailings a week on the Irish Sea and did all it could to boycott the service.

Just fourteen weeks after the start of the new service, on 7 July, Welsh Irish Ferries Limited ran out of cash and the *Ugland Trailer* was returned to her owners. It was two years before the matter of outstanding charter fees was resolved while the company remained under receivership. The problems faced by the new company were twofold. Firstly, a short and fast crossing was preferred by the shippers who could make up the lost mileage quickly by road; secondly the fares that were charged had to compete with the shorter crossings from Pembroke Dock and Fishguard. Fuel and crew costs were three times higher on a nine hour crossing than they would be on a three hour one. The 'shortest passage' rule had already been demonstrated by European Ferries when it moved its Larne service from Fleetwood to Cairnryan, allowing one ship to fulfil the jobs of four with a focus in Northern Ireland on Larne at the expense of Belfast. Rapid expansion of the new service had led to a two ship service from Cairnryan to Larne.

In July, the *Ugland Trailer* was used to deputise for the P&O Freight ferry *Pointer* on the Ardrossan and Belfast service. The Bristol Commercial Ferries proposed service from Avonmouth quickly withered on the vine and was not heard of again.

Early in 1984 Belfast Car Ferries announced the creation of the new subsidiary company Belfast Freight Ferries with the objective of starting a freight service between Heysham and Belfast. The company was established jointly with Scruttons (NI) Limited, the Irish stevedoring company. The new venture was designed to allow freight traffic to be siphoned away from the *Saint Colum I* at Liverpool to allow that service to focus on the accompanied car trade and, of course, the move would prevent anyone else setting up at Heysham. The *Stena Sailer* was taken on charter and duly arrived at Belfast in early March only to be blocked by the unions as she was registered overseas. Once manning levels had been agreed, the service was able to start with three departures from each port, a service which quickly gained support from both sides of the Irish Sea.

The *Antrim Princess*, under the command of Captain Thomas Cree, suffered an engine room fire shortly after leaving Larne on 9 December 1983. The ship had a complete power failure and started to drift westwards towards the shore in deteriorating weather. The sea was such that lifeboats could not be launched with any degree of safety. The *Glasgow Herald*, 10 December 1983, reported the news:

> 106 passengers and 23 crew from the stricken Sealink ferry *Antrim Princess* were winched to safety by RAF helicopters… Shortly after leaving Larne at 10.30 am a fire broke out in her engine room. The captain flashed a May-Day message and ordered passengers to don life jackets. Two other vessels, the *Europic Ferry* and the *Northella*, a naval vessel, rushed to her aid and attempted to fix a tow line, but without success. Throughout the day the master of the *Antrim Princess* and 30 crew members stayed on board to try to salvage the ferry which had a full load of cars and lorries. Later an Admiralty tug arrived from the Clyde to tow the *Antrim Princess* to the safety of Belfast Harbour but last night the vessel had lost power again and helicopters were hovering nearby to take off the remaining crew if necessary.

Passengers were full of praise for the helicopter crews. The *Antrim Princess* was repaired and back in service at the end of the month. However, the ship's anchors had been released when she was finally taken in tow off the island of Muck which is just off the coast of Islandmagee; these had to be recovered before the ship could resume service. The *St David* moved north to deputise from 14 December onwards.

Irish Continental Line's *Saint Patrick II* deputised for *Saint Colum I* at Liverpool from mid-December 1983 until early January. She then stood in for the B&I Line ships *Connacht* and *Leinster* at Holyhead and finally allowed the *Leinster* to relieve the *Innisfallen* at Pembroke Dock. Meanwhile Sealink's chartered *Stena Normandica*, working between Fishguard and Rosslare, was flagged-out to Bermuda in a bid to save operating costs.

Sealink UK Limited continued to operate at a loss. Between 1980 and 1984 £100 million had been invested in Sealink UK Limited, but it still lost on average £2.5 million during each of the five years in this period. During the denationalisation auction for the company, valid bids were received from offshore-based Sea Containers Limited, from Common Brothers of Newcastle-upon-Tyne and from a consortium led by the National Freight Corporation, which included senior management from Sealink UK Limited and James Fisher & Sons of Barrow. European Ferries had been disqualified by the Monopolies and Mergers Commission after it had submitted an earlier bid for £80 million and P&O was prevented by its bankers from pursuing any interest in the sale.

Of the 37 Sealink ships nearly half, valued at £80 million, were leased and not owned by Government. The remaining assets, with an estimated value of £60 million, were owned by Government and included various harbours and other shore installations. The announcement of the successful bid was made by the Secretary of State for Transport, Nicholas Ridley, as recorded in *Hansard*, Vol 64, 18 July 1984:

> I have today given my consent under section 1(2) of the Transport Act 1981, to the sale of Sealink UK Ltd, by British Rail to a subsidiary of Sea Containers Ltd — British Ferries.
>
> The British Railways Board invited tenders, through its advisers Morgan Grenfell and Co Ltd for the purchase of the whole of the board's interest in Sealink UK Ltd. Three proposals were received with conditions attached.
>
> The chosen purchaser submitted the bid with the highest value, of some £66 million. The British Railways Board has been advised by Morgan Grenfell and Co Ltd that the price fairly reflects the value of the business, and this view is supported by my own advisers, Hill Samuel & Co Ltd.
>
> Sea Containers, an international sea freight company with its headquarters in London, has wide experience in freight shipping. It has made a number of constructive proposals for improving Sealink's business. It has agreed on firm contractual commitments to maintain rail-linked passenger services. The parties are already in negotiation on new long-term freight contracts for train ferry and Freightliner services.
>
> Sea Containers has said, first, that it intends to maintain the existing business and to safeguard the rights of employees, including their pension entitlements, which will be protected. It further plans additional capital expenditure to expand the

business and increase its profitability. I know that the company will be seeking early discussions with Sealink's trades unions.

Sea Containers has stated its intention to obtain a listing for the company on the Stock Exchange in due course, and that it would expect at that time to give employees an opportunity to purchase shares on favourable terms. Meanwhile, it is planning profit-sharing schemes for all employees.

Arrangements have been made to ensure that the contribution of the Sealink fleet to national defence will not be prejudiced by the sale.

*P&O Ferries' Ardrossan and Belfast service was operated by **Belard** (1979) from the end of 1985 – she is seen at Belfast off Queen's Island.*

(Author)

This sale is a successful end to the policy transferring Sealink to the private sector which we agreed with the British Railways Board in 1980, and debated in the House in 1981. The price is good, and the sale makes good industrial logic. Customers and passengers of Sealink will benefit from the continuation of competition in the ferry market. Above all, it will be good for those who work in Sealink, who will now join a progressive and expanding group with the substantial resources necessary to make a real success of this important enterprise.

The outcome was not the most satisfactory one. That the price was low reflected the economic downturn that prevailed in the early 1980s, and selling Sealink to a company with no experience of the ferry industry was not a preferred solution. Sea Containers, with its American founder and President, James Sherwood, had no experience in short-sea operations, functioned as an offshore company with headquarters on the South Bank at London, and had no capability that would help take a large ferry company forward to compete head-to-head with European Ferries and other operators working in the markets around the British Isles.

A new livery was exhibited on four Sealink ships as they returned from refit before the sale. This was all-white with a pale blue band and the italic word 'SEALINK' in blue on the hull. The funnel was a wishy-washy blue with a peculiar wavy yellow line across it which was supposed to represent the cuff bands of an officer. Only the **Stena Normandica** wore the new livery on the Irish Sea in 1984, the other ships retaining the old livery but with the twin arrow logo painted out leaving plain red funnels with black tops.

Keeping up with the trend, the side-loading car ferries of the Isle of Man Steam Packet Company had the words 'ISLE OF MAN STEAM PACKET' written along their hulls lest anyone should forget who owned such outdated and strange craft. The B&I Line also joined in with full route descriptions written on its ship's hulls, the **Leinster** looking particularly stupid at Pembroke Dock with the wording 'Dublin-Liverpool, Dublin-Holyhead' written across her side.

The **Innisfallen** (ex-**Leinster**) stood down from Pembroke Dock and Rosslare sailings in October 1984 ready for her new owners in Italy. Her place was taken by Irish Continental Line's **Saint Patrick II**, although the former **Leinster** reappeared again, the sale having fallen through.

Managing owner Irish Shipping was in financial crisis at this stage, having fallen foul of some loss-making charters in the Far East, and the merger of Irish Continental Line and B&I was proposed as a cost cutting exercise. Events were to overtake this idea. In mid-November Irish Shipping Limited was placed in the hands of the receiver by the Irish Government and Irish Continental Line and Belfast Car Ferries assets were frozen. Neither Irish Continental Line nor Belfast Car Ferries could be put on the market until spring 1986 while various tax issues were clarified. The half share in Belfast Freight Ferries was then sold to Scruttons which became sole owners of the company. The B&I Line, meanwhile, remained in Government ownership, but was weighed down by increasing losses year by year.

But the surprise news at the end of the year was that the Isle of Man Steam Packet Company was planning to sell its two elderly steam turbine side-loaders, **Manx Maid** and **Ben-my-Chree**, and replace them with the Maltese-owned ferry **Tamira**, formerly the **Free Enterprise III**. She had been sold by European Ferries three months earlier to George Zammitt, Mira Shipping Company. On return to the UK she was given the traditional name **Mona's Isle**. There then started a series of issues that hindered progress with conversion of the 'new' ship for Manx duties. The first was the realisation that all the certifying exemptions of **Free Enterprise III** had been lost to the new owners and she was treated by the regulating agency as a new ship to the British registry. The second was that she needed to be adapted for her new service with considerable additional accommodation built onto the boat deck aft with compensating permanent ballast forward. The **Tamira** had been bought for just £600,000 but received alterations costing £2 million. Local naval architects Burness Corlett & Partners of Ramsey were appointed to design and oversee the conversion work.

At the same time, it was announced that the Steam Packet company would pool its resources with Sealink British Ferries and close its long-standing Liverpool service in favour of a passenger route from Heysham. In what was effectively a merger of the two interests, the Steam Packet company held 60% of the share capital and Sealink the remaining 40% including 1.5 million in a new share issue. It was proposed that the **Mona's Isle** work alongside the **Antrim Princess** and that the **Manx Viking** be used elsewhere. The **Antrim Princess** was to be chartered to the Steam Packet company, while the freighter **Peveril** was chartered for six months in April 1985 to Belfast Freight Ferries, with a Steam Packet crew, as replacement for **Stena Sailer**.

Belfast Car Ferries sailing brochure for 1985.

[Author's collection]

The Steam Packet was not yet out of the woods, though. The new Steam Packet company now had to make a £2 million profit in its first year or Sealink could acquire an additional 2% shareholding as compensation. The company was already liable for the refit of the **Manx Viking** at a cost of £0.6 million.

Unfortunately, the outcome of the alterations to the **Mona's Isle** was a ship with a cargo deadweight capacity of little over 200 tons (vehicles and passengers). This was less than a quarter of the cargo deadweight capacity available to the ship under European Ferries ownership. Bearing in mind that passengers counted towards deadweight, in those days estimated at a rate of 18 persons to the ton, there was little tonnage left over with a full complement of 1200 passengers on board. Somebody had made a serious error of judgement and the company lawyers were briefed to deal with this issue starting with enquiries targeted at the naval architect's office in Ramsey. **Mona's Isle** was also found to have serious problems docking with an underpowered bow thrust unit so that she often needed assistance, but that had also been the case when she was the **Free Enterprise III**. The **Antrim Princess**, it transpired, was not available for Heysham duties, but **Manx Viking**, which should have moved to the south coast with the intended name **Earl Henry**, was retained on duty.

1 April, the start date for the new service, found **Manx Viking** ready to go on overhaul and renew her passenger certificate. **Mona's Isle** was unable to get on the linkspan at Heysham because it was blocked by **Stena Sailer**, her crew on strike as the ship was about to be replaced by **Peveril**. The 'new' service thus commenced with the side-loaders **Mona's Queen** and **Lady of Mann** in charge, although these were soon needed elsewhere.

The 'new' **Mona's Isle** made her maiden voyage from Douglas to Dun Laoghaire but she was then able to start at Heysham, albeit with a gross underuse of her vehicle decks. Even the turbine steamer **Ben-my-Chree** was reactivated for the TT Races festival. Interestingly, the Scottish link from Douglas transferred from Ardrossan to Stranraer; co-owner of the Steam Packet company, Sea Containers, then owned the latter port and offered cheaper berthing fees.

In July, Vice Chairman of the Steam Packet, Ewen Corlett, who had been responsible for the conversion of **Mona's Isle**, resigned from the Board. Shortly afterwards the **Mona's Isle** was aground in the approach channel to Heysham, her problems ongoing. The ship was withdrawn from service in October and offered for sale. Her place was taken by **Antrim Princess**. A sorry tale indeed!

At Fishguard, Sealink finally bought the **Stena Normandica** from Stena Line A/B and renamed her **St Brendan**. At Stranraer the **Stena Sailer** was chartered for the overhaul periods while ships received the new British Ferries livery.

At the end of 1985 P&O Ferries bought the six year old **Mercandian Carrier II** from KS Merc-Scandia XXIV of Copenghagen and renamed her **Belard** as replacement for the **Pointer** on the Belfast and Ardrossan route. **Belard** offered a total of 784 lane metres stowage on two decks. **Pointer** in turn was renamed **St Magnus** for use on the P&O Orkney and Shetland services. The **Belard** was put under the ownership of POETS Fleet Management Limited and registered at Manchester, her ownership being transferred in 1990 to Northern Ireland Trailers (Scotland) Limited. The **Pointer** was then sold to owners in Malta and renamed **Zebbug**.

B&I Line lost more than IR £10 million in 1984 and in 1985 persuaded Sealink British Ferries to collaborate on services from Holyhead with **St Columba**. The Irish Government was so disappointed in the losses made by the B&I Line that it put a management company in charge to try and reverse the ferry company's fortunes. The company also threatened to move its Dublin terminal to Dun Laoghaire as an economy measure.

New companies had found it extremely difficult to break into the Irish Sea trades. Seaspeed Ferries had succeeded in the 1970s, but only while the company held the Ford Motor Company contract to export trade cars to Ireland. Welsh Irish Ferries Limited tried to persuade shippers to forsake the shorter and established crossings from Fishguard and Pembroke Dock for a much longer and time-consuming passage to and from Barry. In hindsight the company could never have won such an argument.

Belfast Car Ferries Limited and Belfast Freight Ferries were subsidiaries of existing and successful companies and both succeeded where others had failed. The Belfast Steamship Company had failed because of inappropriate and outdated tonnage on the Liverpool and Belfast car and passenger service, while British Rail/Sealink had lost money on the freight service between Heysham and Belfast for which the economic margins had been small. Both these companies had offered a two-ship service whereas their successors used only one ship. At Heysham, the new service offered by Belfast Freight Ferries also benefited from freight traffic augmented by shipments that would otherwise have been booked on the car ferry from Liverpool when that ship was carrying full loads of private cars.

CHAPTER 6
1986-1990 - A PERIOD OF STAGNATION

*The Steam Packet company's **Mona's Isle** arriving at Heysham on 17 September 1985 with a full complement of passengers but with just a quarter of her garage space occupied.*

(Author)

No significant investment was made during James Sherwood's first twenty months in charge of Sealink British Ferries in any of his Irish Sea services. This may have been a reflection of the low economic margins to be made in the Irish routes; Sherwood continued to rely on drafting in ships from elsewhere to fill gaps as needs must. Nevertheless, he invested in the loss-making Channel Island services, perhaps unwisely, bringing ships up to cruise ferry status when all the islanders wanted was a reliable and economical service for themselves and their tourists.

New ships were being provided at Harwich and Dover where profits were more easily made. Sea Containers had purchased the chartered **Stena Normandica** for further service between Fishguard and Rosslare, despite earlier having stated that the ship had outlived her usefulness on the route and that larger and more efficient tonnage was needed.

Sherwood's only personal intervention had been to attend a Steam Packet Board meeting at Douglas in August 1985 to insist that the wayward **Mona's Isle** be sold at the end of the season.

The **Mona's Isle** finally left Birkenhead in March 1986 with the new name **Al Fahad**, flying the Saudi Arabian flag, and bound for a new career in the Red Sea pilgrim and migrant worker trade. In the meantime, a legal challenge was issued on behalf of the Steam Packet company against Burness Corlett & Partners regarding their role as naval architects in the conversion of the ship. This was eventually settled out of court in 1990 for a sum just short of £700,000, an amount barely enough to cover the legal fees accrued in the interim.

Otherwise, Sherwood's complacency on the Irish Sea was essentially the saving grace for the B&I Line which was losing money year by year. But losses were not an essential component of Irish Sea services and Belfast Car Ferries continued to enjoy buoyant returns while Belfast Freight Ferries was also bringing in the money. P&O and Townsend Thoresen were both content with the trade on offer and happy to await the inevitable upturn in business once the Irish political problems had been resolved.

The status quo was retained at Fishguard, Holyhead and Stranraer throughout 1986. It was planned to integrate both the British & Irish and the Sealink British Ferries refit periods but further industrial problems at B&I meant that the multi-purpose train ferry **Vortigern** had to be brought in to cover for the **St Brendan** at Fishguard. The **Innisfallen** finally closed the Rosslare and Pembroke Dock service on 5 January and later worked alongside **St Brendan** during the summer season. At Holyhead the **St Columba** was given a major upgrade in April, while accommodation aboard **Leinster** was also improved, both ships were covered while they were away by the **St David**. **Connacht** was also upgraded shortly afterwards. The **Leinster** and **Connacht** reappeared in a new and distinctive, but rather unusual, livery which included a dark blue zone over the entire ship across the stern quarters to create a rather odd truncated appearance. The **Connacht** maintained the Dublin and Liverpool route and the **Leinster** served between Dublin and Holyhead, the latter in conjunction with Sealink British Ferries. **St David** spent the summer at Stranraer working alongside **Galloway Princess** and **Darnia**; vehicle carrying increased by 10% on this route during the year.

By early July a second ship was required for the Sealink British Ferries/B&I service at Fishguard. The **Innisfallen** remained under maintenance at Liverpool, and the Ostend car ferry **Prins Philippe** was chartered for three weeks to work alongside **St Brendan** until the **Innisfallen** was ready to take up duty on the joint service between

St Columba (1977) in full Sealink British Ferries livery is seen leaving Holyhead.
(Bernard McCall)

The B&I ferry *Leinster* (1981) arriving at the Salt Island Berth, Holyhead in August 1992.
(Author)

The B&I ferry *Connacht* (1978) arriving at Pembroke Dock whilst covering a refit in early 1988.
(Bernard McCall)

***Tynwald** (1967), formerly the **Antrim Princess**, took up duty on charter to the Steam Packet company from April 1986.*
(Bernard McCall)

Rosslare and Fishguard. **Innisfallen** was put on the market during the summer and was sold in the autumn.

The **Antrim Princess** was registered at Douglas on 16 March in preparation to being renamed **Tynwald** and painted in full Steam Packet livery a few weeks later. The cargo ship **Peveril** was retained on charter by Belfast Freight Ferries on the Heysham and Belfast service although that company had made it known they were looking for a larger ship. The two remaining side-loading ferries were rostered to work between Liverpool and Douglas twice a week in the summer season, with trips to Fleetwood, Belfast, Dublin and Stranraer operated also from Douglas.

The **Stena Searider** was chartered for use on the Cairnryan and Larne service by Townsend Thoresen until late March. The service otherwise remained in the hands of **Europic Ferry** and **Free Enterprise IV**, although crews of both ships refused to sail between late-March and mid-May in support of a manning dispute at Felixstowe. The **Gaelic Ferry** was sold out of the fleet during March.

On 10 July 1986 a 'new' **Ionic Ferry** sailed from Cairnryan for the first time while the **Free Enterprise IV** stood down after the morning return trip and then returned to Dover. The **Ionic Ferry** was none other than the **Dragon** in a new guise, transferred from the Townsend Thoresen routes from Portsmouth. Renamed **Ionic Ferry**, and with the large passenger accommodation block removed from above the garage deck aft, she was a worthy successor and offered garage space for both commercial and private car traffic while offering comfortable, although somewhat dated, passenger accommodation. As converted, she could carry 60 standard 12m commercial vehicles or trailers.

In early September the **Peveril** completed her charter to Belfast Freight Ferries and returned to Liverpool for attention, preparatory to taking up duties for her owners in October between Liverpool and Douglas. Belfast Freight Ferries replaced her with two ships, firstly the chartered Dutch-flagged freight ferry **Niekerk**, with an option to purchase, and which was owned by JH Templaars Sheepvaart BV. She had been built in 1971 as the **Starmark** for German owners, had twin screws and a service speed of 17½ knots and offered 636 lane metres of vehicle and trailer space. Originally, she had passenger accommodation for up to 30 persons but this was not certificated within the charter to Belfast Freight Ferries. Shortly afterwards, on 1 October, the **Saga Moon** commenced on the service.

Saga Moon was owned by the Aug Bolten, Wm Miller, Nachfolger and offered 760 lane metres of stowage space. She had been completed as **Lidartinduand** in 1984 for the Traderline A/S.

Another new freight ferry service started at Heysham in November running between Heysham and Warrenpoint. The company behind the new route was Merchant Ferries and their **Merchant Trader** was rostered to leave Heysham at 0600 hours sailing twelve hours later on the return voyage. She offered three return sailings per week and quickly developed new traffic which was supported from both the north and south of Ireland.

Both **Merchant Trader** and Merchant Ferries were owned by Cenargo Broking Services Limited of London, the **Merchant Trader** had previously been chartered to the Royal Fleet Auxiliary as **Sir Lamorak**, as part of a contract the company had won to supply a new airfield in the Falkland Islands. However, she was no newcomer to Heysham, having served between Heysham and Belfast under the Sealink banner in 1980 as **Lune Bridge**. Cenargo was an international company based in London with offices in Cyprus and the United States. Its traditional business had been the tanker charter market but it had moved into bulk freight handling and was keen to become involved in the short-sea ferry industry. It owned the **Scirocco**, formerly the **Keren** (ex-British Rail **St Edmund**) which it had chartered to the Royal Fleet Auxiliary but which was later on charter in the Mediterranean; all other ships had the prefix 'Merchant' to their names, while the deep-sea ships were all managed by Denholm Ship Management. The financial model for the company operations was based to a large degree on loans and mortgages such that the company worked with an extraordinarily small capital base, a model which required careful balancing of the books and exchange of assets and debts as required.

Manx Viking finished on 30 September 1986 and sailed to Barrow-in-Furness to await a buyer. Her roster was taken over by **Peveril** the following day. The two side-loading motor ships, **Mona's Queen** and **Lady of Mann**, finished for the summer in mid-September. The **Saint Patrick II** deputised for **Saint Colum I** on the Liverpool and Belfast passenger service in early October.

The big news in December 1986 was the purchase of European Ferries by P&O for £448 million. European Ferries had been led by Roland Wickendon who was succeeded by Keith Wickendon until his death in an air crash in July 1983. Keith Wickendon, who had been MP for Dorking, had invested heavily in property in the United States, but the company was left exposed when that property market collapsed as the price of oil slumped; P&O had earlier acquired a 21% interest in European Ferries. Plans of integrating the Irish Sea services were not announced at the time of the take-over, but there were obvious implications for Pandoro at Fleetwood, Townsend Thoresen at Cairnryan and P&O at Ardrossan.

Ionic Ferry (1967) formerly the Dragon, seen arriving at Cairnryan on 1 August 1986 during her fourth week of service on the Larne service as successor to Free Enterprise IV.

(Author)

The Ionic Ferry proudly featured on the cover of the 1986 brochure for the Townsend Thoresen Cairnryan and Larne service.

(Author's Collection)

Saint Killian II hit the news on Christmas Eve when she was disabled off the Cornish Coast by an engine room fire on passage from Le Havre to Rosslare. She was eventually towed safely into Plymouth with 296 passengers on board seemingly none the worse for their experience.

Ominously, Sea Containers Limited reported a net loss for 1986 of US $50 million, compared with a net profit the previous year of US $40 million. The company reported substantial losses from Sealink British Ferries due to a variety of causes, but in hindsight these were excuses that covered uninspired management and a constantly changing vision.

In 1987, B&I chartered the French registered ferry **Senlac** from Dieppe Ferries from mid-June until September. Various ships stood in for Sealink British Ferries' **St Brendan** which suffered a number of mechanical failures during the year. Relief vessels included **Stena Sailer**, **Darnia**, **St David** and **Earl Harold**. **Earl Harold** stood in when **St Columba** was absent on overhaul, and carried out the same duty at Stranraer, while **Darnia**, **Galloway Princess** and **St David** were each away in turn. The side-loader **Mona's Queen** stood in for the **Tynwald** on the Isle of Man service from Heysham. At Cairnryan the **Viking Trader**, of similar ilk to Pandoro's **Bison** and **Buffalo**, was brought up from the South Coast to cover for the refits of **Europic Ferry** and **Ionic Ferry**.

During early 1987 an announcement was made that the Swansea and Cork passenger and accompanied car service was to be resumed by a new company to be sponsored by local and national government in Ireland and local interests in South Wales. The new company, Swansea-Cork Car Ferries, advertised in the press that it would start the service on 16 April with three sailings per week, with a fourth sailing provided in the peak season between May and September. A mid-week return between Cork and Roscoff was also proposed in conjunction with Brittany Ferries. The Polish ship **Rogalin** was chartered and renamed **Celtic Pride**; she retained her Polish crew for the season. The **Rogalin** was owned by the Polish Baltic company (Polferries) and had been built in 1976 as the **Aallottar** for the Silja Line.

The Irish Continental Line along with Belfast Car Ferries Limited was finally sold by the receiver of Irish Shipping Limited in March 1987. A deal amounting to Irish £15.5 million had been agreed with a consortium from the Irish financial industry, with the objective of the new company, to be called Irish Continental Group, continuing in business much as before. During the year Irish Continental Line was rebranded Irish Ferries.

Friday 6 March 1987, and the loss of the **Herald of Free Enterprise** at Zeebrugge (Chapter 1), had many serious implications for the ferry industry. Surprisingly neither shippers nor passengers were deterred from ferry crossings by the tragedy as trade and travel continued with little effect on the subsequent summer tourist traffic, this despite press speculation that modern roll-on roll-off ferries were inherently unsafe. The outcome of the subsequent inquiry and the recommendations to the industry that were fed through later in the year impacted both the management, standing operational procedures and the safety features built into vehicle ferries. It would eventually shorten the careers of a number of ships serving under the Red Ensign.

P&O, as the new owner of European Ferries, which included Townsend Thoresen, set about distancing itself from the **Herald of Free Enterprise** and the Townsend Thoresen brand. By May almost all the Townsend Thoresen ships had received pale blue funnels adorned with the P&O house flag. Haste to adopt the new funnel colours was such that the house flag on the **Ionic Ferry** was so small it was hardly visible, and that on the starboard side of the **Europic Ferry** had the fly of the flag facing forward and looked thoroughly bizarre. Painting out the orange hulls and former owners name was not so easy and this took place over the ensuing months as opportunity arose. **Ionic Ferry** was in the news on 3 June when she ran aground on a falling tide at Larne. She was refloated 10 hours later but had to be withdrawn temporarily for repairs to a bent propeller.

In April 1987 the **Merchant Trader** was replaced on the Heysham and Warrenpoint freight service by the larger capacity **Merchant Isle**.

Galloway Princess (1979) back from refit and heading down Loch Ryan bound for Larne.
(Author)

Viking Trader (1977) made her first visit to Cairnryan on relief duties in 1987, before returning to Townsend Thoresen's Portsmouth and Cherbourg route.
(Author)

Celtic Pride (1976) started on Swansea and Cork duties in April 1987 for a consortium led by local councils on both sides of the Irish Sea.

63

Europic Ferry (1967) leaving Cairnryan on 26 August 1987 with a hastily added P&O flag on a newly painted P&O blue funnel – the flag, all that was available in the rush to rebrand Townsend Thoresen, was back to front!

(Author)

Merchant Venture (1978) replaced the *Merchant Trader* on the Warrenpoint service for Merchant Ferries in April 1987.

(Author)

Belfast Freight Ferries newly acquired *Spheroid* (1971) arriving at Heysham in the new company livery.

(Author)

*The former Harwich and Zeebrugge train ferry **Cambridge Ferry** (1963) was used in various roles on the Irish Sea towards the end of her career. She is seen laid up in the River Fal between two such roles.*

(Bernard McCall)

Her registered owner was Proofbond Limited (V Ships UK Limited) of Douglas, Isle of Man. She had been built in 1978 for Italian owners and offered 650 lane metres of vehicle and trailer space on two decks and had accommodation for 12 drivers. Shortly after she started work on the Irish Sea her name was changed to **Merchant Venture** and she was registered under the ownership of Cenargo Navigation Limited (managed by Crescent Shipping), of Douglas. Meantime, Belfast Freight Ferries purchased the **Niekerk**, gave her the name **Spheroid** and registered her at Douglas. She retained the dark blue hull and funnel of her former owner but the Scruttons house flag, a red 'S' on white ground, was added to the funnel. Scrutton, Sons & Company had owned ships in the late eighteenth and early nineteenth century and two of these had carried the name **Spheroid**. **Saga Moon** received the same livery, but was registered at Gibraltar.

Yet another new company started on the Irish Sea, this time between Rosslare and Pembroke Dock, starting in early May. The imaginatively named Ro-Ro Ferries, backed by Irish haulage company Shannahans, chartered the cargo ship **Marine Evangeline** from SNCF Dieppe Ferries and placed her on a daily service with departures from Rosslare at 2030 and return from Pembroke Dock the following afternoon at 1430 hours. She had 590 lane metres of vehicle space. In December the ship was returned to Dieppe and the service ceased in the face of the return of the B&I Line to the route after it had closed at Fishguard.

On September 30 1987, the **Saint Colum I** stood down on the Liverpool and Belfast service and was relieved by the **Saint Patrick II** from Irish Ferries, formerly Irish Continental Line.

At Holyhead the **Stena Sailer** supported the **St Columba** with additional freight sailings during the peak summer period. Towards the end of the year commercial traffic at Fishguard warranted an additional freight ship and the former Harwich train ferry **Cambridge Ferry** was brought out of lay up on the River Fal.

The year 1988 started with the termination of the working agreement between the B&I Line and Sealink British Ferries. This was followed by the closure of the B&I Line service between Liverpool and Dublin to release the **Connacht**, which was put up for sale although, in the meantime, she transferred to the Rosslare and Pembroke Dock route. Pandoro transferred its Dublin freight ships, **Tipperary** and **Buffalo**, from Fleetwood to Liverpool as a response to the closure of the passenger car and freight service previously operated by **Connacht**.

The passenger service was then reopened by Sealink British Ferries who put the **Earl William** on a daily return between Liverpool and Dun Laoghaire, commencing in early April. **Earl William** was suited to both overnight and daylight crossings as she had ample cabin accommodation and the ship soon became popular on the crossing. At Liverpool she shared the Belfast Car Ferries berth at Brocklebank Dock and used the Langton Dock entrance to and from the Mersey. The roster for the season was departure from Liverpool at 2330 hours for an eight hour passage, returning from Dun Laoghaire at 1030 hours. She missed 13 sailings in August due to problems with the variable pitch mechanism on her two propellers. **Earl Granville** stood in for her refit period in November but this ship found few favours with the travelling public.

The Isle of Man ferry **Tynwald** developed stability problems due to failure of ballasting equipment in the summer and this put her passenger certificate in jeopardy. Amazingly, it was agreed with the regulatory authority that a water bowser could be carried on the main vehicle deck and stowed each voyage to best suit the ship's stability, but it was stressed that the situation must be remedied as soon as practicable. Needless to say, the bowser was sent ashore shortly afterwards!

With **Connacht** established on the Rosslare and Pembroke Dock service, the **Prins Hamlet**, from DFDS, worked as relief during March and April. **Prins Hamlet** relieved **Connacht** for refit and later while **Connacht** stood in for **Leinster** at Holyhead. In June it was announced that **Connacht** had been sold to Brittany Ferries with delivery in

Earl William (1964) was placed on a new Liverpool and Dun Laoghaire service following the withdrawal of B&I from Liverpool and Dublin. She is pictured emerging from refit at Cardiff.

(Bernard McCall)

the autumn as a new ship for their service between Portsmouth and St Malo; she was given the name **Duchess Anne**. B&I had now undertaken every cost cutting measure conceivable and was leaving itself with just one ship to run two routes. The chartered **Saint Patrick II** was again brought in to run the Pembroke Dock service to Rosslare – the survival of the company now remained in the balance.

Winter reliefs included the **Seafreight Highway** from Dover standing in for the **St David** at Stranraer and later displacing **Stena Sailer** at Holyhead, the latter moving to Fishguard. At the end of the year the **Stena Sailer** was bought by Sealink British Ferries and renamed **St Cybi**; her port of registration was changed to Nassau in Grand Bahama Island. Another new visitor was Fred Olsen's **Bolette** which was chartered by the Tynwald government to cover the TT race period in case a seamen's strike, that was already affecting P&O and Sealink British Ferries, engulfed the Isle of Man company ships. **Bolette** served between Holyhead and Douglas from late-May until mid-June.

Earl Granville (1973) came round from the Channel Islands routes to deputise for Earl William in November 1988 but her timekeeping was poor.

(Author)

The normal round of winter relief duties included the train ferry *St Eloi*, from Dover, which was used at both Stranraer and Holyhead. On return to Dover the ship was renamed *Channel Entente*. At Holyhead, the B&I ship *Leinster* was relieved by *The Viking* on charter from Sally Line. B&I were finally able to announce a trading profit, albeit of only £1.8 million, for the year 1988, this to the great relief of many as this news secured at least the short-term future of the company. The *Cambridge Ferry* was rostered to support the *St Brendan* during the summer peak season on the Fishguard and Rosslare service.

The *Tipperary* was transferred to North Sea duties in the winter and the *Bison* moved from Fleetwood to Liverpool to replace her on the joint Dublin service with B&I, working alongside *Buffalo*. The Fleetwood and Larne service was maintained by the *Puma* and the *Viking Trader*, the latter now on permanent transfer to Pandoro. *Viking Trader* arrived in full P&O colours – dark blue hull and funnel with the P&O flag on the funnel. Her bow door had been welded shut before she started at Fleetwood as a consequence of her annual survey. A dock strike at Liverpool later in the year had *Bison* and *Buffalo* working between Pembroke Dock and Dublin for a short while.

Before the main season started in 1988, the Isle of Man company invested £2.6 million in a major refit and upgrade for its side-loading ferry *Lady of Mann*. The car deck was extended to accommodate 30 more vehicles and the passenger accommodation was totally refurbished. The ship was adorned in a new livery which included a large medallion type logo on the front of the superstructure with red stripes leading aft along the superstructure. Her sister, *Mona's Queen*, went into the summer season with only essential remedial work carried out.

The new Swansea-Cork service finished on 6 January 1989, despite good loadings over the two year tenure of the *Celtic Pride*. This was brought about by the withdrawal of state aid from the Irish Government, although an offer was made, it was too late to find a suitable ship ready for the all-important summer season. Swansea Cork Ferries pledged to find a ship for the 1990 season.

B&I, meanwhile took the *Earl Harold* on a six month charter to operate the Rosslare and Pembroke Dock service in place of the chartered *Saint Patrick II*. The *Earl Harold* was painted in full B&I livery, her port of registration changed to Nassau and, after a comprehensive overhaul, she started on the route on 5 April complete with an Irish crew. She was supported by the Cypriot registered cargo ship *Oleander* for the peak season in order to divert commercial traffic away from the *Earl Harold* and let her concentrate on the accompanied car traffic. At the end of the six month charter *Earl Harold* was sold to Greek owners and her place at Pembroke Dock taken for the winter months by the Faroese ferry *Norröna*.

In November 1989 the Irish Ferries' ships were relieved by Brittany Ferries' *Armorique* which then moved to Liverpool to stand in for the *Earl William*.

As early as March 1989 frustration with the performance of James Sherwood and Sea Containers was such that the Swedish Stena Line bought an 8% holding in the company with a view to eventually acquiring the ferry business. At the same time Tiphook plc let it be known that they were interested in the container side of the business. This placed Sea Containers on the defensive which did little to promote much needed investment in the Sealink British Ferries side of the business. In May, Stena Line A/B and Tiphook plc formed a consortium under the name Temple Holdings Limited which made an offer of US $824 million for Sea Containers, of which nearly US $400 million was for the Stena Line interest in Sealink British Ferries. This bid and a subsequent increased bid were both rejected by Mr Sherwood and his directors.

One positive move made by Sea Containers was the five year charter of the *Visby* announced in the autumn, as a replacement for the *St Brendan* on the Fishguard and Rosslare service. *St Brendan* had long been outmoded and required a second ship in support during the summer months. She was sold to Italian interests at the end of the year. Her replacement, the *Visby*, was built in 1980 for Gotandlinjen (Gotlandsbolaget) but became superfluous to her owners needs when they lost the contract to trade between Nynäshamn near Stockholm and Visby on the island of Gotland. She was an impressive

*Pandoro's **Bison** (1975) seen off the Poolbeg Light in April 1993 in full B&I Line livery for the joint service between Liverpool and Dublin.*
(Author)

*The **Viking Trader** (1977) now in full Pandoro colours, departing Fleetwood on 9 May 1990 with a full load of trailers on the upper vehicle deck. (Author)*

*The dining saloon aboard **Viking Trader** (1977): she could accommodate 30 drivers although she held a passenger certificate for 80.*

(Pandoro Limited)

vessel with a speed of 20 knots which could reduce the Fishguard and Rosslare passage time to just 3½ hours. Her Swedish owners operated her with a capacity for 2000 passengers and 517 cars or 54 commercial vehicles or trailers, although deadweight restrictions limited full use of the available garage space.

On the negative side, Sealink British Ferries announced the closure of the profitable Liverpool and Dun Laoghaire service from 8 January 1990, with the incumbent **Earl William** being listed for sale. In February, **Earl William** was used as relief to the **Saint Colum I** which was away on annual overhaul. In another strange move the **St Cybi** was to be replaced at Holyhead by **Earl Granville** in a cargo-only mode.

On 31 January, the **St Columba** was disabled by an engine room fire on passage to Holyhead on the morning sailing from Dun Laoghaire. Fire fighters were flown in from Anglesey and the fire extinguished, while tugs brought the stricken ferry into Holyhead where she berthed twelve hours after leaving Dun Laoghaire. Her place was taken by **Darnia** from Stranraer and then by the **Lady of Mann** from Douglas working alongside **St Cybi** which had been brought back from Stranraer. **Earl Granville** was then sent to Stranraer to give support during the overhaul period; she had a temporary passenger certificate for just 80 persons and was succeeded on the route by **Cambridge Ferry** which was better suited to the commercial traffic on offer. The Boulogne ship **Horsa** arrived at Holyhead next and when **St Columba** retuned in mid-March, **Horsa** took over the freight sailings from **St Cybi** which then went for overhaul. Thereafter, the **Horsa** ran alongside the **St Columba** until the end of April. **Horsa** returned to the link after her own refit and worked with **St Columba** throughout the summer period.

On 15 January 1990, Sea Containers finally announced its acceptance of yet another attempt by Temple Holdings to purchase the greater part of its business, this time for £568 million. £247 million of this sum was to come from Stena Line for Sealink British Ferries. James Sherwood recommended to his shareholders that they accept the offer and Sealink British Ferries became part of the Stena Line group of companies, although Sea Containers retained its 41% interest in the Isle of Man Steam Packet Company. The deal included the ports of Fishguard, Holyhead and Stranraer.

Shortly afterward Stena Line pledged a £178 million investment package in Sealink. Stena, of course, was no newcomer to the Irish Sea and the other Sealink regions as it had long been involved in a number of charters and ship sales to Sealink and other operators around the British Isles. Interestingly, Sea Containers was prohibited by the contract of sale to operate in UK waters in competition with Stena using any vessel with a speed of less than 30 knots.

In February the Chief Executive Officers of Stena Line A/B, Mr Dan Sten Olsson and Mr Lars-Erik Ottoson, met with the Sealink Board working under Managing Director Mr Charles Lennox-Conyngham. It was resolved that Stena Line would appoint a supervisor but until then the Sealink management was to continue as before.

The **Visby** arrived at Fishguard ready to take up duty in February 1990. The largest ship on the Irish Sea services was greeted by fanfares on both side of the channel. She was intended to be named **Fandango** as part of Sea Containers 'F' nomenclature until

Felicity (1980), the last of the ships to be given one of James Sherwood's preferred names beginning with F, seen arriving at Fishguard under the Swedish flag.

Munster (1970), in full B&I Line colours, built originally as *Prins Oberon*, seen on the approach to the Pembroke Dock terminal.

it was realised that the name of one of its Dover vessels, *Fantasia*, translated into the French vernacular with unfortunate connotations! The *Visby* was consequently given the more refined name of *Felicity*, an undistinguished name that neither had any connection with her new duties nor with any ship that had served before her at Fishguard.

B&I fought back against the new challenge from Sealink by chartering the Singapore registered *Cruise Muhibah* to take over the Rosslare and Pembroke Dock route. The onetime *Prins Oberon* in the Lion Ferry A/B fleet had, since 1986, served Feri Malaysia running a two week long circuit between East and West Malaysia. With her swimming pool stripped out and minus other luxury adornments she commenced at Rosslare on 27 April 1990 under the name *Munster* and registered at Dublin. She displaced the chartered Faroese ferry *Norröna*. The *Munster* offered nearly 500 lane metres of garage space, but like *Norröna* before her, she could only really be viewed as a stop-gap if the Irish company was ever to prosper. The charter was through a Dublin agency and was initially for a two year period with a subsequent option to purchase. While refitting at Dublin a pair of exotic looking snakes emerged from a compartment when

*Just painted in the new Steam Packet company white livery, the Bahamian registered **King Orry** (1974) seen departing Heysham for Douglas in January 1991.*

(Author)

it was opened following a small fire. The hapless reptiles were speedily removed by veterinary officers from Irish Customs who later identified the pair as harmless and indigenous to Malaysia! In the early autumn, B&I was put up for sale by the Irish Government – bids were received from P&O with whom the company partnered the Liverpool and Dublin cargo service, Irish Ferries and Maersk Line.

At Cairnryan the **Ionic Ferry** and **Europic Ferry** were relieved in February and March by the Cypriot freighter **Roseanne**, which carried a small number of drivers on the service to Larne. At the end of the year the freighter **Gunilla**, normally on Ramsgate and IJmuiden duties with Anglo-Dutch Ferries, was chartered to cover the refit periods for the **Bison** and **Buffalo** on the Liverpool and Dublin service.

In February 1990, the Isle of Man Steam Packet Company announced that it had purchased the **Channel Entente** from Sea Containers for about £4.3 million (US$7 million) as a replacement for **Tynwald**. **Tynwald** finished duty on 18 February and the **Channel Entente** took her first sailing to Heysham the following morning, albeit delayed by poor weather. **Channel Entente** had been registered at Nassau before she was delivered to the Steam Packet Company. Sea Containers agreed to waive the redemption fee for the unused charter period for **Tynwald**, which did not comply with incoming stability rules, and she was then put on the market and sold in April to Italian owners. In June, Sea Containers, attempted unsuccessfully to buy the outstanding shares in the Isle of Man Steam Packet Company, ruffling a few feathers on the island in doing so!

The viability of a number of older ships such as **Tynwald** and **Earl Harold** had been greatly reduced as they did not comply with the new post-**Herald of Free Enterprise** 'stability in damaged condition' regulations. Many of the vehicle ferries dating from the early 1970s could have been altered but at prohibitive cost and with significant reduction in cargo deadweight capacity. Sale of these ships to foreign-flag buyers had become the preferred option. Among other new requirements aboard British ferries was the issuing of consecutively numbered boarding passes to foot passengers in order to ensure a proper tally on the passenger complement (still at 18 passengers to the ton cargo deadweight).

At the end of the 1990 summer season the side-loader **Mona's Queen** was laid up eventually to be sold while the newly refurbished **Lady of Mann** enjoyed continued service. The **Channel Entente** was renamed **King Orry** in December but she retained her Bahamian registry. During her autumn refit she received a new hoistable mezzanine deck which could carry an additional 60 cars. **King Orry** started on a new routine of Douglas and Heysham sailings coupled with a Saturday return from Douglas to Liverpool so allowing up to five hours shopping time for the islanders.

Swansea Cork Ferries Limited was back in business in 1990, again with a grant from the Irish Government. Irish Ferries had previously been offered the same grant, which it turned down, stating that the route was not viable even just for the peak summer season. The **Ionian Sun**, formerly B&I's **Innisfallen** and before that **Leinster**, was chartered for the summer period by Swansea-Cork Ferries and commenced service on 9 May 1990. **Ionian Sun** was owned by Strintzis Lines Mediterranean Shipping Company of Piraeus, and while at Swansea she retained her Greek crew. The ship offered accommodation for 1100 passengers with cabin accommodation for 440, and had space for up to 255 accompanied cars. The **Ionian Sun** was welcomed back to her old route although she was not always able to keep up to schedule. She now offered a swimming pool, cinema and a disco, a far cry from her former B&I days!

A second and third ship joined the Merchant Ferries service to Warrenpoint from Heysham when Crescent Shipping (managers for Cenargo Navigation Limited) purchased the Italian cargo ships **Salahala** and **Emadala**. They were almost identical sisters built in 1977 and 1978 respectively and had been managed by Gilvani Societa di Navigazione per Azoni on services in the Eastern Mediterranean. They were given the name **Merchant Valiant** and **Merchant Victor**

Merchant Victor (1978) along with sister Merchant Valiant were important for the growth of Merchant Ferries; Merchant Victor is seen arriving at Heysham.

(Author)

and retained their registration at Hamilton, Bermuda. The pair were equipped with twin controllable pitch propellers and a bow thrust unit and they had a service speed of 16 knots; each ship carried a crew of eighteen. The **Merchant Valiant** and **Merchant Victor** could carry 52 standard 12 metre trailers plus two 15 metre units and 33 trade cars, they could also accommodate 12 drivers. The ships were valuable additions to the route and demonstrated how traffic had grown since the service commenced in November 1986.

Business was also good for Belfast Freight Ferries which had chartered the **Bassro Star** from Norwegian owners Bassro Star K/S to provide additional capacity. The ship was a single screw vessel and was found to be difficult at berthing in inclement weather conditions. Interestingly she had been built in 1976 as **Seaspeed Dora** for the new Seaspeed Ferry Company Limited service from Felixstowe to the Mediterranean, although she was sold two years later (see Chapter 4). A medium-term solution to the under-capacity on the Heysham and Belfast route was attained when **Spheroid** was taken off duty to receive a new midships section increasing her capacity from 636 to 728 lane metres.

In September, Belfast Car Ferries announced the closure of its Liverpool and Belfast passenger and vehicle service. It had been trying unsuccessfully for some time to find a replacement for the **Saint Colum I** on the service, the ship having become outmoded and expensive to maintain. The final sailing took place on 14 October 1990 and shortly afterwards **Saint Colum I** sailed for Piraeus to take up duties in the Greek islands as **Demitrious Express**.

Before the year was out Stena Line announced its proposals for 1991 under the new banner 'Sealink Stena Line'. These included moving the Dover ships **St Anselm** and **St Christopher** to the Irish Sea and the disposal of **Darnia** at Stranraer. **Darnia** would in any case have required sponsons fitting to comply with the post-**Herald of Free Enterprise** damage stability requirements. The **St Columba** was to be converted into a luxury cruise ferry to attract trippers during the off-peak periods and accommodation aboard the **Felicity** was to be upgraded. There was considerable disruption at the end of the year with delays caused by heavy weather which also caused the loss of a truck that was washed overboard from **St Cybi** while on passage from Dublin to Holyhead.

The Stena Line investment programme was welcome news. The five year period up to and including 1990 had been one of stagnation on the Irish Sea with a distinct lack of vision and inadequate investment coming from Sea Containers while B&I had merely been struggling to survive. The Pandoro services held their own and traffic had built up both on the joint Liverpool and Dublin service with B&I Line and the route between Fleetwood and Larne. The frequent P&O service between Cairnryan and Larne was well patronised but the economic growth of Northern Ireland was still hindered by terrorist activities and had not realised anything like its full potential. New operators Belfast Freight Ferries and the Cenargo-owned Merchant Ferries were both enjoying expansion while gaining a firm hold on the central Irish Sea freight traffic. The 1990s looked set for better trading conditions, but time alone would tell.

Belfast Freight Ferries soon expanded its operation from the one-ship operation by Spheroid (1971), seen here at Belfast.

(Author)

CHAPTER 7
OF FOREIGN FLAGS, FAST FERRIES AND ECONOMIC GROWTH

Stena Caledonia (1981), formerly St David, seen on the approach to Stranraer off the Pier on Wednesday 17 April 1991.

(Author)

The Sealink Stena Line reshuffle at the start of 1991 went ahead at breathtaking speed. **Darnia** finished at Stranraer on 21 February and was handed over to her new owners ten days later at Bremerhaven. Thereafter, each ship emerged from winter refit with the new company name on the hull and with a new corporate Stena Line name – first to be dealt with was the **St Anselm**, formerly on the Dover and Calais service which, as **Stena Cambria**, stood in for the **Felicity** at Fishguard from mid-November 1990, and then **St Columba** at Holyhead in January. She then moved to Stranraer on relief duties in mid-March. The Irish Sea ships were renamed:

- **St Anselm**, from Dover, renamed **Stena Cambria** for the Holyhead and Dun Laoghaire service
- **St Columba** renamed **Stena Hibernia** for the Holyhead and Dun Laoghaire service
- **Felicity** renamed **Stena Felicity** for the Fishguard and Rosslare service
- **Galloway Princess** renamed **Stena Galloway** for the Stranraer and Larne service
- **St David** renamed **Stena Caledonia** also for the Stranraer and Larne service
- **St Christopher**, from Dover, renamed **Stena Antrim** for the Stranraer and Larne service

While all this was going on, the **St Cybi** and **Cambridge Ferry** worked together at Stranraer until **Stena Antrim** was available in June (she was only released from Dover in April). The **Horsa**, now **Stena Horsa**, was back at Holyhead for a brief period once more before the sale-listed **Earl William** could be reactivated to replace her, and until the **Stena Antrim** was available. Also, at Holyhead the **Leinster** was relieved by **Munster**, while **Norröna**, from Smyril Line, was again chartered to maintain the Pembroke Dock link; it was announced in January that Irish Ferries Group was the preferred purchaser of B&I Line.

The gap left by the closure of Belfast Car Ferries' service between Liverpool and Belfast was filled by P&O with a new cargo only service starting on 5 August 1991. P&O was able to secure a six month charter of **Merchant Venture** from Cenargo/Merchant Ferries. It had been intended that she would run between Liverpool and Dublin alongside **Bison** and **Buffalo**, but at that time Dublin was unable to handle the additional ship. Clearly Merchant Ferries considered that the charter fee would exceed any traffic lost to the P&O service, be it to Dublin or Belfast. In the event, the **Merchant Venture** mimicked the service previously operated by **Saint Colum I** with six round trips per week between Liverpool and Belfast. Merchant Ferries' **Merchant Victor** was then chartered briefly for use between Ramsgate and Ostend but returned to the Irish Sea in September working alongside **Merchant Valiant**.

In 1991, **Celtic Pride** returned to the Swansea and Cork route with occasional Cork and Roscoff duties fitted into her schedule for Brittany Ferries. The service started on 1 March with financial backing from the Irish Government and her season on the Irish Sea ended on 28 October. She was back on the seasonal link in 1992, but this time there were no additional services between Roscoff and Cork. In November 1992 the operating company was bought for £1.1 million by the Greek-owned Strintzis Lines Mediterranean Shipping Company which planned to introduce a new ship on the link in 1993.

In June 1991, a new company trading as Dublin Ferries introduced the chartered **Fichtelberg** and **Roseanne** on the Dublin and Liverpool route in direct competition with Pandoro. The Irish haulier Shannahans was the prime mover behind the new company, having

Stena Antrim (1981) formerly the Dover-based St Christopher, seen at Larne on the morning arrival from Stranraer.
(Author)

Norse Lagan (1968) seen leaving Belfast on passage for Liverpool. She offered a service for both commercial traffic and accompanied cars and their passengers.
(Author)

previously been involved with a service between Pembroke Dock and Rosslare (see Chapter 6). **Roseanne** normally served on Irish Ferries Continental services from Rosslare during the summer months. She was replaced by sister ship to **Fichtelberg**, the **Gleichberg** in August and the service increased to two sailings per day from each port; the ships had been built in 1975 for Deutsche Seereederie Rostock GmbH. In September, they were painted in Dublin Ferries livery along with the company name on the ship's hulls and renamed **Spirit of Dublin** and **City of Dublin** respectively. Within a short time Pandoro reduced its four sailings per day to just two because the bulk of the Irish-based trade quickly migrated to the new company – despite its German registered ships!

Belfast Freight Ferries chartered the **Schiaffino** to supplement sailings between Heysham and Belfast alongside **Spheroid** and **Saga Moon**.

Another new company started in November 1991 under the title Norse Irish Ferries. This company was financed by a consortium of haulage companies and the Grover Star Shipping Corporation of Norway. The former **Hansa Link** from the Malmo and Travemunde circuit maintained by Nordo Link was chartered to the new company from Dutch owners, Wagenborg Shipping BV, and renamed **Norse Lagan**. She offered three round trips per week between Liverpool and Belfast. This resulted in P&O withdrawing the **Merchant Venture** from Liverpool and Belfast duties on 21 December 1991.

The **Norse Lagan** was originally built for Canadian owners in 1968 and was lengthened from 147 metres to an incredible 187 metres in 1990. She had a passenger certificate for 400 and commenced carrying passengers in April 1992 with departures from each port every other night. Alternate sailings were taken by the cargo only **Transgermania**, built in 1976 for German owners, with daily departures maintained from both ports. The **Transgermania** was found to be too small for the traffic on offer and was replaced in April by the cargo-only **Norse Mersey**, formerly **Stena Searider**, on charter from Stena Line A/B. This ship had a certificate for 200 passengers, mainly accommodated on pullman type seating, and was given a new non-smoking lounge and a bar. She initially had a black hull but this was later changed to dark blue with the company name on the hull. She had a plain dark blue funnel. So successful was the company that within just two years of the service starting it had attained an 18% share of the total Irish Sea roll-on roll-off freight traffic. Its success was underpinned by reliability of its service.

In December 1991, it was finally announced that the Irish Government had sold B&I Line to the Irish Continental Group for Irish £8.5 million. While the Government wrote off the B&I Line accrued debt of Irish £36 million, the new owners pledged an Irish £30 million investment programme for its new acquisition. Part of this programme was the replacement of the chartered **Munster** on the Pembroke Dock and

Stena Searider (1969) was chartered by Norse Irish Ferries, given a bright yellow hull and renamed Norse Mersey.
(Iain McCall)

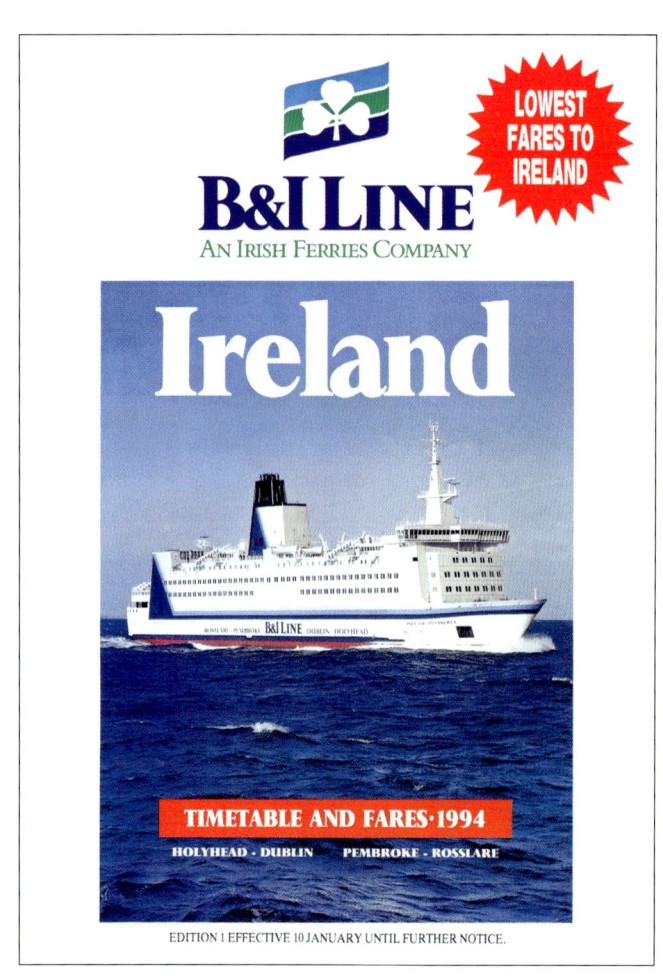

*The newly chartered **Isle of Innisfree** (1986) featured regularly on advertising for the B&I Line, here seen on the 1994 timetables and fares brochure.*

(Author)

Rosslare service with the **Stena Nautica**, to be chartered from Stena Line A/B. **Stena Nautica** was the sister to the **Stena Invicta** already working on the Dover Strait, and she was regarded as a better equipped ship with which to compete directly with the Sealink Stena Line service between Rosslare and Fishguard. Stena, it would seem, was more interested in the charter fee than any likely loss of business although it was increasingly seen that Stena Line UK operated quite separately from its Swedish parent.

The new ship, renamed **Isle of Innisfree**, offered 600 lane metres of vehicle space plus room for a further 152 cars and she had a certificate for 2000 passengers. She started work at Pembroke Dock at the end of March, allowing the **Munster** to stand down ready to be returned to her owners. Meanwhile the Irish Continental Group maintained the **Saint Killian II** and **Saint Patrick II** on its Rosslare to Le Havre and Cherbourg routes, and both ships were in need of replacement in the medium future.

In early December 1991, Dublin Ferries were brought to a standstill by a strike at Dublin Cargo Handling over manning of a new crane. Both the **City of Dublin** and **Spirit of Dublin** were laid up at Dublin while the competition, Pandoro/B&I Line, who used different shore agencies, reaped the benefit of the extra trade. Unfortunately, the power of an Irish Union was enough to bring the new shipping company down, and with outgoings continued through to January and with no income to pay them with, the company ceased to trade and was obliged to return the two ships to their owners. Irish trade unions were more aggressive than their English counterparts and nearly brought the B&I Line to its knees in the 1980s. Nevertheless, the English trade unions were still a strong force to be considered, particularly when a company planned change that might put jobs at risk.

The year 1991 had seen the onset of serious economic decline in the Republic of Ireland which, coupled with the Troubles in the north, had a serious impact on trade across the Irish Sea. The recession was so deep that construction work stopped at the new Dublin Dockyard city development where half completed office blocks lay under silent

***Saint Killian II** (1973) arriving at Cherbourg on 2 June 1990, was one of two ships operated by Irish Ferries on its Continental services at the time of the take-over of B&I Line.*

(Author)

Stena Hengist *(1972), seen as **Hengist**, finished on the Boulogne service in December and came to the Irish Sea on relief duties between January and April 1992.*

(Bernard McCall)

cranes that swung gently to the breeze. The Irish countryside was also affected and was littered with abandoned housing developments where half completed buildings were left open to the weather awaiting funds to progress.

The newly redundant **Stena Hengist** had closed the Boulogne service and arrived for duty at Holyhead on 9 January 1992. The ship was sister to, and former running mate with, the **Stena Horsa**, which as **Horsa** had served at Holyhead for much of the 1990 summer season (see Chapter 6). **Stena Hengist** served as relief vessel working between Holyhead and Dun Laoghaire and then between Stranraer and Larne, returning to Holyhead in mid-March ready for hand over to her new owners as **Romilda**; the **Horsa** had already been sold to Greek owners in February. Closure of the Boulogne link was one of the cost-cutting measures implemented by Stena Line which for the second year running had incurred a massive loss on its British-based ferries (1992 was the first year the company made a profit with its British investment). **St Cybi** was sold after relief work at Holyhead in December 1991 and **Cambridge Ferry** left the fleet for further service in the Mediterranean in April 1992. During the summer, **Stena Galloway** was brought to Holyhead when the **Stena Cambria** broke down. The **Stena Galloway** commenced service on 23 July and stayed on the route until mid-August.

In March 1992, the **Europic Ferry** was replaced on the Cairnryan and Larne service by the **Pride of Ailsa**, formerly **Pride of Sandwich** and built in 1972 as **Free Enterprise VI**. **Pride of Ailsa** took her maiden Irish sailing from Larne on 13 March when **Europic Ferry** stood down for refit. On 18 June **Pride of Ailsa** was joined by sister **Pride of Rathlin**, formerly **Pride of Walmer** and built in 1973 as **Free Enterprise VII**. The second ship displaced the **Ionic Ferry** which was sold for further trading in the Mediterranean. The 'new' ships were extensively rebuilt and lengthened in 1985, the modifications requiring large stability sponsons to be added to the central part of the hull. Both ships were brought to the North Channel in order to provide suitable competition to Stena's upgraded Stranraer and Larne service. The **Europic Ferry** returned to Cairnryan on 2 April, with the new corporate name **European Freighter**, ready to commence two round trips a day, weekdays only, for commercial vehicles and trailers. She retained a passenger certificate for 160 but normally only carried a few tens of drivers.

At Holyhead, the freighter **Auersberg** was chartered during the summer of 1992 to cream the freight traffic away from the **Stena Cambria** and **Stena Hibernia**.

Sea Containers returned to the fray on 1 June 1992 under the trading banner *Seacat Scotland*, which offered a new fast ferry service between Belfast and Stranraer with the catamaran **Seacat Scotland**. Competition with Stena Line was permitted according to the sale contract of Sealink British Ferries provided any vessel used by Sea Containers had a speed of at least 30 knots; the service speed of the **Seacat Scotland** was 36 knots. The brand-new fast wave-piercing catamaran **Seacat Scotland** inaugurated the service on 1 June with the objective of wooing passengers away from the airlines – there was no Belfast City Airport in those days and the airport, Aldergrove, was a long way out of town. The new catamaran offered up to six round trips per day, dropping to just four at slacker periods including the winter months. The voyage time was just 90 minutes from berth to berth; the vessel could accommodate 450 passengers and up to 80 accompanied cars. This was the first fast service on the Irish Sea and was well patronised from the start despite the bumpy ride and frequent cancellations during inclement weather.

From the end of 1992, the **Belard** was transferred from the Ardrossan and Belfast service to Ardrossan and Larne. P&O claimed they had been forced out of Belfast by increasing harbour dues. The change offered a shorter passage time and consolidated the P&O services at Larne; the management of the ship was transferred at the same time to Pandoro.

The year 1993 saw the former Sealink ships emerge from refit with a new 'Stena Sealink Line' banner on their hulls. The move was one step closer to the ships being marketed as just Stena Line with the Sealink

75

Pride of Ailsa (1972) docking at Larne, clearly showing the stability sponsons added during the reconstruction of the ship in 1985.
(Author)

adjunct dropped altogether. Stena Line stated that the Sealink brand was hard to sell given all the 'ups and downs' of its past history. A row developed at Holyhead due to Sea Containers demanding slots for another new Seacat service, this time to Dublin. Both Stena Line, owners of Holyhead port facilities, and Sea Containers blamed the other for the differences and the dispute remained unresolved.

B&I Line's new *Isle of Innisfree* swapped places with the *Leinster* after the Easter break. The larger ship had earlier tested the linkspans at both Holyhead and Dublin and her move to the Dublin service was seen as a sensible means of developing traffic on that route. During her annual refit the *Leinster* was renamed *Isle of Inishmore*, distancing the company from the traditional names of the B&I Line and its difficult past few years. *Saint Killian II* stood in during the refit period but had to use the new deep-water berth where strong winds across this exposed site often hindered arrivals and departures. With the bigger and better-appointed ship now based at Holyhead, a veritable price war commenced between B&I and Stena, a conflict that did no favours for either company.

At Cairnryan the *European Freighter* was withdrawn from her ten sailings a week to Larne in April 1993 and sold for further service in Greek waters. As the former *Europic Ferry* she was the last of the Transport Ferry Service ships to remain in service under the Red Ensign. However, in their first year on the link, the *Pride of Rathlin* and *Pride of Ailsa* had greatly improved patronage of the service by providing a far higher standard of passenger accommodation and larger vehicle space for all the commercial traffic on offer as well as accompanied cars. Peter Donkin, general manager of P&O European Ferries Irish Services reported a growth in commercial traffic of 13% and in passengers of 29 % between January and August 1993 compared to the same period the previous year. However, Stena Line at Stranraer were losing business and reduced the *Stena Galloway* to freight only during the summer.

The Strintzis Line-owned Swansea Cork Ferries opened the summer season with the newly renamed *Superferry* on 5 March 1993. This vessel was larger than her predecessor, *Celtic Pride*, and offered capacity for 1400 passengers and up to 370 accompanied cars. She had been built in 1972 as *Cassiopeia* and later used as the *Izu Maru 3* for a service between Tokyo and Tokushima. In 1991 she was bought by Strintzis Line and converted for use in the Adriatic as *Ionian Star*. At Swansea she had a Greek crew and Polish catering staff.

Merchant Ferries' *Merchant Victor* and *Merchant Valiant* were replaced in spring 1993 by the Norwegian-owned sisters *Jolly Bruno* and *Jolly Giallo*. The pair was built in 1977 and 1978 for Stena Ocean Line Limited and K/S A/S Stewa II of Oslo respectively. At the same time the Mersey Docks & Harbour Board purchased a 50% share in Merchant Ferries in order to develop a new service to Dublin from the Twelve Quays development at Birkenhead, once that facility was completed.

The *Jolly Giallo* was renamed *Merchant Bravery* and registered under the ownership of Cenargo Navigation Limited while her port of registration was changed to Nassau. The *Jolly Bruno* was initially registered in Italy under the ownership of Proofbond Limited but this changed to Cenargo shortly afterwards when she was registered as *Merchant Brilliant* also at Nassau. Both ships received new bow thrust units, high lift rudders and new stern doors before entering service between Heysham and Warrenpoint. They had two vehicle decks and could accommodate 105 standard commercial units, 40% more capacity than offered previously by *Merchant Victor* and *Merchant*

Pride of Rathlin (1973) approaching Larne on passage from Cairnryan on 9 September 1992.
(Author)

Ionic Ferry (1967) seen leaving Cairnryan towards the end of her career under the Red Ensign.
(Author)

Valiant. **Merchant Brilliant** entered service between Heysham and Warrenpoint in 29 August 1993 and her sister **Merchant Bravery** on 31 August. **Merchant Venture** was retained at Heysham to work supplementary sailings as required and the Fleetwood service that had been operated for the past couple of years was closed, leaving both **Merchant Victor** and **Merchant Valiant** available for redeployment.

In November 1993, the **Merchant Valiant** was chartered by P&O as a replacement for the **Belard** on the Ardrossan and Larne cargo route. The **Belard** was then chartered to the Isle of Man Steam Packet Company for a new service in the North Sea under the trading name Mannin Line Limited. **Merchant Victor** was chartered to the Crowley group.

Belfast Ferries charter of **Schiaffino** came to an end. The ship was renamed **Sally Eurobridge** and dispatched on a new charter to Irish Ferries for the summer to relieve commercial traffic from the **Saint Killian II** and **Saint Patrick II** on the Continental services from Rosslare, this year also with three sailings per week from Cork.

The freight ferry **Peveril** became wholly owned by the Isle of Man Steam Packet Limited in December 1992 when her demise charter from James Fisher at Barrow came to an end. **Lady of Mann** had to be withdrawn for repairs after hitting the breakwater at Douglas during the 1993 TT festival in early June. As a consequence, the **King Orry** was supported by **Seacat Scotland** from Stranraer and Caledonian MacBrayne's **Pioneer** working from Gourock, while Belfast Freight Ferries' **Saga Moon** worked in support from Heysham.

Belfast Freight Ferries bought **Stena Topper** in March 1993 and renamed her **River Lune**. She started in service the following month and offered space for 93 standard commercial units, some 50% greater capacity than each of the two existing ships, **Spheroid** and **Saga Moon**.

The service by **Seacat Scotland** was supplemented by **Hoverspeed Great Britain** on the Stranraer and Belfast route operated by Sea Containers in the summer onwards. **Hoverspeed Great Britain** was the first of the larger 74 metre long ships to be built by Incat at Hobart. She lost her anchor in rough weather in mid-September on passage to Stranraer and missed a number of sailings until it could be replaced. She was transferred to Dover in November but was expected back at Belfast in January 1994.

European Freighter (1968) seen leaving Cairnryan on her maiden voyage under her new name on the 1045 sailing to Larne, Thursday 2 April 1992.
(Author)

As the year progressed it became clear why Stena Line had obfuscated over port usage at Holyhead by Sea Containers. At midday on 1 July 1993, a new catamaran, named **Stena Sea Lynx**, a name contrived to sound like Stena Sealink, arrived at Holyhead on her delivery voyage from Hobart, Tasmania. After final fitting out, docking tests at Dun Laoghaire and further trials in the Irish Sea, she took her maiden voyage from Holyhead at 0700 hours on 15 July 1993. She was owned by Buquebus International of Argentina, but registered in Nassau and taken on an initial 18 month charter. She had been ordered by Condor Ferries as a consort for **Condor 10**, but that order was cancelled and the vessel was completed for Buquebus.

Meanwhile, Styg Bystedt, Technical Director for Stena Rederi and his Chief Executive Officer, Dan Sten Olsson, announced at a press conference at Holyhead an order worth £128 million for two jumbo-sized high speed ferries designed in house by Stena. The first of these was destined for Holyhead and to be ready for the summer season in 1995, although delivery was actually delayed into 1996. Known as the Stena HSS, somehow standing for High Speed Sea-Service, the vessels would be able to carry 1500 passengers and 375 cars at 40 knots in all weathers on a hull 124 metres long with a beam of 40 metres.

Seacat Scotland *(1991) arriving at Belfast on 8 June 1997. She had a white hull in her first year of service during 1992 and adopted the dark blue colour scheme in later years.*
(Author)

Belard *(1979) leaving Larne in April 1993, she was transferred to Pandoro when she moved from her base at Belfast to work from Larne.*
(Author)

Stena Cambria *(1980) arriving at Dun Laoghaire in April 1993 with the new 'Stena Sealink Line' script on her hull – she was formerly the **St Anselm** on Dover and Calais duties.*
(Author)

The 'cruise ferry' **Stena Hibernia** *(1977) approaching Holyhead in April 1993.*

(Author)

By the end of September Stena Line reported that the **Stena Sea Lynx** had operated at 87% capacity for cars and 77% for passengers, clearly a good result for any new service. The fast service had not impacted the conventional ferries and they too had enjoyed growth, fuelled partly by the ongoing economic recovery in both Ireland and Great Britain. At last, the Irish recession was over – the era of the Celtic Tiger was about to begin.

Pandoro announced orders for two new and larger ships to maintain the Dublin and Liverpool service then operated by **Bison** and **Buffalo**. The design service speed of the new ships was 22 knots, 4 knots faster than the existing ships on the route, and this would cut the voyage time to 6½ hours. Pandoro had earlier served notice on B&I that it would withdraw from the partnership with them at the end of the year, allowing Pandoro to move from the Dublin Ferryport to a new facility being constructed on the North Wall just downstream from the East Link Toll Bridge.

In August 1993 the **European Clearway** was 'sold' by P&O European Ferries to Pandoro so that she could start a new three-times-a-week service between Rosslare and Cherbourg in direct competition with Irish Ferries. The service commenced on 6 November 1993. A sister to the ill-fated **European Gateway** (see Chapter 5), the **European Clearway** and her two other sisters were not lengthened like the **European Gateway**, and had remained on services to France and Belgium with a capacity for just 46 commercial units and a passenger certificate for 107 drivers and passengers.

Irish Ferries announced the purchase of **Pride of Bilbao** towards the end of 1993. The former **Olympia** of the Viking Line, was on charter to P&O as **Pride of Bilbao**, and employed between Portsmouth and Bilbao and Portsmouth and Cherbourg with 28 months of the charter to run. The idea was that by April 1996, when the charter ended, the ship would be available to replace both the **Saint Killian II** and the **Saint Patrick II** on the Continental services. However, there were three further options open to P&O which could extend the charter period for a further 6½ years.

At Holyhead the hearing on the behaviour of Stena Line Ports towards Sea Containers reported that Stena had been 'entirely negative'.

*Isle of Inishmore (1978), ex-***Leinster***, seen leaving Dublin on 20 April 1993 on one of her last sailings to Holyhead before being transferred south to Rosslare.*

(Author)

Stena immediately responded by offering sensibly timed berthing slots to Sea Containers, an offer that was not taken up.

By the end of 1993 the wave piercing catamarans had demonstrated that they could attract new clientele without severely eroding traffic from existing conventional ferry services. Premium fares were charged to counter loss of economies of scale, and to help pay towards higher fuel consumption per ton of cargo deadweight. The **Seacat Scotland** at Stranraer and **Stena Sea Lynx** at Holyhead were popular with business people travelling from city centre in Ireland to UK port with reasonable road and good rail connections to large hinterlands. So pleased were their owners that the Stranraer service had been increased by the addition of the **Hoverspeed Great Britain** and Stena Line planned to introduce the larger 78 metre **Stena Sea Lynx II** on the Holyhead and Dun Laoghaire route and move the **Stena Sea Lynx** to Fishguard and Rosslare duties. Gareth Cooper, Managing Director of Stena Sealink Line underlined their success and commented 'the introduction of new and innovative tonnage, provided it was reliable and punctual, would immediately lead to success'.

Merchant Brilliant (1979) on the approach to Heysham – she commenced on the Heysham and Warrenpoint service in August 1993.

*Caledonian MacBrayne's little ferry **Pioneer** (1974) was used to help out in the TT festival in 1993, with sailings between Gourock and Douglas.*

(Author)

***Hoverspeed Great Britain** (1990) joined **Seacat Scotland** on the Belfast and Stranraer high speed service in 1993.*

(Bernard McCall)

Buffalo (1975) approaching Dublin off the Poolbeg Light on Friday 23 April 1993.

(Author)

The normal round of relief ships appeared for the 1994 overhaul period with **Norröna** covering for Stena. At Cairnryan the **Pride of Ailsa** and **Pride of Rathlin** were relieved by **European Endeavour**, one of the sisters of the **European Clearway** working between Rosslare and Cherbourg. The **European Endeavour** (built as **European Enterprise** in 1978) came north from Dover to stand in for the big passenger and freight ferries while they went in turn for annual refit, but the freighter offered only basic passenger facilities and required a slightly longer crossing time.

The big ferry **Isle of Innisfree** damaged the linkspan at Holyhead in January causing disruption of services which brought **Saint Killian II** onto a Dublin and Liverpool cargo only service for a while until repairs could be carried out at Holyhead.

The Isle of Man Steam Packet Company was next to join the fast ferry revolution. On 28 June 1994, the chartered **Seacat Isle of Man** (ex-**Seacat Boulogne**, ex-**Seacat France**) took up duties for the Steam Packet company as a replacement for **Lady of Mann** which retired to Birkenhead on 27 June to lay alongside the redundant **Mona's Queen**. The 'maiden' voyage of the **Seacat Isle of Man** was from Douglas to Fleetwood, but she also served Belfast, Dublin and of course Liverpool. She finished the season on 26 September with traffic recorded as 15% up on the previous year when **Lady of Mann** was in charge.

Lady of Mann was reactivated in January 1995 to stand in for **King Orry** while that ship was away at Birkenhead for her annual refit. The Isle of Man Steam Packet Company had been working hard to upgrade the onetime **St Eloi** to satisfy the SOLAS regulations in order to register the ship at Douglas yet retain her full passenger certificate. The final work was carried out during her refit and the ship returned to service with a plate bearing the word Douglas welded on to her quarters where once it had said Nassau. The Bahamian flag was folded up and put away once and for all, and **King Orry** finally became a proper 'Isle of Man boat'.

The Caledonian MacBrayne ferry **Claymore** was used to provide an Ardrossan and Douglas link on summer Saturdays, outward to Douglas, and returning to Ardrossan on Sundays. This link, operated in conjunction with the Steam Packet company, was repeated in 1995 although loadings were generally poor.

Hoverspeed Great Britain did not return to Stranraer in 1994 as she was deployed on Folkestone and Boulogne duties, but **Seacat Scotland** continued to work between Belfast and Stranraer giving four return sailings a day. She went on charter work based at Qatar in November and was replaced by **Seacat Isle of Man**. Meanwhile Stena was building new port facilities at Dun Laoghaire and Belfast to accommodate its new generation HSS vessels. **Stena Sea Lynx** transferred to Fishguard starting on 30 June shortly after the new **Stena Sea Lynx II** commenced at Holyhead on 22 June. The difference between the two vessels was that the older one could accommodate 400 passengers and 80 cars whereas the **Stena Sea Lynx II** could carry 600 passengers and 120 cars. **Stena Sea Lynx II** was chartered from her builders, Incat in Tasmania, and she too was registered at Nassau.

European Clearway (1975) inaugurated the new service between Rosslare and Cherbourg for Pandoro in November 1993.

(Author)

King Orry (1974) at last upgraded to SOLAS requirements and finally registered at Douglas. She is seen leaving Heysham for her home port on 19 September 1995.
(Author)

Superferry recommenced her Swansea and Cork service on 2 March 1994 and was scheduled to continue through until mid-January before retiring for refit.

But the big news, in the late spring of 1994, was the announcement by Irish Ferries that the B&I Line had placed an order with Dutch shipbuilders for a new vessel to replace the chartered *Isle of Innisfree* on the Holyhead and Dublin route. The new ship was designed to offer 80% greater vehicle space with accommodation for 1700 passengers and would be equipped to allow a reduction in passage time from 4 hours to just 3½ hours. The cost of the project was stated to be Irish £46 million.

Pandoro finally split from B&I on 1 June 1994. The *Bison*, which previously had an Irish crew and B&I livery, was repainted in P&O colours. During her winter refit her upper vehicle deck was widened by 2 metres either side and she was given stability sponsons along her hull to conform with new SOLAS regulations. *Bison* was also given a new passenger lounge and a number of additional passenger cabins. Sisterships *Buffalo* and *Puma* also needed to comply with SOLAS by 1999 but no work was carried out on these ships.

On return to Pandoro, the *Bison* was again altered during the summer by the addition of a new third uppermost vehicle deck abaft the accommodation superstructure. A new stern ramp to the upper deck was also provided; the work provided space for an additional 20 trailers. *Bison* was given a Pandoro crew and deployed on the Fleetwood and Larne service alongside the *Viking Trader*, the pair offered twelve round trips per week. The *Puma* moved to Liverpool to join *Buffalo* on the Liverpool and Dublin North Wall route which also offered twelve round trips a week.

In addition, a third ship, the Polish-owned *Arcade Eagle*, was chartered to supplement the Dublin route. She was replaced later in the year by the *Atlantic Freighter*, owned by Marine Atlantic of Canada, and a sister to P&O Ferrymasters *Elk* operating in the North Sea. The chartered Ardrossan and Larne ship, *Merchant Valiant*, included a run between Larne and Fleetwood most weekends during winter 1994/1995. In May, the *Atlantic Freighter* was replaced by *Norsky* on charter from North Sea Ferries; her port of registry was changed from London to Hamilton, Bermuda. *Norsky* was originally built for the Fleetwood and Dublin route as the *Ibex*, and shortly after her return to the Irish Sea her name reverted once again to *Ibex*.

The North Sea Mannin Line service operated by *Belard* had lost £2 million in the twelve months to April 1995 and the Isle of Man Steam Packet Company was obliged to close the service. The *Belard* was chartered to Pandoro on 15 May for a period of 4½ months. *Belard* moved back to her old service between Larne and Ardrossan while *Merchant Valiant* became available to cover the summer refit periods of the Pandoro fleet. As the charter of *Merchant Valiant* ended she was purchased by P&O and sent for her own overhaul during which she received new rudders, a second bow thrust unit and was given the new corporate P&O animal name *Lion*. *Lion* took up duty again on 21 October. The Rosslare and Cherbourg vessel *European Clearway* was renamed *Panther* during her summer refit.

The *Sea Cat Isle of Man* returned from a lucrative charter to Condor Ferries (Channel Islands) and commenced her Isle of Man season on 24 May 1995. *Lady of Mann* was reactivated for the TT festival before retiring back to Birkenhead again, but she left the Mersey in July to take up a charter based at Madeira, returning in mid-November. After a six year period of inactivity at Birkenhead the side-loader *Mona's Queen* was finally sold for further service in the Philippines. At the end of the year the Steam Packet company announced it would not be chartering a Seacat for 1996 on the grounds of high cost and instead would be using *Lady of Mann*.

Norse Mersey was returned to Stena Line by Norse Irish Ferries in mid-January 1995 and her place was taken on the Belfast and Liverpool route by the chartered Panamanian registered *Vomero*. This ship had a pronounced sheer and a bright yellow hull and was quickly dubbed 'The Banana Boat' on both sides of the Irish Sea. Her charter was expected to cover the period up and until the delivery of the new cargo-only *Norse Mersey* building in Italy and due for delivery in May. The new *Norse Mersey* was built at a cost of £20 million and was described as the first dedicated freight roll-on roll-off ferry built for the Irish Sea for two decades. She was chartered from Levantina Trasporti Srl of Bari, Italy, and was never actually owned by Norse Irish Ferries. The ship was also given a yellow hull and carried the Norse Irish company name on her hull in white lettering, the latter not always easy to see. She was 174 metres long by 25 metres breadth, had a service speed of 19 knots and offered 1900 lane metres of stowage. She ran a cargo only service every other night with accommodation for drivers only, with *Norse Lagan* carrying commercial vehicles as well as accompanied cars and passengers on alternate nights.

On 1 January 1995 the B&I Line brand disappeared and was replaced by Irish Ferries so that the Continental and Irish Sea services came under one umbrella. The ships adopted a new livery with a twisted emblem in shades of green on the hulls but carrying the same funnel markings as before. The charter of *Isle of Innisfree* was not renewed and she was returned to owners Stena Line at the beginning of March. The new ship, also named *Isle of Innisfree* was due in service in May with *Saint Patrick II* standing in during the interim. New terminal buildings were constructed at both Holyhead and Dublin ready for the new ship. Additional calls were planned at Roscoff from Rosslare by *Saint Killian II* and *Saint Patrick II*. The Continental services had been experiencing a downturn in trade at the expense of Brittany Ferries which ran services between Cork and St Malo as well as Cork and Roscoff.

Once again *Norröna* was acting relief for the Stena Sealink refit season. On 20 March, *Stena Sea Lynx* commenced working between Fishguard and Rosslare while *Stena Sea Lynx II* took up sailings between Holyhead and Dun Laoghaire with a delayed start to the season due to rough weather. However, from late May until mid-June the *Stena Sea Lynx* was back at Holyhead deputising for the larger *Stena Sea Lynx II* which had suffered an engine failure. Construction work on dedicated linkspans for the new HSS craft was progressing well at all four ports, Holyhead, Dun Laoghaire, Belfast and Stranraer, with new passenger facilities also at Holyhead.

Pandoro   Sailing Schedule

Northern Ireland Fleetwood – Larne Service

Departure Day(s)	Departure From	Departure Time	Arrive At	Arrival Time	Unloading
Monday	Fleetwood	2200	Larne	0600	On arrival
	Larne	2200	Fleetwood	0600	On arrival
Tuesday to Friday	Larne	1000	Fleetwood	1800	On arrival
	Fleetwood	1000	Larne	1800	On arrival
	Fleetwood	2200	Larne	0600	On arrival
	Larne	2200	Fleetwood	0600	On arrival
Saturday	Fleetwood	1000	Larne	1800	On arrival
	Larne	12 Noon	Fleetwood	2000	On arrival
	Fleetwood	2200	Larne	0600 (Sun)	On arrival
	Larne	2200	Fleetwood	0600 (Sun)	On arrival
Sunday	Larne	1100	Fleetwood	1900	On arrival
	Fleetwood	1800	Larne	0200 (Monday)	0600 (Monday)

Quay to Quay Bookings for Driver Accompanied and Unaccompanied Movements
Telephone: Fleetwood 0253 777111
           Larne 0574 260511

Southern Ireland Liverpool – Dublin Service

Departure Day(s)	Departure From	Departure Time	Arrive At	Arrival Time	Unloading
Monday	Liverpool	2300	Dublin	0700 (Tues)	On arrival
	Dublin	2300	Liverpool	0700 (Tues)	On arrival
Tuesday to Saturday	Liverpool	1100	Dublin	1900	On arrival
	Dublin	1100	Liverpool	1900	On arrival
	Liverpool	2300	Dublin	0700	On arrival
	Dublin	2300	Liverpool	0700	On arrival
Sunday	Liverpool	1900	Dublin	0700 (Mon)	On arrival
	Dublin	1100	Liverpool	2000	On arrival

Quay to Quay Bookings for Driver Accompanied and Unaccompanied Movements
Telephone: Liverpool 051-933 5620
           Dublin 010-353-1-745001

ALL VEHICLES TO ARRIVE AT QUAY 1 HOUR BEFORE SAILING TIME, OR 2 HOURS BEFORE IF ANY DANGEROUS CARGO CONTENT.

Pandoro Ltd., Dock Street, Fleetwood, Lancashire FY7 6HR. Tel: Fleetwood (0253) 777111 Telex: 67166 PD-FWD-G Fax: (0253) 777111

Pandoro timetable issued summer 1994.

(Author's Collection)

***Lion** (1977) formerly Merchant Ferries' **Merchant Valiant** seen arriving at Larne under Pandoro ownership.*

(Author)

***Saint Patrick II** (1973) showing off the new Irish Ferries livery at Rosslare on 26 April 1995.*

(Author)

*The new **Isle of Innisfree** (1995) seen leaving Dublin off the Great South Wall in October 1996.*

(Author)

On 23 May 1995, the new *Isle of Innisfree* took her maiden commercial voyage with the 0900 hours sailing to Dublin. This allowed *Isle of Inishmore*, one-time *Leinster*, to return to Pembroke Dock and Rosslare duties on 23 May releasing *Saint Killian II* for the Continental routes, the latter including a new Cork and Roscoff link. In September Irish Ferries confirmed an order for a second new ship of larger capacity than *Isle of Innisfree*.

In mid-summer, Belfast Freight Ferries sent the *Saga Moon* to the Tees Dockyard for lengthening by 18 metres. She was back in service in October. Meanwhile, also in October, Merchant Ferries closed their service from Heysham to Warrenpoint in favour of Heysham and Dublin in a move to focus on the trade to the south of Ireland.

Business at Cairnryan had grown such that a third ship was deployed on the P&O service to Larne from late September 1995. The *European Endeavour*, previously used on relief duties at Cairnryan moved north to start work in support of *Pride of Ailsa* and *Pride of Rathlin* with the remit of diverting some of the commercial traffic away from the passenger ships.

Stena Sealink moved its Northern Irish terminal from Larne to Belfast on 12 November. This coincided with *Stena Cambria* deputising for the two Stranraer ships. The move allowed all the Stena services to be concentrated at Belfast in anticipation of the new HSS craft joining the fleet in 1996. *Stena Cambria* was replaced at Holyhead by *Stena Traveller*, a large and modern dedicated freight ship with accommodation for 120 drivers. She inaugurated another new route, that between Holyhead and Dublin, so allowing commercial vehicles better road access than available at Dun Laoghaire, a seaside town which had always sought to limit the number of commercial vehicles through traffic to and from the harbour.

As the year 1995 ended, Stena Sealink Line ceased to exist and was replaced by the new trading name Stena Line. This final link with the British Railways Board ended and Stena Line became a new household name throughout Britain and Ireland. The final changes to the former railway fleet started to appear with the winter refit season when ships emerged in full Stena Line livery. To complete the change, and eradicate Sealink once and for all, the *Stena Sea Lynx* was renamed *Stena Lynx*, and the *Stena Sea Lynx II* was likewise renamed *Stena Lynx II*.

Following the recession in the early 1990s, economic expansion was enjoyed later on both sides of the Irish Sea with greatly enhanced commercial traffic between the island of Ireland and Great Britain (see Figure 1 Chapter 1). This partly reflected the ceasefire that had been negotiated successfully between the loyalist and republican groups in late summer 1994 with the hope for stability in Northern Ireland. Freight only ships grew in capacity, existing ships were enlarged, while new ships were designed to accommodate both private accompanied cars as well as large numbers of commercial vehicles. The ferry industry had enjoyed this expansion although some companies, notably the former B&I Line and Irish Ferries, had struggled to keep up with increasing demand. In the days of B&I this was because of under-capacity, and subsequently as Irish Ferries due to ageing ships that were unable to compete head on with Brittany Ferries' modern vessels on the Irish services to France.

Of course, P&O and Stena Sealink had also to deal with competition from the Channel Tunnel beneath the Dover Strait, once this was opened to traffic in May 1994. The response from the ferry companies was to provide merged services and larger and faster ships with a 'user friendly' service. The trend for larger ships was mirrored on the Irish Sea, even B&I keeping up with the newly commissioned *Isle of Innisfree* and an order confirmed for a second and larger ship of a similar design. The other development was the high speed ferry, a development designed to attract business people and others who would have been otherwise tempted to use the burgeoning airline network. The initial Seacats developed in size and in their ability to ameliorate an erratic and bumpy ride in a moderate swell. Stena was set to introduce its new HSS craft in 1996 with a totally new concept of sea travel that was to be trialled on the Irish Sea.

European Endeavour (1978) seen on her morning departure from Larne to Cairnryan in May 1996.
(Author)

Given all the new development in ferry technology there had also been an unprecedented investment in port infrastructure. New twin level linkspans had been commissioned at most ports throughout the five year period to 1995, while ever larger marshalling areas were built to speed the process of loading and unloading and so reduce ship turnaround times. Approach roads were installed in order to take traffic away from urban areas near each port and in one case, that of Dun Laoghaire, the main cargo service was transferred to Dublin in order to avoid restrictions on the numbers of commercial vehicles allowed through that seaside town.

There remained only one ship on the Irish Sea that still had the traditional single crew manning system. That, unsurprisingly, was the *Lady of Mann* which belonged to the ultra-conservative Isle of Man Steam Packet Company despite its 42% ownership by Sea Containers. All other vessels were manned for 24 hour operation through rotation of crews, while there was an enhanced engineering and maintenance presence that undertook routine jobs at sea which would otherwise have been carried out between trips in port.

Ships continued to be modified and enlarged to suit changing patterns of trade. New ships were even designed with the potential to be lengthened, Irish Ferries new *Isle of Innisfree* being one of these. Others, such as Pandoro's *Bison*, were so radically modified by lengthening, the addition of new passenger accommodation and, in the case of the *Bison*, by the construction of an uppermost third vehicle deck, that they were barely recognisable in their new form. Many modified ships required stability sponsons to be added along the ship's hull, *Bison* being no exception, but others also needed sponsons in order to satisfy the incoming SOLAS regulations and so qualify to retain existing passenger certificates.

Lady of Mann (1976) in her heyday.
(Author)

CHAPTER 8
THE FAST FERRY FASHION

Stena Cambria (1980) was the first ship on the Irish Sea services to be repainted in the full Stena Line livery.

(Author)

A major setback was the breaking of the ceasefire when the IRA bombed Canary Wharf in London in February 1996 and part of the centre of Manchester in June. Confidence in trade in the North of Ireland waned once more. However, political progress had been made and there remained a vision of peace and stability, eventually to be turned into reality by the Good Friday Agreement in 1998. At last the road blocks disappeared, the barricades around the police stations and the gated entrances to shopping streets in cities and major towns were slowly removed while the army Land Rovers that cruised the streets in pairs became less evident.

At the start of 1996, Stena Line was comfortably established both at Belfast and at Dublin. The move to Belfast had increased the voyage time by 45 minutes but had given access directly to the city, whereas that to Dublin had allowed commercial vehicles access to the improved road system at Dublin rather than the streets of Dun Laoghaire. As the ships came back into service from their winter refits they appeared smart and business-like in their new Stena Line livery. First to be repainted was the **Stena Cambria**, which had gone for refit in October 1995 and was back in service the following month acting as relief while other ships went for the same treatment. One ship that was slow in adopting the new livery was **Stena Felicity** which retained the old Stena Sealink Line colours until March 1996 when she was relieved by **Stena Londoner** from Newhaven. Her charter from her Swedish owners was then extended until 1997.

The planned introduction of the two revolutionary HSS craft, one on the Dun Laoghaire and Holyhead route and the other deployed between Belfast and Stranraer, was well advanced. This included the transfer of some ships and existing high speed catamarans away from the Irish Sea. **Stena Hibernia**, for example, was renamed **Stena Adventurer** in anticipation of her moving to the Dover Strait once the HSS was established at Holyhead – a move which in the event never took place. Redeployment of the former Dover ships **Stena Antrim** and **Stena Cambria** was also on the cards. Following her spell of relief work **Stena Cambria** left Holyhead for Dover starting work in the Dover Strait in mid-February. **Stena Cambria** was destined to transfer to Newhaven in the summer.

The first new HSS craft, named **Stena Explorer**, arrived at Holyhead from her builders in Finland on 21 March 1996. The shore facilities were completed on time despite damage to part of the linkspan at Holyhead when a supporting pontoon sank. Crew familiarisation and final preparation of the craft allowed a maiden commercial voyage to Dun Laoghaire to take place on 10 April. **Stena Lynx** was now redundant and transferred to Newhaven. **Stena Adventurer** remained on duty at Dun Laoghaire in support of the new vessel until the end of September when she was withdrawn and put up for sale as lying at Belfast. She was briefly in service between Belfast and Stranraer on relief work before she was sold.

The HSS type craft were large vessels and were powered by four steerable water jets driven by gas turbine machinery which gave them a design service speed of 40 knots. Like conventional ships they also had two sets of bow thrust units. They were certificated to carry up to 1200 passengers and could accommodate 375 cars or 50 commercial vehicles along with 120 cars.

On 28 February 1996, the **European Trader**, sister to the **European Endeavour** already working on the Cairnryan and Larne route, arrived at Cairnryan to relieve the **European Endeavour** and then the **Pride of Rathlin** while those ships underwent their annual refits. P&O announced that they too would be operating a fast craft later in the year with a chartered single hull vessel capable of accommodating 600 passengers and 160 cars. On arrival of the new vessel the **Pride of Ailsa** was programmed to stand down while the **European Trader** would remain in service.

Stena Felicity (1980), a big ship in an even bigger sea, completed her annual refit in March 1996 and returned to service in full Stena Sealink Line colours.

(Author)

On 12 June, the new fast craft duly took up duty at Cairnryan. Named ***Jetliner***, the vessel was a 95 metre long ship capable of 35 knots with a scheduled crossing time to Larne of just 60 minutes, as opposed to the conventional ferry which took 2 hours and 15 minutes. She had been built as one of a pair, named ***Djursland***, as partner to sister ***Kattegat*** for the Grenaa to Hundested domestic Danish service. She was released to P&O on charter before her completion. Her arrival in service allowed ***Pride of Ailsa*** to be destored on 15 June and handed over to her new Egyptian owners at Belfast two days later.

The arrival of the ***Jetliner***, just three months after her charter had been agreed, was quite a coup for P&O. The new HSS destined for the Stena Line Belfast and Stranraer route, ***Stena Voyager***, had been delayed as the linkspan at Stranraer was yet to be completed. The ***Stena Voyager*** eventually took her maiden voyage on 21 July 1996, and P&O and Stena faced each other head on to attract patronage for their new fast services. The HSS now in service, ***Stena Antrim*** stood down at Belfast on 1 October and sailed south to Newhaven, while ***Stena Caledonia*** and ***Stena Galloway*** continued to operate with reduced passenger certificates. In November the ***Stena Voyager*** was obliged to reduce speed while in Belfast Lough and her schedules were retimed accordingly. This was a consequence of wash problems along both shores of the Lough causing damage to small boats and shore installations. ***Jetliner*** broke down in late November with gearing problems. New parts had to be manufactured and the ship was off service until 8 March 1997. However, her performance remained erratic thereafter and ***Jetliner*** became something of an embarrassment to her operators.

Sea Containers still maintained ***Seacat Scotland*** on its Belfast and Stranraer high speed service. Sea Containers were also the preferred candidate to operate a new service between Ballycastle and Campbeltown, much along the lines of the Western Ferries service between Red Bay and Campbeltown in the early 1970s (see Chapter 3). The Caledonian MacBrayne ferry ***Claymore*** had been identified for the new service should Caledonian MacBrayne be awarded the contract but the Scottish Office made it clear that Caledonian MacBrayne would have to sell the ***Claymore*** to whichever company was awarded the contract for the new service. In the event the service was awarded to Sea Containers which bought ***Claymore*** from Caledonian MacBrayne later in the year at a heavily marked down price which was reported to be less than £1 million.

The trading name for the new operation was announced as Argyll and Antrim Steam Packet Company. ***Claymore*** was scheduled to run two return trips a day between Campbeltown and Ballycastle with a passage time of three hours starting in summer 1997. The service duly commenced on 1 July 1997 with Sea Containers committed to a minimum of three years on the route. The service closed for the winter on 19 October. In the winter months the ***Claymore*** was chartered back to Caledonian MacBrayne to cover the annual overhaul season.

New SOLAS requirements were proposed that would help a vehicle ferry to remain afloat with 0.5 metres of water on the lower vehicle deck in a 4 metre sea. Conversion of those vessels that did not comply would require sponsons or transverse watertight bulkheads to be built onto the vehicle deck, with consequent loss of cargo space and deadweight. Older ships such as the two Irish 'Saints' were not considered viable candidates for conversion and the future of Irish Ferries Continental services was reported to be 'at risk'. Irish Ferries also learnt that P&O wished to extend their charter of ***Pride of Bilbao*** for a further 21 months. This meant that this larger and more modern ferry was still unavailable as a potential replacement for both ***Saint Killian II*** and ***Saint Patrick II***.

In late March 1996 it was announced that Sea Containers had taken over the Isle of Man Steam Packet Company with a 58% majority shareholding. This took control of the company away from the island and away from the ultra-conservative former Steam Packet Board. The Board had made a succession of expensive mistakes, not least the ***Mona's Isle*** conversion issue (see Chapter 5) and the loss-making Mannin Line with the ***Belard*** operating on the North Sea. More recently the Board had been in denial over the popularity of the Seacat, refusing to credit that this fast mode of sea travel was what the passengers actually wanted and giving them the ***Lady of Mann*** instead. With Sea Containers in charge, a fast craft was sure to return to Manx waters, but it was too late in the season for a renewed Seacat service for 1996. That summer the ***Seacat Isle of Man*** was working for Color Seacat under the name ***Seacat Norge***. Sea Containers vision was a new general-purpose ship to replace both ***Peveril*** and ***King Orry*** plus two high speed craft, one to operate all year round. By the summer, Sea Containers were in possession of 95% of the Steam Packet shares. ***Belard*** remained laid up at Birkenhead.

Stena Explorer (1995) the first of the HSS craft in service, seen leaving Dun Laoghaire.
(Bernard McCall)

European Trader (1975) joined the P&O fleet running between Cairnryan and Larne at the end of February 1996. She is seen leaving Larne on 10 June 1997.
(Author)

Jetliner (1995) commenced the high speed service between Cairnryan and Larne in June and is seen arriving at Larne.
(Author)

Stena Voyager (1996) arriving at Stranraer from Belfast on 16 May 2005.

(Iain McCall)

At the end of April 1996, a new company called Seatruck Ferries inaugurated a freight service between Heysham and Warrenpoint. The chartered Romanian freight vessel **Bolero** offered six return sailings each week. Seatruck Ferries was formed by a group of investors and shipping interests keen to restore the link between Heysham and Warrenpoint. On 21 July, the service was increased with the introduction of the **Riverdance**, formerly **Sally Eurobridge**, and onetime **Schiaffino**, to the service. She was chartered from International Trailer Service of Nassau, and eventually bought in October 1998. The name **Riverdance** followed the dance theme set by the chartered **Bolero**, although now with a very Irish flavour.

Merchant Ferries had abandoned the Heysham and Warrenpoint route in 1995 when that company moved from the Northern Irish port to Dublin, ostensibly 'because shippers prefer to work through the capital city', but it was then known that Merchant Ferries was planning a passenger service to Dublin, with two new general-purpose ships. Interestingly, Norse Irish Ferries announced at the same time that they were planning to access similar ships for service between Liverpool and Belfast. In the meantime, the **Norse Lagan** was purchased from her Dutch owners, Wagenborg Shipping BV, and registered in Douglas.

Pandoro made some changes over the summer period in 1996. The chartered **Tidero Star**, built in 1978, was added to the Dublin fleet of **Buffalo**, **Puma** and **Ibex**, to provide four departures from both Dublin and Liverpool each day. **Viking Trader** was renamed **Leopard** and transferred from Fleetwood and Larne to Liverpool and Dublin in exchange for **Buffalo** which returned to the Fleetwood and Larne service. The **Ibex** was again sent away for major surgery to increase capacity and her place was taken by **Commodore Clipper** from the Channel Islands until **Ibex** returned in service at Liverpool on 19 August. The **Ibex** had been given stability sponsons and a new third uppermost vehicle deck along with upgraded passenger accommodation. Although the sponsons reduced the speed of the ship, time in berthing was also reduced as she also had a third bow thrust unit installed as well as an azimuth propeller. A new weekend

Stena Antrim (1981) returned to duties on the English Channel once the Stena Voyager was established on the Belfast and Stranraer route. She is seen arriving at Belfast stern first in May 1996.

(Author)

service started with **Puma** in charge of a round trip from Dublin to Cherbourg in lieu of one trip to Liverpool and back. Pandoro continued to flag ships out to Bermuda with all vessels other than **Leopard** employing Spanish deck crews by summer 1996. The Nassau registered **Lion** had her Spanish crew replaced by Polish seamen in the autumn.

On 17 May 1996, the fast Seacat service resumed between Fishguard and Rosslare alongside the conventional ferry service operated by **Stena Felicity**. Condor Ferries **Condor 10**, a near sister to **Stena Lynx**, had been chartered for the service. The **Condor 10** received a Stena Line funnel but otherwise retained her Condor name and livery. Although **Stena Lynx** had been used at Holyhead earlier in the year supporting **Stena Explorer**, she and **Stena Lynx II** were employed at Dover throughout much of the remainder of the year. **Condor 10** was returned to Condor Ferries in mid-October when **Stena Lynx** arrived fresh from refit to take over again at Fishguard.

Bolero (1985) inaugurated the new service between Heysham and Warrenpoint in April 1996 for Seatruck Ferries.

In mid-September 1996 the **Stena Traveller** was replaced on the Holyhead and Dublin freight service by the **Stena Challenger**. Although the ships were sisters, the **Stena Challenger** had been converted during completion to accommodate 500 passengers, so creating a versatile and multi-purpose vessel that was set to develop the passenger and accompanied car trade directly into Dublin port.

Irish Ferries new ship for the Holyhead and Dublin route was launched on 4 October 1996 and named *Isle of Inishmore*. On 28 October, she broke free from the fitting out berth in a storm and drifted a kilometre upstream before she was recovered; the vessel was undamaged. This vessel had a capacity of 2100 lane metres or 856 cars. Her former namesake, onetime **Leinster**, had earlier been renamed *Isle of Inishturk* to free the name for the new ship. The *Isle of Inishturk* remained on the Rosslare and Pembroke Dock service but was advertised for sale. Her place was taken in 1997 by the *Isle of Innisfree* once she was displaced by the new ship then under construction for the Holyhead and Dublin route. Freight traffic during the summer was such that Irish Ferries chartered the **Purbeck** from Sally Line to operate a single round trip between Holyhead and Dublin as well as a weekend trip from Pembroke Dock to Rosslare with trade cars.

Continuing losses on the Irish Ferries services to the continent forced the closure of all services on 1 November 1996 until the following summer. **Saint Killian II** and **Saint Patrick II** were laid up at Le Havre. The company had lost out to Brittany Ferries which had operated modern tonnage to Ireland over the last few years, but there had also been an overall decline in passenger and accompanied car traffic on the routes between France and Ireland.

Belfast Freight Ferries increased its service to four departures a day from both Heysham and Belfast at the start of 1997. The chartered **Merle** was added to the fleet to work alongside **Spheroid**, **Saga Moon** and **River Lune**. Sister to the **River Lune**, **Merle** was formerly the **Sally Euroroute** and before that the **Bazias 3**. The **River Lune** was purchased by the company late in 1996 at a cost of £1.6 million.

Irish Ferries new ship arrived at Dublin from her Dutch builders on 17 February 1997. Named *Isle of Inishmore*, she took her maiden commercial voyage to Holyhead on 2 March allowing *Isle of Innisfree* to take over the Pembroke Dock and Rosslare service from *Isle of Inishturk* on 22 March. The *Isle of Inishmore* was 183 metres long by 28 metres breadth and had a certificate for 2200 passengers. Her four engines sustained a service speed of 21 knots. She was built at a cost of Irish £60 million.

Seacat Norge reverted to the name ***Seacat Isle of Man*** in February and her port of registration changed back from Nassau to Douglas. She recommenced work for the Isle of Man Steam Packet Company on 21 May 1997. The **Belard** was chartered to P&O to act as relief for the three Cairnryan and Larne conventional ships while they were away at refit. The charter lasted seven weeks after which **Belard** returned to lay up at Birkenhead. As **Belard** carried only nine drivers and had only two four berth cabins, drivers were asked to travel on the available passenger ships and collect their vehicle at the other end. A daily service was operated between Liverpool and Douglas in the summer using **Lady of Mann** with the **Seacat Isle of Man** on the service on Wednesdays. In April the company announced plans for the new passenger and vehicle ferry to replace both **King Orry** and **Peveril**. **Belard** replaced **Peveril** on the Heysham and Douglas freight service in April when she returned from her charter to P&O.

The third and last of the Stena Line HSS fast craft, the Dutch registered **Stena Discovery**, took her first commercial voyage from Belfast in March 1997 while the normal incumbent, **Stena Voyager** moved to Holyhead to allow **Stena Explorer** to return to her builders for a major overhaul. **Stena Explorer** returned to Holyhead in time for the **Stena Discovery** to move to her own route between Harwich and Hook of Holland starting on 2 June. The arrival of the HSS at Harwich allowed the **Koningin Beatrix** to stand down preparatory to being transferred to Fishguard as a replacement for **Stena Felicity**. **Stena Lynx** resumed the high speed ferry between Fishguard and Rosslare on 10 March.

Stena Challenger (1990) seen leaving Dublin from the Great South Wall on 2 October 1996.

(Author)

Isle of Inishmore (1996) seen berthing at Pembroke Dock on 3 May 2011.

(Iain McCall)

Isle of Inishturk (1981) formerly Isle of Inishmore, seen arriving at Pembroke Dock on 12 November 1996.

(Author)

Overhaul periods for the HSS ships in 1997 had the new **Stena Lynx III** brought up from Dover to act as relief and maintain the high speed crossings. The **Stena Caledonia** received stove pipe extensions to her twin funnels during her refit in January in an attempt to counteract soot falling on deck. **Stena Galloway** received her overhaul once the **Stena Caledonia** was back in service.

Pandoro transferred the **Leopard** to a new Dublin and Fleetwood service at the start of 1997. The Dublin and Liverpool route was maintained by **Ibex** and **Puma** while the chartered **Tidero Star** was replaced by the **Seahawk** built in 1975 and on charter from Seahawk K/S of Oslo. P&O no longer carried livestock on its services and inevitably a new company started up on the Cork and Cherbourg route specifically for export of live cattle to France. This was Gaelic Ferries, which chartered the **Purbeck** from Truckline at Poole in October 1997 to provide three round trips per week.

The **Saint Killian II** opened the Rosslare and Continental sailings for Irish Ferries on 26 March 1997. The **Saint Patrick II** remained laid up at Le Havre alongside **Isle of Inishturk**. **Saint Killian II** did not comply with the latest SOLAS requirements and it was announced that this would be her last season on the Continental services. She retired to lay up on 29 September 1997. This year the roster had been complex with services to Cherbourg, Le Havre and Roscoff from both Cork and Rosslare. Also at Cork, Strintzis Lines' **Superferry** resumed the service to Swansea on 14 March 1997 for the summer and autumn season. Both Irish Ferries and Strintzis were actively looking for replacement ships for their services to continue into 1998.

On 27 June 1997, **Koningin Beatrix** took her first commercial voyage on the Irish Sea. Due to severe gales closing Fishguard, the ship sailed from Pembroke Dock to Rosslare working initially alongside **Stena Felicity** in order to clear traffic due to irregular sailings. On 3 July **Stena Felicity** sailed for Bremerhaven pending a decision on her future use. The **Koningin Beatrix** was re-registered at London in mid-August for the duration of her charter to Stena Line UK from Stena Line BV. On 3 August **Koningin Beatrix** struck the breakwater at Rosslare during a storm. She sailed for Dublin in the night to discharge passengers and vehicles before proceeding to Birkenhead for repairs. She was back in service on 8 August.

The new ships building for use by Norse Irish Ferries had a capacity for 330 passengers, including 220 berths, and 2100 lane metres of stowage space on three decks. The lower deck was only used on passage to Belfast when trade cars were stowed below, and private cars used the upper vehicle deck both ways. The design speed was 22 knots and each ship was planned to complete a return trip from the new Twelve Quays berths at Birkenhead to Belfast once the Birkenhead facility became operational in 1999. The new vessels, **Mersey Viking** and **Lagan Viking**, were chartered from their builders Visentini, with an option to purchase after two years. The **Mersey Viking** was registered under the ownership of Francesco Visentini and the **Lagan Viking** from an associate company Levantina Trasporti srl, with both ships registered at Bari. The **Mersey Viking** took her inaugural commercial sailing from Belfast on 23 July 1997. She worked alongside the **Norse Mersey** which offered accommodation

Stena Lynx III (1996) at Rosslare on 8 June 2009.

(Iain McCall)

Stena Caledonia (1981) seen leaving Belfast on Sunday 8 June 1997 sporting her new funnel extensions.
(Author)

Leopard (1977) now registered in Hamilton, arriving at Dublin from Fleetwood, and seen off the Great South Wall.
(Author)

for 64 drivers. The new **Lagan Viking** entered service on 16 November with a maiden commercial voyage from Belfast. **Norse Mersey** stood down once **Lagan Viking** was in service and was chartered to P&O Ferrymasters for its Teesport to Gothenburg service.

Bolero came off charter in mid-year and was replaced on the Seatruck Ferries service between Heysham and Warrenpoint by Merchant Ferries **Merchant Victor**. Sister to the **Riverdance**, the **Merchant Victor** was renamed **Moondance** when she was purchased by Seatruck shortly afterwards.

P&O's **Jetliner** service was increasingly unreliable as the year 1997 progressed. While **Pride of Ailsa** was away for refit, the **Leopard** was drafted in from Pandoro in exchange for the smaller capacity **European Trader**, the ships returned to their own routes in late June. **European Endeavour** underwent a partial rebuild in the summer to raise the headroom on her upper deck to 5 metres. She was away from the service for five weeks during which no replacement vessel was provided.

On 12 June 1997 the Isle of Man Steam Packet Company inaugurated a new passenger and car ferry service between Liverpool and Dublin using **Lady of Mann**. This provided full time employment for the ship which had been displaced from much of its summer work by **Seacat Isle of Man**. The voyage time between Liverpool Princes Pier and the Dublin Ferryport was scheduled as 6½ hours with a departure from Liverpool at 0830 hours and returning from Dublin at 1630 hours. On Wednesdays the **Seacat Isle of Man** took over and operated the service with a 4½ hour crossing that proved popular with the travelling public. Nevertheless, the **Lady of Mann** was reported to be taking good bookings with the car deck usually two thirds occupied. From 3 November the service was reduced to four sailings per week by **Lady of Mann**, increasing again over Christmas but ceasing thereafter so that **Lady of Mann** could cover the 1998 refit season.

Seacat Scotland was replaced at Belfast in October by **Seacat Danmark**. The former vessel was sent for refit prior to taking up charter work in South America.

Merchant Ferries became wholly owned by Cenargo again in late summer when the Mersey Docks company sold its 50% share in Merchant Ferries back to Cenargo. The sale centred on a deal whereby Cenargo would use its two new ferries, then building in Italy, on a new Liverpool and Dublin route. The new ships were designed with 2000 lane metres capacity, cabin accommodation for 112 passengers and a certificate to carry up to 250 passengers. New terminals were then under construction both at Birkenhead (Twelve Quays) in the river and within the dock system at Liverpool.

In November 1997 Irish Ferries announced the charter of the **Normandy**, formerly **Stena Normandy** and built originally in 1982. She was also at one time the **St Nicholas** on Sealink's Harwich and Hook of Holland route. The **Normandy** was owned by Rederi AB Gotland and the charter period was for 21 months. The **Normandy** started work on the Irish Sea as relief to the **Isle of Innisfree** at Pembroke Dock in February 1998 and she then stood in for the **Isle of Inishmore** at Holyhead. Meanwhile, **Saint Killian II** was placed on the For Sale list alongside **Saint Patrick II**.

At the end of 1997, P&O Ferries completed the flagging-out of its Irish Sea fleet in line with that already carried out by Pandoro. A call for voluntary redundancies left the remaining sea-going staff transferred to P&O in Bermuda, and all the ships were registered at Hamilton. The animal names were changed to corporate European names:

Lion renamed **European Highlander** for the Ardrossan and Larne service
Bison renamed **European Pioneer** for the Fleetwood and Larne service

Saint Killian II (1973) seen arriving at Rosslare Harbour on Thursday 4 October 1996.
(Author)

Koningin Beatrix (1986) seen leaving Fishguard on Friday 17 July 1998.
(Author)

Mersey Viking *(1997) seen in the Mersey on departure from the Twelve Quays Terminal.*

(Author)

Moondance *(1978) seen at Warrenpoint.*

Buffalo renamed **European Leader** for the Fleetwood and Larne service
Ibex renamed **European Envoy** for the Liverpool and Dublin service
Leopard renamed **European Navigator** for the Liverpool and Dublin service
Puma renamed **European Seafarer** for the Liverpool and Dublin service
Panther renamed **European Pathfinder** for the Rosslare and Cherbourg service

Stena Lynx resumed at Fishguard on 12 March 1998 after covering the HSS refit periods at both Holyhead and Stranraer. **Stena Caledonia** was also in service between Holyhead and Dun Laoghaire while **Stena Explorer** was off duty.

The Isle of Man company sold the **Belard** in January 1998 and reactivated the **Peveril** which started work on 13 January on the Heysham and Douglas freight service working alongside **King Orry**. The **King Orry** emerged from refit in the spring in full Sea Containers livery complete with dark blue hull. The same treatment was applied to **Lady of Mann** before she came back into service later in the year.

In 1998 the Sea Containers (Isle of Man company) Liverpool and Dublin service was reopened by **Superseacat Two** on 12 March 1998, and not by **Lady of Mann** which remained laid up. The Superseacats were larger than their twin-hulled predecessors and were monohulls with a service speed of 38 knots. They were 100 metres in length and had a capacity for 774 passengers and 175 accompanied cars. **Superseacat Two** offered a passage time of 3 hours and 50 minutes with two round trips a day at peak periods. The vessel was registered at La Spezia and carried an Italian captain in addition to a normal Seacat Scotland crew.

Seacat Isle of Man *(1991) is seen leaving Heysham.*

(Bernard McCall)

Seacat Danmark (1991) seen arriving from Douglas at Princes Pier, Liverpool on Sunday 7 June 1998.

(Author)

Normandy (1982) seen at Rosslare on 26 August 2005.

(Iain McCall)

European Pioneer (1975) seen leaving Larne shortly after she was renamed and flagged out to Bermuda.

(Author)

The usual round of refits and reliefs took place with ships moving from one roster to another to cover for absentees. P&O Stena Line's **Stena Cambria** was brought up from Dover to cover for the **Koningin Beatrix** in January, then the two Stranraer-based ships, **Stena Galloway** and **Stena Caledonia** and later the **Stena Challenger** at Holyhead during April. Similar moves allowed the P&O Pandoro ships to be dealt with during the early part of the year. **Pride of Rathlin** returned from service on 23 January 1998 with a reduced passenger certificate for 610 persons, registered in Hamilton, Bermuda with a foreign crew. **European Trader** had also been reregistered at Hamilton in February.

Stena Lynx (1993) seen arriving at Fishguard on Friday 17 July 1998.

(Author)

King Orry (1975) in full Sea Containers livery, seen leaving Heysham in June 1998.
(Author)

The big news in January 1998 was the takeover of Scruttons plc, owners of Belfast Freight Ferries, by Cenargo at a cost of £15½ million. This move allowed pooling of resources between Merchant Ferries and Belfast Freight Ferries. Cenargo had four general-purpose passenger and freight ferries on order at the Astilleros Espanoles Seville, the first two of which had been named **Dawn Merchant** and **Brave Merchant** and these were destined for the new Liverpool and Dublin passenger and freight service. Late delivery of these ships put the start date for the service back into 1999. The **Dart 4** was chartered from Dart Line to support **Merle**, **Spheroid** and **River Lune** on the Heysham and Belfast route while the **Saga Moon** ran to Dublin alongside **Merchant Bravery** and **Merchant Brilliant**. The **Merchant Venture** was away on charter in the North Sea. **Dart 4** was returned to her owners in February 1999 when the new Liverpool and Dublin service finally got under way.

The **Claymore** resumed her Campbeltown and Ballycastle service on 8 May 1998. She was then withdrawn from 2 to 15 June for a charter to Honda to cover that company's interests in the Isle of Man TT races, much to the annoyance of regular travellers and shippers. From 19 June she offered two return trips a day from Ballycastle until the end of the season on 11 October.

In May the **Seacat Scotland** returned from her winter charter in South America. She replaced **Seacat Danmark** on the Belfast and Stranraer service which then took up duty on the Isle of Man Steam Packet Company (Sea Containers) routes. On 6 July 1998, the new Steam Packet general purpose ferry **Ben-my-Chree** arrived at Douglas for the first time from her builders Van der Geissen de Noord in the Netherlands. She wore a unique livery with the three legs of Man on her red funnel. With a passenger certificate for 500 there was criticism that there was insufficient seating and berths available for

Lady of Mann (1976) seen arriving at Princes Pier, Liverpool on Sunday 7 June 1998 with Sea Containers dark blue hull and plain black topped red funnel.
(Author)

Claymore (1978), owned by Argyll and Antrim Steam Packet Company and seen while on charter to Honda for the Manx TT Races arriving at Heysham on Sunday 7 June 1998.

(Author)

The new 'Isle of Man boat' Ben-my-Chree (1998) arriving at Heysham from Douglas on 15 May 2005.

(Iain McCall)

that many people. The ***Ben-my-Chree*** has virtually no crew cabin accommodation and was designed for a crew change every twelve hours. The new ship started service in freight mode on 11 July, and replaced the ***Peveril*** on her overnight run from Heysham. ***Peveril*** left Heysham to lay up at Birkenhead on 13 July having taken her last commercial sailing on 10 July.

The ***Ben-my-Chree*** was unable to cope with the passenger demand during the school holidays and ***King Orry*** was retained in service until 28 September 1998. ***King Orry*** was sold for £2 million in October and was renamed ***Moby Love***, leaving the Mersey on 23 October under the Italian flag.

Norse Irish Ferries' ***Lagan Viking*** and ***Mersey Viking*** started to operate a day sailing between Liverpool and Belfast on Tuesdays, Thursdays and Saturdays from 10 March 1998.

The ***European Leader***, formerly ***Buffalo***, was lengthened by 15 metres and stability sponsons added during the early summer at a cost of £4½ million. The work included upgrading and enlarging accommodation to cater for 80 drivers. Her place at Fleetwood was taken by the chartered ***Lembitu***, owned by the Estonian Shipping Company, and newly completed as the second of four sisters.

The ***Stena Lynx*** was returned to her owners Buquebus in December 1998 and the ***Elite***, again renamed ***Stena Lynx III*** arrived from Dover to replace her. She stood in for the HSS refits at Holyhead and Stranraer before commencing on the Fishguard and Rosslare service alongside ***Koningin Beatrix*** on 12 March 1999.

On 8 April 1999, ***Superseacat Three*** started on the Dublin and Liverpool service for Sea Containers. She replaced ***Superseacat Two*** which took over the Manx routes until Easter after which ***Seacat Isle of Man*** was available. On 11 January the ***Seacat Danmark*** maintained a new passenger service between Belfast and Heysham, allowing easy access to the M6 Motorway and cutting short the long road journey otherwise needed to Cairnryan or Stranraer. ***Seacat Scotland*** continued to serve between Belfast and Stranraer, but only once a day, and offered in addition two round trips each day to Troon.

Irish Ferries planned to introduce its own fast craft between Dublin and Holyhead in July 1999. Named ***Jonathan Swift***, she was designed to accommodate 800 passengers and 200 accompanied cars on a crossing timed at 1 hour and 50 minutes. The aluminium catamaran was under construction at Fremantle, Australia. With ***Normandy*** working the continental services from Rosslare, the ***Saint Patrick II*** was sold as laying at Le Havre to Greek owners in May, and the ***Saint Killian II*** was sold in December for use on the Black Sea.

In due course, Irish Ferries became embroiled in a longstanding patent dispute over the hull design of its fast craft ***Jonathan Swift***. Stena Rederi claimed that her design infringed their patent for preventing hogging and sagging of multihull vessels calling at UK ports. The House of Lords ruled that the ship only 'accidentally or temporarily' visited UK waters and as such it did not infringe the patent (even though the ship lay over at Holyhead for three hours twice a day). Stena conceded and dropped the case.

Seatruck's two sisterships ***Riverdance*** and ***Moondance*** were improved at the start of 1999 by the replacement of their lorry lifts by fixed internal ramps. This reduced loading times at the terminals at Warrenpoint and at Heysham.

Damage to the HSS ***Stena Explorer*** at Dun Laoghaire in mid-February brought ***Koningin Beatrix*** out of refit to operate the Holyhead route, although she did not fit the Dun Laoghaire linkspan and sailed instead to Dublin. After a week on the service she left to resume her annual refit. In the meantime, the ***Rosebay*** was brought in from Harwich to maintain the Fishguard service until the ***Stena Lynx III*** was available to take over towards the end of April.

The new, but long delayed, Merchant Ferries' passenger and freight service between Liverpool and Dublin commenced on 1 March 1999. The drive-through ferries ***Dawn Merchant*** and ***Brave Merchant*** offered a freight only service from mid-February. With this new capacity available to Dublin, the ***Merchant Brilliant*** and ***Merchant Bravery*** transferred to the Heysham and Belfast route to work alongside ***Merle*** and ***Spheroid*** under the Belfast Freight Ferries banner. The smaller ***Saga Moon*** and ***River Lune*** were put on the Merchant Ferries Heysham and Dublin route.

Superseacat Three *(1999) seen approaching Dublin off the Poolbeg Light on 19 April 1999.*

(Author)

Dawn Merchant (1998) in the River Liffey arriving at Dublin on Monday 19 April 1999, seen during her third week of duty on the new Dublin and Liverpool service.

(Author)

The new Merchant Ferries ships, known as 'the Race Horses', were named after the famous horses Dancing Brave and Dawn Run and the passenger accommodation celebrated horse racing with, for example, the Jockey Club bar and the Finishing Post restaurant. The two ships offered a 7½ hour voyage with sailings from each port every night and five daytime sailings as well. There were two hoistable ramps facing opposite directions so that vehicles could be driven directly up to the upper vehicle deck on embarking and off down the other ramp at disembarkation. The ships had a massive stern ramp which was 17 metres wide while the bow door width was just 5 metres. They could accommodate 250 passengers in two berth cabins and reclining seats in the Grandstand Lounge. In addition to accompanied private cars the vehicle stowage provided for 120 trailers.

In March 1999, P&O announced that it had ordered a new ferry to replace **Pride of Rathlin** on the Cairnryan and Larne service. The order had been placed with Mitsubishi Heavy Industries, Japan, for delivery in summer 2000. The design speed was 23 knots and the new ship would offer a reduced passage time of 1¾ hours. Shortly afterwards an order for a second ship from the same builders was announced, the second vessel was intended to replace the **European Leader** on the Liverpool and Dublin service. Of similar dimensions, the second ship was designed with 2000 lane metres stowage and accommodation for just over 400 passengers.

In late February, the sale of Swansea Cork Ferries was announced by Strintzis Lines. The Irish investment company Briar Star Shipping Limited had bought the company for Irish £2.1 million. **Superferry**

Brave Merchant (1998) seen leaving Dublin for Liverpool off the Poolbeg Light.

(Author)

Jonathan Swift (1998) seen approaching Dublin off the Poolbeg Light on 4 June 2009.

(Iain McCall)

again operated between Swansea and Cork, this year under the Maltese flag, and the service commenced on 15 March 1999. On 26 June the chartered Greek ferry **Venus**, owned by Ventouris Ferries, started a new freight only route between Cork and St Malo with three sailings per week. The **Venus** had been built in 1976 as the **Dana Gloria** for DFDS. The French service was advertised under the banner St Malo Cork Ferries under the auspices of Swansea Cork Ferries when passenger berths became available in the summer. The key to the new service was the abandonment of livestock export from Ireland by the newly formed Gaelic Ferries, providing a ready-made niche for the **Venus**. However, on 25 November the **Venus** was withdrawn following an inspection of the ship by French authorities.

Cenargo plc announced the purchase of Norse Irish Ferries during the spring with completion of the deal in late summer 1999. Cenargo had previously added Belfast Freight Ferries to its portfolio and Norse Irish Ferries complemented its existing business in the Irish Sea. As from 1 October Belfast Freight Ferries and Merchant Ferries were merged into one unit. The **Merchant Venture** was chartered to P&O in September to provide additional sailings on the Fleetwood and Larne route while the **Merle** was returned to her owners.

The Argyll & Antrim Steam Packet Company operated the **Claymore** on her short summer season between Ballycastle and Campbeltown once again in 1999. However, towards the end of the season, parent company Sea Containers announced that the operation no longer fitted with its fast ferry commitments and that it was losing considerable sums of money on the route (estimated by some to be £½ million in 1999). In February 2000 Sea Containers stated that they had completed the contractual three year period of service and that they would not continue with the route in 2000. The **Claymore** was laid up at Liverpool and listed for sale with an inflated price tag of £1.2 million. She later carrying out a six week charter in the Faroes and returned to lay up at Birkenhead. Three years later, in August 2002, she was sold to Pentland Ferries for use on the Gill's Bay and St Margaret's Hope, Orkney, service.

On 3 July 1999, Irish Ferries' **Jonathan Swift** took her maiden commercial voyage between Dublin and Holyhead. She maintained three round trips per day. **Jonathan Swift** had a capacity for 200 cars and 800 passengers within a cargo deadweight of 400 tons. The vehicle deck offered nine lanes with a further six mezzanine decks. Shortly after the inauguration of the new high speed ferry service, the Irish Continental Group announced that an order had been placed with Aker Finnyards OY for a new ship for the Holyhead and Dublin service. This was planned as the world's largest passenger ferry with accommodation for 2000 passengers and was scheduled to enter service early in 2001. In November the chartered ferry **Normandy** was purchased from Stena Line UK for Irish £13.4 million, underlining the group's commitment to the continental services.

The Stena Line response to the Irish Ferries expansion was to charter **Stena Invicta**, from the merged P&O Stena Line operating in the English Channel, for service alongside **Stena Challenger** on the Dublin and Holyhead service. The **Stena Invicta**, which had been laid up for the previous twelve months, started on 12 December and provided much needed extra freight capacity on the route; she also provided extra passenger capacity for 1750 persons should the HSS **Stena Explorer** be off duty due to poor weather or breakdown. On 7 February 2000, the **Stena Invicta** moved to Fishguard to stand in for **Koningin Beatrix**. The charter of the **Stena Invicta** ended in mid-March and the ship was handed over to her new owners, Colour Line, on 1 April 2000. During her stay on the Irish Sea the ship carried no Stena Line markings and had a plain white hull and white funnel.

The second half of the 1990s had been characterised by unprecedented expansion of trade, a boom that was dubbed the Celtic Tiger. The Republic of Ireland had fully recovered economically and was developing a thriving computer manufacturing industry. The north of Ireland was in full production with political stability providing confidence for investors. A key beneficiary of this economic boom was, of course, the Irish Sea ferry industry which had expanded its capacity to satisfy increased demand. At the same time the tourist trade had bounced back with a massive increase in accompanied car traffic. Prospects for the ferry companies, for the moment, looked good.

CHAPTER 9
THE MILLENNIUM AND INTO THE 21st CENTURY

Stena Caledonia (1981) showing her 'duck tail' sponsons added at her annual refit in February 2000; seen arriving stern first at Belfast on Tuesday 20 May 2008.

(Author)

At the Millennium there were six companies operating roll-on roll-off ferries on the Irish Sea (see also Figure 2 in Chapter 1):

P&O Ferries/Pandoro – direct descendants of Coast Lines subsidiaries Burns & Laird Lines Limited and Belfast Steamship Company Limited

Stena Line UK – the successor to Sealink, British Railways Board/British Rail

Irish Ferries – a company that incorporated the B&I Line under the ownership of Irish Continental Group. B&I Line was the direct successor to Coast Lines subsidiary British & Irish Steam Packet Company Limited and City of Cork Steam Packet Company Limited

Sea Containers established 1965

Cenargo – Merchant Ferries established by Cenargo in 1986, Belfast Freight Ferries established 1984 and Norse Irish Ferries established 1991. Cenargo purchased Belfast Freight Ferries in 1988 and Norse Irish Ferries in 1999

Seatruck Ferries Limited established 1996

There were three large ferries on order: the mega ferry for Irish Ferries Holyhead and Dublin route and two smaller ferries for P&O, one for Cairnryan and Larne and one for Liverpool and Dublin. This investment reflected both the Irish Peace Process which had generated a higher degree of confidence and industrial expansion throughout the island of Ireland, and also the need to provide modern and efficient tonnage in a very competitive market.

On the down side was the ending of duty free sales aboard ships running between Great Britain and the Republic of Ireland. This particularly impacted the economic margins of the fast ferry services in the Irish Sea. As a consequence, the **Stena Lynx III** was returned to her owners, American Fast Ferries Limited, in October 2003 and the Fishguard and Rosslare high speed service was suspended for the winter. **Superseacat Three** continued on the Liverpool and Dublin route for Sea Containers, but instead of two round trips a day ran only one with an additional evening sailing from Liverpool to Douglas and back. Over capacity on the Dublin freight routes, due to competition from P&O and Merchant Ferries, led Stena Line to sell the **Stena Challenger** in April on the condition that she remain on

Normandy (1982) with side stability sponsons seen leaving Cherbourg for Rosslare on Monday 4 August 2003.

(Author)

Celtic Star (1998), registered in Limassol, worked on the Liverpool and Dublin service on charter to P&O from April 2000. She is seen leaving Dublin off the Great South Wall.

(Author)

The new *European Causeway* (2000) commenced service for P&O Irish Sea between Cairnryan and Larne in August 2000 allowing *Pride of Rathlin* to stand down.

Brave Merchant (1998) in the new Norse Merchant Ferries livery seen leaving Dublin off the Great South Wall on 22 March 2002.
(Author)

Lagan Viking (1998) in the Mersey bound for Belfast wearing the new Norse Merchant Ferries livery, the web site address was added later.
(Author)

Ulysses (2000) set a new benchmark for general-purpose ferries when she started on the Dublin and Holyhead route for Irish Ferries in March 2001.
(Author)

the Holyhead and Dublin freight service for the remainder of 2000 on charter back to Stena.

The increasingly stringent SOLAS requirements continued to challenge shipowners. The **Stena Caledonia** received 'duck tail' sponsons at the stern during her refit in February 2001 in order to comply with the latest requirements. **Stena Galloway** was not upgraded. Irish Ferries **Normandy** received side sponsons the following year.

Superseacat Two took over from **Seacat Danmark** on the Heysham - Belfast route for Sea Containers on 18 April. The **Superseacat Two** had been modified in the winter to improve her stability in poor weather; she crossed from Belfast to Heysham in just 4 hours with two sailings each day from both Heysham and Belfast. **Seacat Scotland** remained on the new Belfast and Troon service and closed the Belfast and Stranraer route on 13 March 2000; Stranraer had become difficult for Sea Containers because of a dispute with the local planning authority regarding a new terminal building. Given the rising cost of fuel, Sea Containers added a fuel surcharge to most of its services in the summer. The **Lady of Mann** spent her second summer on charter working in the Azores on whale spotting day cruises.

P&O chartered the **Celtic Star** to support its service between Liverpool and Dublin from 27 March 2000 onwards. She joined the **European Leader** and **European Envoy** as well as the chartered **Celtic Sun** which had joined the fleet earlier in the year. The two Celtic ships were quite different, the **Celtic Star** having been completed in 1998 whereas the **Celtic Sun** dated from 1991 and had previously served as the **Loon Plage** on the North Sea. She was sister to the **Varbola** then on charter to Merchant Ferries. The attraction of the **Celtic Sun** was not so much her freight capacity for 70 trailers but rather her service speed of slightly more than 20 knots. She also carried up to 12 drivers.

The new ferry for Cairnryan building for P&O in Japan was named **European Causeway** at her launch on 20 March 2000. The **Jetliner** was returned to her owners in April when the chartered **Superstar**

Stena Forwarder (2000) seen arriving at Dublin off Poolbeg Light shortly after she entered service.

(Author)

Express moved north from her Portsmouth and Cherbourg route. The **Superstar Express** had been displaced at Portsmouth by an even larger fast craft. The **Superstar Express** was slightly faster than the **Jetliner** with a maximum service speed of 41 knots, and could operate in a 3.5 metre wave amplitude at reduced speeds, rather than 3.0 metres for the older craft. The new craft, built at Fremantle in Australia in 1997, could accommodate 823 passengers and 165 accompanied cars on a cargo deadweight of 340 tons.

On 14 August 2000 the **European Causeway** took her maiden commercial voyage on the Cairnryan and Larne route. She has a service speed of 23 knots but achieved 26 knots during her six week delivery voyage from her builders in Japan. This increased speed over her predecessor, **Pride of Rathlin**, allowed the new ship to provide four return sailings per day. Light and airy accommodation is provided for 410 passengers along with the usual lounges, restaurant, bar and children's area. **Pride of Rathlin** was laid up pending sale before going to Indonesian waters with the new name **BSP III**.

The **European Causeway** was built by Shimonoseki, part of the Mitsubishi group of companies. The hull of the ship comprises a single skin but to compensate there are five longitudinal bulkheads below the main vehicle deck which along with the lateral bulkheads allow compartments to be monitored and isolated should that be necessary in the event of the hull being breached. In addition, there are no flood control doors on the main deck but instead crossflow systems were installed that automatically pump water laterally across the ship should water accumulate at one side of the vehicle deck. The two vehicle decks can be loaded and unloaded simultaneously from twin level linkspans while the lower hold is accessed by a fixed ramp; there is also a hoistable ramp between main and upper vehicle decks, although this is rarely used.

Irish Ferries new super ferry **Ulysses** was floated out of her building basin on 1 September 2000 with a projected start date on the Irish Sea of March 2001.

In October 2000 the replacement for the **Stena Challenger** at Holyhead was announced by Stena. The **Stena Forwarder** building at the Visentini yard at Venice, was due on the Holyhead and Dublin route in March 2001 at which time **Stena Challenger** would be handed over to her new Canadian owners.

The last of the first-generation freight ferries on the Irish Sea, the Isle of Man Steam Packet Company's **Peveril**, was sold in autumn 2000. She had previously served between Heysham and Belfast on the joint P&O and Sealink overnight freight service. The ship saw further service under the Costa Rican flag trading to near South American ports.

Swansea Cork Ferries operated the **Superferry** again in 2000 on its seasonal service between its namesake ports. In 2001, however, the company took the former **Saint Patrick II** on bareboat charter which, with the name **City of Cork** and registered in Malta, operated between 12 March and 6 November that year.

On 1 January 2001, the Merchant Ferries and Norse Irish Ferries interests, now all owned by Cenargo, were merged under the new

Pride of Suffolk (1978) was transferred from Felixstowe to P&O Irish Sea for the Dublin and Liverpool route in September 1991 as the replacement for Celtic Sun.

(Author)

*The Dutch registered **Norbank** (1993) seen arriving at Dublin off the Great South Wall in August 2003.*
(Author)

***Norbay** (1994) was also transferred from the North Sea in March 2002 and maintained the Liverpool and Dublin service for P&O Irish Sea.*
(Author)

***Stena Galloway** (1980) seen arriving at Belfast in 1996. She was sold in March 2002 leaving **Stena Caledonia** to work alongside the high speed **Stena Voyager**.*
(Author)

Stena Europe (1981) at Rosslare.

(Iain McCall)

company title Norse Merchant Ferries. The ships all now wore grey hulls apart from the two Belfast to Liverpool ships which were still in red. The new funnel device was an unimpressive three component wavy triangular symbol on a white funnel. Cenargo's second pair of passenger and freight ferries, **Northern Merchant** and **Midnight Merchant**, were delivered during 2000 and took up service between Dover and Dunkirk under charter to Norfolk Line. It was thought at one time that they might replace the **Lagan Viking** and **Mersey Viking** on the Liverpool and Belfast route as Cenargo had purchased these two ships from their Italian owners in March for US $60 million.

P&O's new ship for the Liverpool and Dublin route, **European Ambassador**, arrived in Liverpool from her builders in Japan on 6 January 2001. P&O confirmed that a third ship, a sister to **European Causeway**, was also under construction in Japan and due for delivery in May 2002.

European Highlander (2002) joined European Causeway on the Cairnryan and Larne service at the start of July 2002.

(P&O)

107

Merchant Bravery (1978) arriving at Dublin from Heysham and seen off the Great South Wall.

(Author)

European Ambassador differed from the **European Causeway** in that she had more powerful engines arranged in a father and son configuration. She also had overnight accommodation with twin and four berth cabins for 222 passengers and pullman chairs for a further 183 passengers. The was also one cabin arranged for disabled passengers. **European Ambassador** left the Shimonoseki yard on 13 December 2000, and was officially named at a ceremony at Dublin on 26 January. She had already entered service taking her maiden sailing from Liverpool to Dublin on 9 January 2001.

Sea Containers transferred the two Superseacats out of the Irish Sea in 2001. **Seacat Danmark** took over the Belfast and Heysham service while the Dublin and Liverpool route was provided by **Rapide**, formerly on the Dover and Ostend route. **Seacat Scotland** maintained the Belfast and Troon route while **Seacat Isle of Man** worked the various services from Douglas to UK ports and Ireland.

The new ship for the Holyhead and Dublin service of Irish Ferries, **Ulysses**, was handed over by Aker Finnyards on 22 February 2001 and arrived for the first time at Dublin on 28 February. She took her maiden commercial voyage from Dublin on 25 March. The ship offers a massive 4070 lane metres of vehicle stowage space, equivalent to 1340 cars or 240 freight vehicles, and can accommodate 1875 passengers. The displaced **Isle of Inishmore** was laid up awaiting a decision on her future, while **Normandy** stood in during the refit period for **Isle of Innisfree** on the Pembroke Dock and Rosslare service before resuming her own seasonal continental duties from Rosslare. In due course the two Isles were swapped, and **Isle of Innisfree** was laid up at Le Havre while the larger **Isle of Inishmore** took up service between Rosslare and Pembroke Dock. **Isle of Innisfree** was later chartered to P&O as **Pride of Cherbourg** and in 2005 sub-chartered to Stena Line for use in the Baltic as **Stena Challenger**. Both **Pride of Bilbao** and **Stena Challenger** remained on charter agreements to P&O lasting until 2007.

With **Ulysses** now in service and advertised as the largest ferry in the world (perhaps the largest capacity ferry in the world) Stena Line started advertising the fastest conventional ferry on the Irish Sea. This was the new **Stena Forwarder** which offered a service speed of 24 knots and reduced the voyage time to just 3 hours. The **Stena Forwarder**, under charter from her Italian builders Visentini, commenced work on 12 April 2001. **Stena Challenger** had finished four days earlier, but **Stena Forwarder** suffered damage on trial docking at Dublin on 8 April and was not able to start commercial sailings as advertised the next day. The HSS **Stena Explorer** was left in charge while **Stena Forwarder** visited dry dock at Birkenhead.

The **Stena Forwarder** was a stern-loader with no bow door. She had 2100 lane metres of vehicle stowage with a further mezzanine deck for 75 cars. She had a certificate for 1000 passengers and offered 75 cabins with a total of 308 berths. The ship was officially named at a ceremony at Dublin on 26 April.

On 30 March 2001 the **European Pathfinder** was replaced on the Cherbourg and Rosslare service by the **European Seafarer**. This replacement ship offered greater freight capacity on a route where traffic was growing. On 19 April the **European Pathfinder** replaced the **European Trader** on the Cairnryan and Larne service. The **European Pathfinder** had a large shelf welded aft of the main vehicle deck in order to better fit the local linkspans. The following month the **European Trader** was sold, leaving near sisters **European Endeavour** and **European Pathfinder** to work alongside the new **European Causeway**. The **European Trader** went to a company called Taygran Shipping for service to the Outer Hebrides in competition with Caledonian MacBrayne. However, by the autumn, the new company was in the hands of the receiver and the **Taygran Trader**, as she had become, was laid up at Leith and advertised for sale, latterly working in the Red Sea.

At the start of July 2001, P&O switched its Larne and Ardrossan service to Larne and Troon, having outgrown Ardrossan with its limitation on the size of vessels that it could accommodate. The **European Highlander** (onetime **Merchant Valiant** and later P&O's **Lion**) was renamed **European Mariner** to release her name for the

Seacat Isle of Man (1991) seen arriving at Dublin off the Great South Wall on Thursday 21 August 2003.

(Author)

new ship building in Japan and intended to partner the **European Causeway** at Cairnryan. **European Mariner** was displaced on the route later in the year by **European Navigator** which offered greater capacity.

On 9 September, the **Koningin Beatrix** ran aground at Fishguard Harbour sustaining propeller and rudder damage. She was already booked to go to Falmouth for a new engine crankshaft and **Stena Galloway** came down from Stranraer as relief on 11 September.

In November, P&O split its Liverpool and Dublin service to offer a new route between Dublin and Mostyn on the River Dee. Mostyn offered brand new facilities, long awaited by P&O at Liverpool, and was seen as a positive move for the company to develop its operations. Berth to berth was also much shorter in time as the locking in and out process at Liverpool was obviated. The new **European Ambassador** and the **European Envoy** (former **Ibex**) moved to Mostyn while the Liverpool freight only service was continued by **Celtic Star** and **Pride of Suffolk** which had displaced the chartered **Celtic Sun** from 3 September. The **Celtic Sun** then took up a charter to Norse Irish Ferries running between Heysham and Dublin.

The **Pride of Suffolk** had been transferred to Liverpool from Felixstowe and Rotterdam duties. She had previously been named **Baltic Ferry** when she was in the Townsend Thoresen fleet and had a passenger module added in 1986 which, as **Pride of Suffolk**, had been removed in 1995, converting her back into a freight ship with accommodation for drivers and a few passengers. Dating from 1978 when she was commissioned as **Stena Transporter**, the ship had a large and useful freight capacity.

Pride of Suffolk was renamed **European Diplomat** towards the end of the year. Her tenure on the Liverpool and Dublin service was short-lived and she was again transferred, starting work on 19 January 2002, to the Rosslare and Cherbourg route as a replacement for **European Seafarer**. Before the **European Diplomat** moved to the French service she had her accommodation upgraded to provide berths for 107 drivers and passengers with a new lounge module for lorry drivers fitted on the main deck in front of the superstructure.

European Seafarer went to the Larne and Fleetwood route, displacing **European Navigator** which took over the Larne and Troon service. **European Mariner**, displaced from Troon, was put on short-term charter to the Isle of Man Steam Packet Company from 21 January 2002, in lieu of **Ben-my-Chree** which was away on annual refit. She then covered for **European Pathfinder** between Cairnryan and Larne from 13 February while that ship was repaired following minor fire damage. **European Mariner** was then laid up at Barrow awaiting a decision on her future, however, she was soon back on the Larne and Troon service with **European Pioneer** withdrawn for urgent repairs. During summer 2002 she was chartered to Color Line.

The **Norbank** and **Norbay** were transferred to the Irish Sea from North Sea Ferries cargo service between Hull and Rotterdam. The **Norbank**, Dutch registered and crewed, and **Norbay** registered at Hull, were built in 1993 and 1994 respectively. They have a service speed of 22 knots and can carry 150 freight vehicles or trailers and can accommodate up to 114 drivers and passengers. John Kearsley, Managing Director of P&O Irish Sea commented:

> To ensure that we maintain our high level of service on our Liverpool route, we now plan to introduce these newer and larger ships to enhance the facilities for both our freight and passenger customers.

On 7 January 2002, the **Norbank** and **Norbay** started on the Liverpool and Dublin service and displaced the **Celtic Star** allowing her to start a new route between Liverpool and Larne the next day.

Stena Galloway was withdrawn in March 2002. This was a direct result of a downturn in trade across the Irish Sea coupled with over capacity on most routes. All the Irish trades had been badly impacted by the foot and mouth disease outbreak which restricted the movement of cattle and dairy products throughout much of 2001. **Stena Galloway** was sold to Moroccan owners to serve between Tangier and Cadiz. Her withdrawal left **Stena Caledonia** alone in support of HSS **Stena Voyager**.

On 13 March 2002, the **Koningin Beatrix** was replaced on the Fishguard and Rosslare route by **Stena Europe**. The **Stena Europe**

Superseacat Two *(1997) on charter to the Isle of Man Steam Packet Company, seen leaving Dublin off the Great South Wall on Friday 23 August 2003.*

(Author)

received a £4 million refit before entering service at Fishguard; the work included removal of a number of cabins to increase her garage space to 1300 lane metres. **Stena Europe** had previously been in use in the Baltic and before that had worked alongside **Koningin Beatrix** on the Harwich and Hook of Holland route. She had been built in 1981 as **Kronprinsessan Victoria** for the Sessan Line and was a sister to Irish Ferries **Normandy**. **Koningin Beatrix** was renamed **Stena Baltica** and then took up service between Kiel and Karlskrona.

Swansea Cork Ferries brought the **Superferry** back to its namesake service on 8 April 2002. Now named **Blue Aegean**, she was still marketed as **Superferry** but now registered at St Vincent and the Grenadines. Swansea Cork Ferries announced in due course that they had purchased the vessel for €6.5 million.

Seatruck Ferries, which maintained the **Riverdance** and **Moondance** on the Heysham and Warrenpoint service, were running near to capacity. The company had always been undercapitalised and help finally came in a buyout from the Danish Clipper Group. A full review of the company's prospects concluded that new ships and new routes would be the way forward but no action was taken just yet, although P&O's **European Mariner** was chartered for two months to provide a three-ship service.

The long promised new facilities on the Mersey at Twelve Quays finally opened in mid-June 2002. This allowed Norse Merchant Ferries Belfast service, operated by **Lagan Viking** and **Mersey Viking**, to transfer from Liverpool to the new river berth on Monday 17 June. This shortened the passage time to Belfast by up to 90 minutes with locking in and out at Liverpool no longer part of the journey. The ships were now able to offer daytime services in addition to the normal night time sailing with 12 return trips per week. The Dublin service offered by **Brave Merchant** and **Dawn Merchant** was due to transfer to Twelve Quays in August.

In July 2002, the second new ship for the P&O route between Cairnryan and Larne joined the service. The **European Highlander** was a near sister to the **European Causeway** delivered in 2001, and was built, like her sister, in Japan. The new ship has capacity for 123 freight units and 400 passengers. She took her maiden commercial voyage on 3 July with the 0800 hours departure from Larne. **European Endeavour** was retained on the route and **European Pathfinder** worked on the service as well while **European Causeway** went for refit in mid-July. **European Causeway** returned on 17 July and both **European Endeavour** and **European Pathfinder** stood down. **European Navigator** remained on the Larne and Troon service.

On 12 June 2002 the **European Pathfinder** received damage to a crankshaft whilst on passage between Cairnryan and Larne. Temporary repairs allowed her to continue until 17 July. The **European Endeavour** was sold in July to Trans Europa Ferries and renamed **Gardenia**, and the **European Pathfinder** was also sold, in October, after being laid up at Liverpool. She was renamed **Begonia**, also under the ownership of Trans Europa Ferries and registered at St Vincent. Once again, the two ships were partners, this time working between Ostend and Ramsgate.

From July 2002, the **European Ambassador** operated a weekend return sailing from Dublin to Cherbourg between her normal Dublin and Mostyn roster. This proved popular both with shippers and with the general public and the service was extended into the autumn with the last sailing taking place on 3 November.

Another Irish Sea ferry went south to the English Channel in the summer. Norse Merchant Ferries' **Dawn Merchant** was withdrawn from the Liverpool and Dublin service leaving **Brave Merchant** to offer a reduced service now based at the new Twelve Quays riverside berths at Birkenhead. On 2 September 2002, the **Dawn Merchant** joined her two younger sisters **Midnight Merchant** and **Northern Merchant** on the Norfolk Line service between Dover and Dunkirk. This reduction in capacity on the Liverpool and Dublin route reflected both over-capacity and the downturn in trade caused by the foot and mouth problems that started in 2001.

The **Dawn Merchant** was replaced on the Liverpool and Dublin route by **Norse Mersey**, which started work on 7 September, and was owned by Levantina Trasporti srl. She had previously been on charter to Norse Irish Ferries until 1997 when she worked between Liverpool and Belfast. The freight ferry **Lindarosa**, also owned by Levantina Trasporti srl, was taken on charter to supplement freight sailings between Liverpool and Belfast, starting on 4 September.

On the Heysham and Dublin freight route, the charter of the **Lembitu** ended in the spring and she was replaced by **Varbola**, working alongside **Saga Moon**. The Heysham and Belfast service was in the hands of **Merchant Brilliant**, **Merchant Bravery** and **River Lune**. Meanwhile, **Merchant Venture** was on charter to Gulf Shipping (Norse Island Ferries), running between Aberdeen and the North Isles from 3 September alongside the former P&O Scotland ferry **St Rognvald**. In November the **Merchant Venture** was disabled by engine failure and laid up at Lerwick; she was brought to Birkenhead the following March (2003) and was sold to owners in Dubai in August that year.

Stena Line confirmed in the summer that the new ferry building at Hyundai, a sister to the **Stena Britannica** at Harwich, would be completed as a day passenger vessel to replace the **Stena Forwarder** on the Holyhead and Dublin route.

Lady of Mann again spent the summer in the Azores, this year with air conditioning fitted throughout her public spaces. Sea Containers axed its Belfast and Heysham service before the season started and placed **Seacat Isle of Man** on the Belfast and Troon route until **Rapide** was ready to take over at the beginning of April. **Seacat Isle of Man** and **Superseacat Three** maintained the Isle of Man company services including the Liverpool and Dublin route. At the end of the year the **Rapide** swapped her registration in Luxembourg for the port of Nassau.

Cenargo was in trouble at the end of the year and filed for protection from creditors under Chapter 11 of the United States bankruptcy code. Cenargo International had always relied on loans rather than share capital and intense competition on the Irish Sea coupled with a decline in freight traffic had brought the company to its knees. The protection filed in the United States was challenged by the Lombard, Royal Bank of Scotland Group, owners of the collateral vested in **Midnight Merchant** and **Northern Merchant** which were both on charter to Norfolk Line, and this forced the British registered components of Cenargo into administration. The administrators sought a financial restructuring of Norse Merchant Ferries rather than any attempt to sell the company.

*Stena Transporter (1978) seen leaving the River Stour off Landguard Point on Wednesday 2 April 2003 just prior to moving to Holyhead to replace **Stena Forwarder**.*

(Author)

Norse Irish Ferries reported a loss of over £5 million for the nine month period up to June 2002. **Brave Merchant** was withdrawn from the Liverpool and Dublin service in February and chartered to the Ministry of Defence, later also to Norfolk Line and finally to P&O. She was replaced by the chartered freighter **Lindarosa**, and when **Brave Merchant** resumed service in the Irish Sea on 7 September, she in turn replaced **Norse Mersey** which went off charter. **Brave Merchant** resumed on the Dublin service after a spell of relief work on the Belfast route on 7 September. Her owners, though still in receivership, were in the process of being put on a firmer financial footing. The Heysham and Belfast route was then in the hands of **Merchant Brilliant** and **Merchant Bravery**, while **Varbola** and **Saga Moon** maintained the Heysham and Dublin route.

During 2003 the **Superstar Express** added two round trips a day between Larne and Troon to her schedule, starting on 15 April, and only two trips on the shorter Cairnryan route. This put her in direct competition with Sea Containers which withdrew **Seacat Scotland** at the end of 2002 and replaced her with **Seacat Isle of Man**. In late March **Rapide**, which had earlier closed the Heysham and Belfast

Stena Adventurer (2003) approaching Dublin from Holyhead on Thursday 21 August 2003 in her seventh week of service.

(Author)

111

Ben-my-Chree (1998) arriving at Heysham in her new Steam Packet livery complete with new passenger module before the funnel.
(Author)

service, took over. In addition, the **Superseacat Two** was put on the Liverpool and Dublin service and then on the fast services between Douglas and Belfast from 28 March; she had been laid up throughout much of 2002. **Lady of Mann** was also back in service and spent another summer in the Azores.

But like Cenargo, Sea Containers was also in trouble and had to put the Isle of Man Steam Packet Company up for sale in the spring of 2003. Montagu Private Equity, formerly HSBC Private Equity, a new investment spin off company from the HSBC bank, bought the company for US $233 million (£142 million) with effect from 1 July 2003. The deal included the **Ben-my-Chree**, **Lady of Mann**, **Seacat Isle of Man** and **Superseacat Two**, although the latter remained on charter from Sea Containers. The Steam Packet also took over the management of the remaining Sea Containers route on the Irish Sea between Belfast and Troon which was maintained by the **Rapide**.

P&O too was trying to shed its less profitable routes. In May 2003 it announced a deal with Stena Line involving the sale of seven ships working on the P&O Irish Sea routes between Mostyn and Dublin, Liverpool and Dublin and the Fleetwood and Larne routes plus the intended closure of the short-lived Mostyn and Dublin route. As proposed, this included the almost new **European Ambassador** as well as the former North Sea twins **Norbank** and **Norbay**, although the **Norbay** was then on charter within the P&O group and **Norbank** was yet to be purchased by P&O from Royal Nedlloyd, former partners in North Sea Ferries. On her purchase later in the year, however, she retained her Dutch crew and registration. Stena also proposed a 50% purchase of Larne Port from P&O in order to allow it to expand berth facilities and move the HSS **Stena Voyager** from Belfast to Larne. The entire deal was referred to The Office of Fair Trading and then to the Competition Commission. The outcome was, as reported in the *Irish Times*, 2 March 2004:

> Ferry companies P&O and Stena have reached agreement allowing Stena to purchase part of P&O's ferry operations and some of its assets on the Irish Sea. Stena will acquire P&O's Fleetwood-Larne route, including the three ferries **European Leader**, **European Pioneer** and **European Seafarer**, and the two P&O ferries currently operating on the Mostyn-Dublin route, **European Ambassador** and **European Envoy**. The transaction, which is subject to finalisation of contracts and employee consultation, is anticipated to be completed on April 5th.
>
> The agreement follows the decision by the UK Competition Commission last month to block a 2003 proposal which included the transfer of P&O's Liverpool-Dublin route to Stena. In so doing, the Commission concluded that the transfer of the Fleetwood-Larne route to Stena would not raise competition concerns.

Following the previously announced Irish Sea transaction, consultations commenced with employees about the possible closure of the loss-making Mostyn-Dublin service, of P&O's shoreside operations at the Port of Mostyn and the Fleetwood head office.

In the event the **Norbank** and **Norbay** remained in service for P&O Irish Sea on the Liverpool and Dublin route. **European Navigator** was sold in December 2003 and handed over to her new Jordanian owners on 17 February 2004, while **European Mariner** returned to the Troon and Larne service which again became freight only, the **European Navigator** having previously offered sufficient passenger facilities to attract some private cars and passengers. The deal with Stena was completed for £50million, but with the assets at Mostyn being written off and the disposal price less than the book price of the assets sold, P&O was left with an exceptional impairment charge of about £24 million. At the same time P&O stopped carrying livestock on its Cherbourg route aboard **European Diplomat** and on services into Fleetwood.

Swansea Cork Ferries resumed on 10 March with their own ship **Superferry**. Irish Ferries **Normandy** received a major upgrade before starting her season between Rosslare and Cherbourg.

Stena Forwarder was returned to her owners in April 2003 at the end of her charter. She took her last sailing from Dublin on 13 April already devoid of any Stena Line markings and with a dark blue funnel ready for her new career in Mexico. In her place, the **Stena Transporter** was transferred to Holyhead from Harwich to maintain a freight only service from 14 April, until the new **Stena Adventurer** arrived from her builders in South Korea. The new ship took her maiden voyage on 1 July allowing **Stena Transporter** to stand down and return to the North Sea.

Stena Adventurer offers a massive 3517 lane metres of stowage space for accompanied cars, freight vehicles and trailers which are loaded and unloaded via double deck linkspans at both Holyhead and Dublin. She has spacious accommodation for 1500 passengers on three decks and has a service speed of just over 22 knots. Within twelve months of the introduction of **Stena Adventurer**, Stena Line reported a 40% increase in freight on its Irish Sea services, much of it attributed to the introduction of the new ship.

In 2004 the Belfast and Troon High speed ferry **Rapide** only operated between 12 March and 1 November. Sea Containers stated that the service lost money over the winter. At Fishguard, Stena Line finally bought **Stena Lynx III** and she worked the seasonal service between 8 April and 26 September 2004.

Irish Ferries had their normal round of refits early in the year with **Normandy** deputising at Rosslare and Pembroke while **Isle of Inishmore** covered for **Ulysses** and then had her own refit.

The Isle of Man company's **Ben-my-Chree** had her passenger accommodation extended with a 110 tonne passenger module lifted into place abaft the existing accommodation. This work was carried out at Liverpool in January and fitting out of the new accommodation was completed after the ship had returned to service on 8 February. The work enabled her passenger capacity to be increased.

Norse Merchant Ferries came out of receivership with the formation of the Norse Merchant Group. Trade creditors accepted a 5% pay-out in February, a figure greater than would have been the case if the company had ceased to exist, and a Company Voluntary Arrangement allowed bonds to be issued to cover the various loans the company had taken out. Services on the Irish Sea remained buoyant and it was for this reason alone that the company was able to survive. The company outsourced the technical management of its ships later in the year and changed the registration of **Lagan Viking** and **Mersey Viking** from Bari to Belfast. As a final celebration of the company's survival, it was announced that it had contracted to charter from Visentini, two new ferries to replace the Vikings on the Belfast route. The new ships were designed with a speed of 23 knots with 500

*Stena Nordica (2001), formerly P&O Irish Sea's **European Ambassador**, seen arriving at Dublin off Poolbeg Light on Friday 9 June 2009 when she had become partner to **Stena Adventurer**.*
(Author)

passenger berths. Managing Director Phillip Shepherd stated:

> In addition to overnight pullman seating, the new ships will offer berths for approximately 500 passengers in en-suite cabins. This gives them a passenger capacity of almost double that of our existing ships, **Lagan Viking** and **Mersey Viking**.

The **Lagan Viking** and **Mersey Viking** were planned to switch to Birkenhead and Dublin on the arrival of the new ships, and for **Brave Merchant** to be redeployed. Meanwhile, the **Leili**, sister to **Varbola**, was taken on charter in October 2004 to run alongside **Brave Merchant** and **Lindarosa** on the Dublin and Birkenhead route. The **Merchant Bravery** and **Merchant Brilliant** were sold in October and raised the Jamaican flag while they were chartered back to Norse Merchant Ferries until the new tonnage arrived.

The final outcome of the Stena Line and P&O deal started in 2003 took place on 4 April 2004 when the **European Envoy** took the final sailing on the P&O Irish Sea Mostyn and Dublin service. The **European Ambassador** had earlier transferred to Liverpool, as relief to **Norbay** which was under refit, but she too finished on 8 April. **European Ambassador** was then renamed **Stena Nordica** and deployed in the Baltic while **European Envoy** was renamed **Stena Envoy** and chartered for use between Norway and Denmark. The **European Leader**, **European Seafarer** and **European Pioneer** were renamed **Stena Leader**, **Stena Seafarer** and **Stena Pioneer** and the three ships continued to work the now Stena owned Fleetwood and Larne route. **Stena Nordica** would later return to Dublin to serve alongside **Stena Adventurer**.

With the passenger service from Mostyn now closed, Norse Merchant Ferries resumed carrying passengers aboard the **Brave Merchant** on its Birkenhead and Dublin route on 29 March. **River Lune** returned from a charter to Dart Line and resumed on the Heysham and Belfast freight route at the start of March 2004. This move made up a three-ship service along with the sisters **Merchant Brilliant** and **Merchant Bravery**. **Saga Moon** and **Varbola** maintained the Heysham and Dublin route. From the end of March **Varbola** and **Merchant Brilliant** swapped places.

Seatruck Ferries also joined in the tourist trade for the first time. A round trip on the **Riverdance** or **Moondance** between Heysham and Warrenpoint was advertised at £180 for a car and two people inclusive of cabin and meals. The company warned intending passengers that the ships were essentially freighters and that the stairs aboard the ships were steep and narrow.

The Continental Irish services were not doing so well. Irish Ferries flagged out the **Normandy** to the Bahamas at the end of the year and the ship was crewed by a staffing agency drawing on East European crews. Despite the industrial dispute that rumbled on afterwards the company then flagged out the remainder of its fleet to Cyprus – so much for the ships being 'Ambassadors of Ireland'. At the same time, P&O announced the withdrawal of **European Diplomat** from 19 December on the Cherbourg and Rosslare route.

Shortly after the New Year, Sea Containers announced the withdrawal of the **Rapide** on the Belfast and Troon service. Thereafter, the company announced its total withdrawal from ferry activities, citing airlines that offered cheap deals as the preferred travel option coupled with spiralling fuel costs. At the same time the Isle of Man Steam Packet Company announced that it would not resume its Liverpool and Dublin passenger and car service in 2005.

In 2005 the **Seacat Isle of Man** was chartered to Irish Sea Express, a company founded by Liverpool business associates, and put onto a new Liverpool and Dublin daytime service under the name **Sea Express I**. The service started on 27 April, but the original intention to run two trips a day quickly fell to one round trip and the service ended on 8 October with the company entering administration four days later. The vessel was returned to the Isle of Man Steam Packet Company. During the year the **Superseacat Two** was purchased outright by the Steam Packet Company from Sea Containers and registered at Douglas.

P&O replaced the **Superstar Express** with the slightly larger **Express**, previously the **Cherbourg Express**. She started the seasonal service between Cairnryan and Larne on 16 March 2005 and was in service until 18 September. Shortly before the new fast ferry commenced work, the **European Highlander** reached the headlines when she was blown ashore on 8 January, 100 metres south of the Cairnryan linkspan. She lay broadside onto the beach until she could be towed off the next day to discharge passengers and vehicles; the ship was little damaged by the incident and was soon back in service.

In January 2005, **European Diplomat** was purchased by shipowners O'Flaherty of Wexford for €10 million. Renamed **Diplomat** and given a green funnel, she commenced three round trips a week between Rosslare and Cherbourg starting on 1 February, much as she had before under P&O but this time marketed under the banner Celtic Link Ferries. The company was keen to serve the agricultural and fishing sector with the export from Ireland of live cattle and chilled fish. P&O managed and crewed the vessel for the new owners. An additional weekend round trip to Pembroke Dock was added from 7 March. The ship could accommodate 74 passengers, and in addition to drivers the service was advertised for use by private cars.

Norse Merchant Ferries renamed its Belfast twins **Lagan Viking** and **Mersey Viking** which became **Liverpool Viking** and **Dublin Viking** in order to release the old names for the new Belfast ships building in

*Stena Leader (1975), built as **Buffalo**, retaining the P&O blue livery without company markings after purchase of the Fleetwood and Larne service by Stena.*

Italy. The new pair offer 2276 lane metres of stowage space. In June 2005, however, it was announced that Norfolk Line was in process of buying Norse Merchant Ferries, a process that was completed in November. The company had a reported 27% share of the Irish Sea freight traffic and was valued at £250 million. In the meantime, the new *Lagan Viking* was delivered wearing the old company colours only briefly before being repainted in Norfolk Line livery. The 23 knot *Lagan Viking* took her first commercial sailing from Belfast on 19 July allowing the *Liverpool Viking* to transfer to the Dublin route alongside *Brave Merchant*. The *Lindarosa* left the company, her charter having been completed. In the autumn both *Brave Merchant* and *Dawn Merchant* (the latter previously on charter to Norfolk Line) were sold to a Hong Kong investment group. *Brave Merchant* was replaced by *Dublin Viking* when she in turn was displaced from the Belfast route by the new *Mersey Viking* in November.

Seatruck ordered two new ferries from Astilleros de Huelva in Spain for delivery in 2007. The ships were designed to accommodate 120 trailers. Meanwhile it chartered *Lembitu* in June, previously working for Norse Merchant Ferries, and gave her the name *Challenge* to work alongside *Riverdance* and *Moondance* on the Heysham and Warrenpoint service.

Lady of Mann spent the summer in the Azores again, but while she was away from home she had been put up for sale. On return she sailed to Greece to be converted into a stern-loading ferry for inter-island use. The Steam Packet company announced in October that it had been bought by Macquarie Bank Limited for £225 million so providing a handsome profit to previous owners, Montagu Private Equity.

By the end of 2005 the six ferry operators that existed at the Millennium had evolved, principally through intense competition and declining tourist traffic, into the following operators and services, with Celtic Link Ferries also having become established during the year:

P&O Ferries – Cairnryan and Larne *European Causeway*, *European Highlander*; Troon and Larne *European Mariner*; Liverpool and Dublin *Norbank*, *Norbay*

Stena Line UK – Belfast and Stranraer, *Stena Voyager*, *Stena Caledonia*; Fleetwood and Larne *Stena Leader*, *Stena Pioneer*, *Stena Seafarer*; Holyhead and Belfast *Stena Adventurer*, *Stena Explorer*; Fishguard and Rosslare *Stena Europe*; *Stena Lynx III*

Irish Ferries – Holyhead and Dublin *Ulysses*, *Jonathan Swift*; Pembroke Dock and Rosslare *Isle of Inishmore*; Rosslare and Cherbourg *Normandy*

Norfolk Line – Birkenhead and Dublin *Lagan Viking*, *Mersey Viking* (both on charter); Birkenhead and Dublin *Dublin Viking*, *Liverpool Viking*, *RR Shield* ex-*Leili* (on charter); Heysham and Belfast *Saga Moon*, *Merchant Brilliant* (on charter), *RR Arrow* ex-*Varbola* (on charter); Heysham and Dublin *River Lune*, *Merchant Bravery* (on charter)

Seatruck Ferries – Heysham and Warrenpoint *Moondance*, *Riverdance*, *Challenge* (on charter)

Isle of Man Steam Packet Company – Heysham and Douglas *Ben-my-Chree*; Douglas and Liverpool, Douglas and Belfast, Douglas and Dublin *Sea Express I*, *Superseacat Two*

Celtic Link Ferries – Rosslare and Cherbourg, Rosslare and Pembroke Dock *Diplomat*

The stage was now set for the contemporary era of ferry operation and consolidation of the Irish Sea services. Of the existing players, the rising star was Seatruck Ferries, while Celtic Link was also an established player. The Norfolk Line interests, as it happened, were to be short lived.

Liverpool Viking (1997) in full Norfolk Line colours seen arriving at Dublin.

(Author)

Mersey Viking (2005) seen in the Mersey after she had adopted Norfolk Line colours.

Saga Moon (1984) seen approaching Dublin after Norfolk Line had taken over Norse Merchant Ferries in 2005.

(Author)

CHAPTER 10
THE CONTEMPORARY ERA AND A LOOK BACK AT HOW AND WHY

Oscar Wilde (1987) arriving at Rosslare. She had a unique livery of dark blue hull and white funnel for much of her Irish career.

(Irish Ferries)

The years subsequent to 2005 saw a general consolidation of the ferry industry in the Irish Sea with each company offering its own distinctive service. The fast ferries had become expensive to operate in competition with airlines and were largely withdrawn. The HSS fast ferries were withdrawn in November 2011 at Belfast and October 2015 at Dublin, both high speed routes having been overtaken on the one hand by cheap air fares, and on the other by increasing fuel costs. The Fishguard and Rosslare high speed service operated by **Stena Lynx III** under the banner Stena Express also closed at the end of the season in 2011. The P&O fast ferry **Express** finished her last season on the Cairnryan and Troon to Larne routes in September 2015. However, the Isle of Man Steam Packet Company has retained high speed ferries to work alongside its general-purpose ferry **Ben-my-Chree**, and Irish Ferries maintain a fast ferry, commissioning the **Dublin Swift** in 2018, as a successor to **Jonathan Swift** on the service between Dublin and Holyhead.

In December 2007, the Isle of Man company's **Sea Express I**, the former **Seacat Isle of Man**, was renamed **Snaefell** following lay up since March 2006 after a collision in the Mersey. Her place had been taken by the chartered **Emeraude France**. **Superseacat Two** was renamed **Viking** in January 2008; she survived in the Isle of Man fleet until September 2009 when she was sold to Hellenic Seaways. Her successor was a former United States Navy fast transport which was given the name **Manannan** ready to take her maiden run on 22 May 2009 on the Liverpool service. She is a twin hulled vessel 96 metres in length with a beam of 26 metres and was built by Incat in Tasmania in 1998. She can accommodate 200 vehicles and carries 850 passengers and crew. **Manannan** works between Liverpool and Douglas with trips also to Belfast and Dublin. **Snaefell** finished service in October 2010 and was later sold to Greek owners.

Freight demand was high in the mid-2000s although recession in Ireland was not far off. Celtic Link Ferries took advantage of this boom by introducing a second route between Liverpool and Dublin which again accommodated lorries carrying live cattle. The **Northern Star** (previously chartered to P&O as **Celtic Star** and later renamed **Northern Star**) was chartered to open the new service which commenced on 7 May 2006; she reverted to her old name shortly afterwards. **Celtic Star** was joined by the **Carmen B** which had been built as the Finnish owned **Timmerland** in 1978. This charter was terminated only two months later due to overstretched resources and limited cash; in the meantime, the **Carmen B** had been renamed **Celtic Sun** and had her quarter stern ramp replaced by a full stern access door.

Stena Line added a second ship to the Holyhead and Dublin route; the freight carrier **Stena Seatrader** started on the service on 9 October 2006 working alongside **Stena Adventurer**. The **Stena Seatrader** was previously deployed in the North Sea, and offered 2100 lane metres of vehicle stowage but only limited accommodation for drivers and passengers.

P&O added a third ship, **RR Triumph**, for use on its Dublin and Liverpool route from 17 July onwards.

Swansea Cork Ferries sold **Superferry** in autumn 2006 due to 'an offer that was too good to miss'. Her final sailing was brought forward to 5 October. There was no service the following year although the chartered freight ferry **Victoria**, built in 1980, ran on the route under the banner HJ Line for two months between 21 March and the end of May. The service was poorly patronised from the outset. Swansea Cork Ferries was unable to source a suitable vessel thereafter and ceased to trade.

The Irish Continental Group announced at the start of 2007 that it had purchased the **Kronprins Harald** from Color Line for €55 million. Intended as a replacement for **Normandy** on the Rosslare and Cherbourg or Roscoff routes, the ship remained with Color Line on charter from the Irish Continental Group until September when she

Stena Seatrader (1973) seen leaving Dublin off the Poolbeg Light on Thursday 2 November 2006 during her third week on the Dublin and Holyhead route.
(Author)

Pride of Bilbao (1986), the Irish ferry that never went to Ireland, seen arriving at Portsmouth off the Round Tower on 26 August 2003.
(Author)

European Endeavour (2000) seen leaving Dublin off the Poolbeg Light on Friday 12 June 2009. She was originally built as *Midnight Merchant*.
(Author)

Clipper Ranger (1998) at Heysham. She was launched as *Lembitu*, and was chartered by Norse Merchant Ferries and P&O before she was bought by Seatruck and renamed *Challenge* in 2005.

(Seatruck Ferries)

Dublin Viking (1968) seen leaving Dublin off the Poolbeg Light on Friday 3 November 2006.

(Author)

Riverdance (1977) ashore at Cleveleys in February 2008.

(Blackpool Gazette)

was renamed **Oscar Wilde**. The **Normandy** took her last sailing at the start of November to allow crew training aboard the **Oscar Wilde**, which then commenced duty from Rosslare on 30 November. **Oscar Wilde** accommodated 580 cars and 62 freight vehicles and offered over 1300 overnight berths. P&O extended the charter of **Pride of Bilbao** during the year until September 2010 so providing valuable income to the Irish company. **Normandy** spent the next summer on charter in the Mediterranean before being sold to Far Eastern interests.

P&O also invested in second hand tonnage when it bought the **El Greco** for €57 million and renamed her **European Endeavour**. She was built originally as the **Midnight Merchant** for Cenargo and had been used by Norfolk Line at Dover. She started in service sailing from Liverpool to Dublin on 6 November 2007 as relief to **Norbay** and then **Norbank** while they were away for refit. Thereafter, she was used on the Irish Sea for relief and supplementary work, on the Liverpool and Dublin route, and on Cairnryan and Larne duties. **Stena Nordica** was back in the Irish Sea in the winter period first relieving **Stena Seatrader** at Holyhead which went for a major upgrade on 10 January 2008 and then **Stena Europe** at Fishguard until 11 February. Seatruck Ferries bought Celtic Link's Dublin and Liverpool interests in September 2007 for £6 million. **Celtic Star** was retained on the service and was joined in January 2008 by **RR Challenge**, with **Merchant Brilliant** taking her place on the Warrenpoint service until Seatruck took delivery of the first of its 142 metre long freight ferries ordered from Astilleros de Huelva in Spain. The new ship was named **Clipper Point**, and offers stowage for 120 trailers; she started work on the Heysham and Warrenpoint service in February 2008. Sister ship **Clipper Pace** joined her on 3 March 2009. In addition, during October, the **RR Triumph** and **RR Arrow** were purchased from Elmira Shipping principally for charter work, and in December the sisters **Challenge** (originally **Lembitu**) and **Shield** were also bought, the latter pair with a price tag of €34 million. All four ships had previously been on charter to various operators on the Irish Sea, their previous names respectively: **Lebola**, **Varbola**, **Lembitu** and **Leili**. The **RR Triumph** was later renamed **Clipper Racer** and the **RR Challenge** became the **Clipper Ranger**.

Celtic Link Ferries still had the Rosslare and Cherbourg service operated by **Diplomat**. In December 2007 the company bought the quasi-sister ship **Finnforest** from Striomma Turism & Sjofart AB and chartered it back to them; she carried 155 trailers.

The year 2008 started badly as economic recession in Ireland deepened. Plans for a joint development of Cairnryan port by both P&O and Stena were abandoned as having become too expensive, despite Stena wanting to move from Stranraer and P&O to develop its port facilities. At Liverpool, P&O chartered the **Equine** from Cobelfret to replace the chartered **Global Freighter** which had been brought in to satisfy extra demand on the Dublin service.

The weather was atrocious in the early part of 2008. Norfolk Ferries had twice switched **Dublin Viking** to the Birkenhead and Belfast service to allow her slower counterparts on that route to catch up on schedule on the shorter Dublin route, once in January and once again in March.

On the evening of 31 January 2008 Seatruck Ferries' **Riverdance** was nearing the end of her voyage from Warrenpoint to Heysham when she was hit broadside by an extraordinarily large wave. The consequent roll to starboard shifted some of the cargo and the vessel developed an alarming list, reported to be approaching 60° at one stage. Gale force winds pushed at the ship which suffered a generator failure and at 1945 hours a Mayday call was made. A helicopter rescue of the five passengers and nine of the crew was successfully carried out as she drifted towards the Fylde coast. Shortly before 2200 hours she was aground on Cleveleys beach and at 0500 hours the next morning the force of the gale at high tide pushed the ship broadside up onto the beach. The rest of the crew were then winched safely off the ship which later became a constructive total loss and was broken up where she lay. The Marine Accident Investigation Branch maintained that the **Riverdance** had been travelling too slowly in a rough following sea and this, coupled with poor cargo distribution including that of heavy loads of scrap iron on trailers, made the ship unstable.

Seatruck had been short of vessels since they began operating the Dublin and Liverpool service. To make matters worse, **Moondance** was out of service for almost four months after grounding at Warrenpoint on 29 June and damaging her rudder. The Marine Accident Investigation Branch report, in this case, highlighted lax procedures and complacency as the main cause of the mechanical failure that led to the grounding. Back in service in November, **Moondance** was transferred to a new Clipper Denmark route in the Baltic, but returned to Liverpool three weeks later as the new service had failed to attract patronage. **Moondance** was sold for further service with Turkish owners at the end of the year.

Clipper Point (2007) was the first of a series of four similar ships built in Spain for Seatruck Ferries.

(Seatruck Ferries)

Stena Nordica (2001) replaced *Stena Seatrader* on the Dublin and Holyhead route in December 2008.

(Author)

Stena Adventurer (2003) seen leaving Dublin off the Great South Wall on 12 June 2009, wearing the new owner's logo adopted after her annual refit earlier that year.

(Author)

*The newly renamed **Anglia Seaways** (2000), formerly **Maersk Anglia**, with a DFDS funnel but still carrying the pale blue hull colour of Norfolk Line but without lettering, is seen at Heysham.*

(Wikimedia Commons)

Newbuild **Clipper Point** had been due to start work for Seatruck during the previous June, but was only now on its way from the builders in Spain; her three sisters equally delayed. In the meantime, a complex roster of charters, including the **Phocine** from Cobelfret, kept the company going. **Clipper Point**, which can accommodate 120 trailers within 1830 lane metres of stowage space, finally arrived and took her maiden commercial voyage from Warrenpoint on 23 March 2008; she made the return voyage in the evening the following day. The **Phocine** was then returned to Cobelfret. At the same time the company announced the order of a further four freight ferries, again Heysham-max with a length of 142 metres but with four vehicle decks connected by fixed ramps. The order was placed with Flensburger Achiffbau Gesellschaft in Germany.

Stena Nordica returned to the Irish Sea on 4 November 2008, initially to stand in for **Stena Europe** while that ship went for its annual overhaul. Thereafter **Stena Nordica** moved to the Dublin and Holyhead route on 4 December to replace the **Stena Seatrader**. This change provided additional passenger capacity on the route with **Stena Nordica** working alongside **Stena Adventurer**. A new style and bolder logo was adopted and appeared on the hull of **Stena Adventurer** after her refit in March 2009. **Stena Transporter** was again used to deputise for her while she was absent. Meanwhile, **Stena Seatrader** was renamed **Seatrade** for use by Ventouris Ferries in Greece.

Between April and the end of June 2009, **European Endeavour** was again in use deputising for **Norbay** and **Norbank** during those ships' refit periods. **Norbay** then deputised at Cairnryan for the refits of **European Causeway** and **European Highlander**. Thereafter, **European Endeavour** was attached to the Dublin and Liverpool service acting as third ship alongside **Norbank** and **Norbay**.

From January 2009 Stena cut its HSS **Stena Voyager** service from Belfast to just two round trips a day due to high operating costs. At the same time it increased the schedule for the conventional ferry, **Stena Caledonia**, from one to two round trips. This reflected the position at Holyhead and Dun Laoghaire where the HSS **Stena Explorer** had already reduced to one trip a day when **Stena Nordica** came on service. At Fishguard **Stena Lynx III** still maintained two round trips day, but for the summer season only.

An unfortunate incident happened aboard **Stena Voyager** on 29 January when a chemical tanker broke loose and broke through the stern doors to overhang the sea. The driver had not applied the hand brake and the shackles holding the vehicle were insufficient to hold it as the trim changed on accelerating out of Loch Ryan. The vessel was carrying 152 passengers and put back to Stranraer.

Despite the economic depression and downturn in trade on the Irish Sea, a second conventional ferry was added to the Belfast and Stranraer service. The former **SeaFrance Manet** (one time **Stena Parisien** and built in 1984 for SNCF as **Champs Elysees**) was purchased to work alongside **Stena Caledonia**. The ship was given a major internal upgrade and entered service on 11 November 2009 under the name **Stena Navigator**.

Norfolk Line transferred the 1680 lane metre **Maersk Exporter** and **Maersk Anglia** from the North Sea to Heysham and Dublin or Belfast in March and June 2009 respectively, and **Maersk Importer** followed in September. They collectively replaced **West Express**, formerly **Merchant Bravery**, and the **Shield** and **Arrow**.

On her return to Seatruck, **Shield** replaced **Clipper Ranger** on the Heysham and Dublin service and **Arrow** went to lay up in Liverpool.

Stena Hibernia (1996) served on the Heysham and Belfast route until September 2012.

(Stena Line)

Arrow later replaced **Shield** which was chartered to DFDS. **Shield** returned in August to lay up. **Saga Moon** was sold to Mexican owners in December 2009 for €1.8 million. She was renamed **Santa Marcela**.

Seatruck's new **Clipper Panorama** commenced service on 25 January 2009, joining sister **Clipper Point** on the Heysham and Warrenpoint service. The new **Clipper Pace** commenced service between Liverpool and Dublin on 3 March 2009, while the fourth and last ship in the series, **Clipper Pennant**, started on the Liverpool and Dublin service on 13 October. An interesting feature of these ships was the use of two engines on daytime sailings to provide a speed of 22 knots, but only one engine on overnight passages which were carried out at a reduced speed of 15 knots with consequent saving in fuel costs. With the new ships in service **Arrow** and **Moondance** were laid up at Liverpool, although **Arrow** became third ship on the Heysham and Warrenpoint service in October. **Clipper Racer**, formerly **RR Triumph**, was chartered out for use in the Mediterranean. On 17 May 2010, Seatruck inaugurated a new route between Heysham and Larne with **Clipper Ranger**, offering twelve return sailings per week. This was doubled up from 6 October when sistership **Arrow** joined the new service.

A new consortium led by West Cork Tourism under the name Fastnet Line was created in 2009 to reopen the Swansea and Cork route. The new enterprise bought the passenger and vehicle ferry **Julia**, which had been built in 1982, for €6.3 million with the help of a mortgage from a Finnish Bank. She remained in Finland until 2010 and then took up service between Swansea and Cork from 10 March, the route having previously been abandoned in 2006.

Celtic Link Ferries expanded its routes again when it linked up with LD Lines to sub-charter that company's brand-new **Norman Voyager**. The ship was deployed onto a new Cherbourg and Portsmouth service with a weekend return between Cherbourg and Rosslare. The vessel was owned by Epic Shipping and chartered to LD Lines. The first sailing took place from Cherbourg to Portsmouth on 4 October 2009 and the **Norman Voyager** made her first call at Rosslare three days later. Loadings on the Portsmouth and Cherbourg link were so poor that the service was quickly suspended and the vessel put onto the Rosslare and Cherbourg route with three return sailings a week. **Diplomat** took the final advertised sailings to Portsmouth and then went to Waterford to lay up. **Diplomat** was then chartered in April to Marine Express, Puerto Rico, and shortly afterwards the **Finnforest** was also chartered for work in the Adriatic based at Naples.

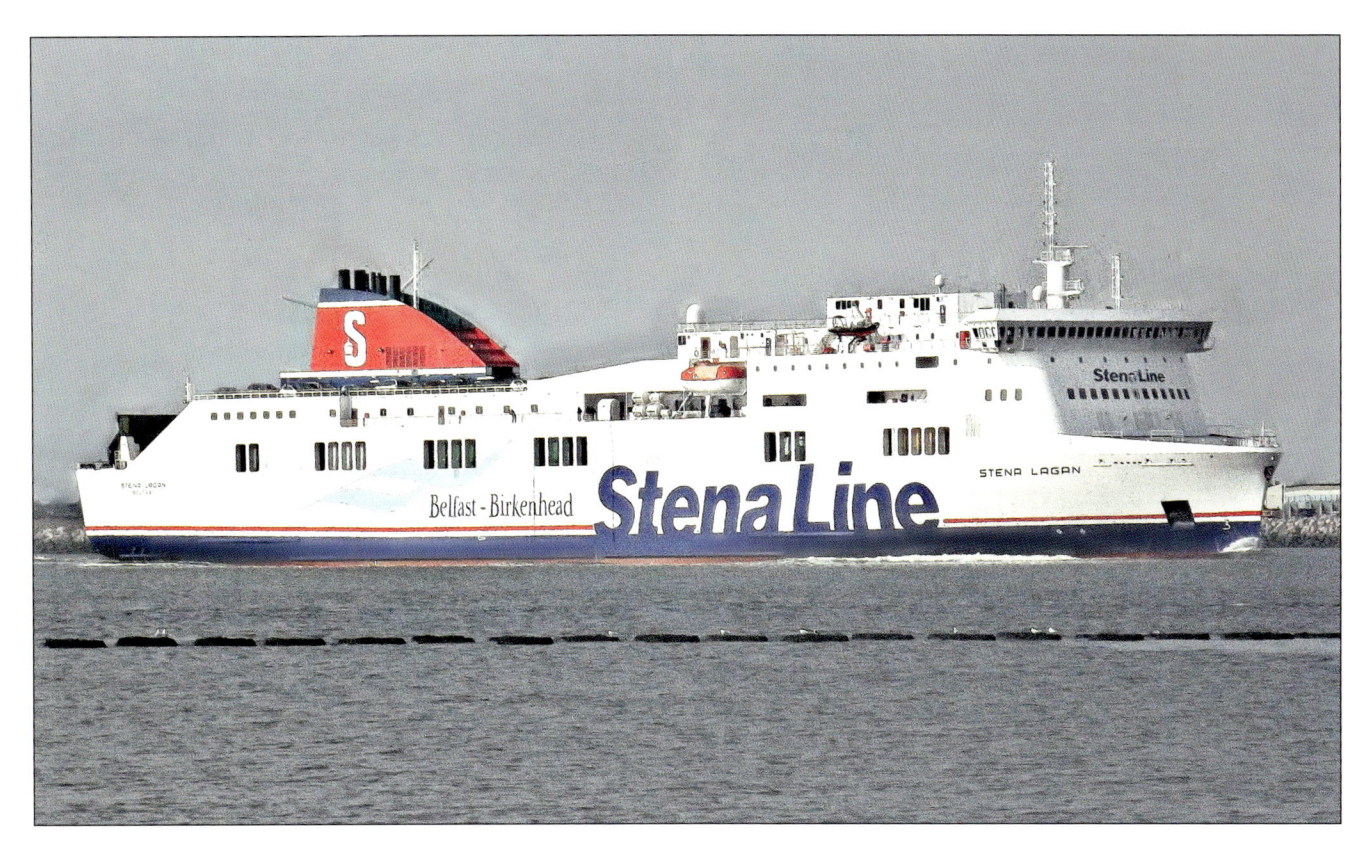

Stena Lagan (2005), formerly Lagan Viking, seen coming up the Mersey off New Brighton on arrival from Belfast.

(Wikimedia Commons)

Stena Superfast VII (2001) was one of two identical ships chartered to serve between Belfast and the new Stena Line quay at Cairnryan.

(Stena Line)

In December 2009, the sale of Norfolk Line to DFDS was confirmed, subject to sanction by the monopolies interests in the European Union which granted the go ahead for the deal the following July. The survival of the fittest very much ruled during the recession which had now become global. P&O Ferries were relieved to learn that they would not be due for rationalisation during the reorganisation of owners DP World, which was in serious financial trouble but was too big for anything other than piecemeal takeovers. A further reflection of the downturn in trade saw HSS **Stena Explorer** in use at Dublin for only two months in 2010, with **Stena Lynx III** brought in from Fishguard to extend the season, the latter being far cheaper to operate.

In April, DFDS chartered the **T Rex** to cover for overhauls of its Dublin ships. **T Rex** was formerly the **Dawn Merchant** and had worked on the same route between 1999 and 2002. Sister ship **European Endeavour** was chartered to cover the remaining refit period for the Birkenhead ships during August. As vessels returned from overhaul later in the

Seatruck Precision (2012) seen leaving Dublin off the Great South Wall was delivered in July 2012 and in September she was renamed ***Stena Precision*** while on charter to Stena Line.

(Seatruck Ferries)

Stena Horizon (2005) seen off Rosslare on arrival from Cherbourg, was formerly Celtic Link Ferries ***Celtic Horizon***.

(Wikimedia Commons)

year, they were given a unified corporate branding under the title DFDS Seaways. This included dark blue hulls with the company name in white and dark blue funnels carrying the white Maltese cross emblem. New names with the suffix 'Seaways' were applied; **Lagan Viking** and **Mersey Viking**, for example, were renamed **Lagan Seaways** and **Mersey Seaways** respectively. Others adopted regional names, the Heysham-based **Maersk Exporter** became the **Scotia Seaways** and **Maersk Importer** the **Hibernia Seaways**, while **Maersk Anglia** became **Anglia Seaways**.

In mid-May 2010 the chartered **Celtic Star** was replaced on the P&O Liverpool and Dublin route by **Norcape**, better known in the Irish Sea in her younger days as the **Tipperary**.

In October 2010 the **Pride of Bilbao** was returned to Irish Continental Group after her extended charter to P&O. She was promptly sold to St Peter Line for use in the Baltic.

As the global recession began to bottom out in 2010, some significant changes were announced by Stena Line during December. The first

Stena Superfast X (2001) served on the Dublin and Holyhead route between March 2015 and January 2020.

(Stena Line)

was the closure of the loss-making Fleetwood and Larne route employing **Stena Pioneer**, **Stena Seafarer** and **Stena Leader**. **Stena Pioneer** took the last sailing on 23 December. **Stena Seafarer** had also been used as relief on other services and was again in use in the New Year when she stood in for **Stena Europe** at Fishguard and then **Stena Caledonia** at Belfast. The decision had been taken to close the Fleetwood and Larne service following mounting losses on the route coupled with the advanced age of the ships which were increasingly prone to mechanical failure. The second change was the announcement that Stena had bought the DFDS services including the ships operating on the Heysham and Belfast and on the Birkenhead and Belfast routes, more than compensating for the closure of its existing service between Fleetwood and Larne.

The Irish Competition Authority and the UK's Competition Commission looked closely at the closure of Fleetwood and Larne and the purchase of the Heysham and Birkenhead to Dublin services by Stena Line. The issue was whether the closure of the Fleetwood and Larne route was a prior part of the overall deal to lessen the impact on competition or whether it was coincidental. Stena Line were loud and clear that it was pure coincidence! In the end the deal was allowed through and the three former Pandoro ships, **Stena Pioneer**, **Stena Leader** and **Stena Seafarer** were sold for further use under the Latvian flag based in Ukraine. In July 2011, the **Scotia Seaways** was renamed **Stena Scotia** and the **Hibernia Seaways** became the **Stena Hibernia**, while the Birkenhead ships adopted the names **Stena Lagan** and **Stena Mersey**. The latter pair were initially chartered from DFDS but were bought outright in 2012.

Stena Line chartered the Tallinn Group ferries **Superfast VII** and **Superfast VIII** which were renamed **Stena Superfast VII** and **Stena Superast VIII** and re-registered at Belfast. After an extensive conversion the sisters inaugurated a new route between Belfast and a brand-new facility north of P&O's port at Cairnryan called Old House Point. The service started on 21 November 2011. **Stena Navigator** stood down on the old route to Stranraer on 16 November, followed by **Stena Caledonia** and the HSS **Stena Voyager** four days later. The two conventional ferries were sold and the HSS **Stena Voyager** went to Sweden in April 2013 to be dismantled. Stranraer, of course, was now no longer a ferry port. The charter of the two Superfast ships was extended in February 2014 for a further five years.

In January 2011, DFDS announced its withdrawal from the Irish Sea with the closure of its Birkenhead and Dublin service and the Heysham and Belfast service at the end of the month. The **Liverpool Seaways** was redeployed by DFDS in the Baltic and the **Dublin Seaways** was sold to Stena North Sea Limited and renamed **Stena Feronia**, while **Anglia Seaways** was chartered to Seatruck to open its new service between Heysham and Dublin, Seatruck quick to capitalise on DFDS's loss. The **Stena Feronia** was later used for relief work on the Birkenhead and Belfast service.

In April 2011 the Macquarie Bank sold its interests in the Isle of Man Steam Packet Company to Banco Espirito Santo. There was no outward change to the management or operation of the shipping company.

In July 2011, the **European Mariner** stood down on the P&O Larne and Troon service and was replaced by the larger **Norcape**. The **European Mariner** was sold for demolition. The tenure of the **Norcape** was short, and on 26 November she was aground at the entrance to Troon Harbour and withdrawn for repairs while the service was suspended. The repairs were not carried out and on 8 December it was announced that the Larne and Troon freight service would close with all remaining traffic diverted to Cairnryan and Larne. On 12 December the **Norcape** left Larne for Turkey to be broken up.

Celtic Link Ferries now dominated the freight traffic between Cherbourg and Rosslare while Irish Ferries **Oscar Wilde** focussed more on the tourist traffic. Celtic Link Ferries needed to acquire a larger ship to meet increasing demand. In October 2011, the Italian-owned **Cartour Beta** was chartered, and later purchased, to replace

European Seaway (1991) first came to Cairnryan and Larne service to relieve European Causeway and European Highlander in 2017.
(Author)

Stena Performer (2011) was returned to Seatruck by Stena Line in August 2018 after being employed on the Heysham and Belfast route for six years.
(Stena Line)

the **Norman Voyager**. The new ship was renamed **Celtic Horizon** and was of Visentini origin and of similar design to the **Stena Lagan** and **Stena Mersey**. At the same time the **Diplomat** and **Finnforest** were sold for demolition.

At the start of November, the new Fastnet Line, operating the **Julia** between Swansea and Cork, was put into receivership and the **Julia** was laid up. The service did not resume and **Julia** was sold in 2012 for use as an accommodation ship.

Seatruck Ferries received its four new 2166 lane metre ferries **Seatruck Progress**, **Seatruck Power**, **Seatruck Performance** and **Seatruck Precision** from their German builders between November 2011 and July 2012. The **Clipper Panorama** was given the name

Seatruck Panorama in December 2011 and *Clipper Pace* was similarly dealt with shortly afterwards. *Seatruck Performance* and *Seatruck Precision* were renamed *Stena Performer* and *Stena Precision* in September 2012, on bareboat charter to Stena for its Heysham and Belfast service instead of *Stena Hibernia* and *Stena Scotia* which were sent to work for Stena Ro Ro.

The final piece of consolidation was the purchase of Celtic Link Ferries by Stena Line in February 2014 when the *Celtic Horizon* became the *Stena Horizon* as from 31 March 2014. This was an important acquisition by Stena as it gave that company its first foothold in the Ireland-France sector. Traffic on the Birkenhead and Belfast route was booming and *Stena Hibernia* was drafted in to provide supplementary freight only sailings alongside *Stena Lagan* and *Stena Mersey*.

In November 2013 Irish Ferries announced the charter of the *Cartour Epsilon* via a subcharter from GNV Caronte & Tourist at Civitavecchia, Italy. The ship, completed only in 2011, was to provide two extra round trips between Holyhead and Dublin and offers 2860 lane metres of stowage space and accommodation for 500 persons including 68 four berth cabins. *Cartour Epsilon* commenced work on 19 December. From 14 January 2014 the ship added a weekend return trip from Dublin to Cherbourg to her new roster and on 14 February she was bought outright by Irish Ferries Limited and renamed *Epsilon*. In March 2019 the *Epsilon* was sold back to Caronte and Tourist and chartered back to Irish Ferries.

On 9 March 2015 the *Stena Nordica* and HSS *Stena Explorer* were replaced on the Dublin and Holyhead service by *Stena Superfast X*, a sistership to the two similarly named ships based at Belfast. She was previously operated as *Dieppe Seaways* for DFDS on the English Channel. The new ship offered nearly 2000 lane metres of cargo stowage and accommodated 1200 passengers. In January 2020 she was replaced by the newly built *Stena Estrid*.

In June 2016 Irish Continental Group signed a contract with Flensburger Schiffbau-Gesselschaft in Germany for a cruise ferry to accommodate 1885 passengers, with 435 cabins and to provide over 3000 lane metres of vehicle stowage. The contract price was €144 million and delivery was set for May 2018. She was intended as a replacement for *Epsilon*. Construction of the ship was greatly delayed and she was only launched on 19 January 2018. The new ship, named *W B Yeats*, was the first in Irish Ferries fleet to be equipped with exhaust scrubbers.

Jonathan Swift took her final sailing between Dublin and Holyhead on 24 April 2018. Her successor, *Dublin Swift* started on 27 April, her initial sailing the previous day being cancelled due to poor weather.

In June 2017, the relief ship for the *European Causeway* and *European Highlander* at Cairnryan was the Dover based *European Seaway*. This was the first time that this ship had been used in this capacity and it reflected her increasing downtime on the Dover-based services as new and more efficient tonnage had become available. *European Seaway* was in service at Cairnryan from 4 May until 19 June. She returned to Cairnryan as relief in 2019.

In May 2018 the Isle of Man Government nationalised the Isle of Man Steam Packet Company. This seemingly retrograde move was made because of government dissatisfaction with the Isle of Man company's offer of future services and, perhaps, a lack of trust in the company. Nationalisation was seen as necessary in order that Government could dictate future service requirements.

In August 2018 the *Stena Performer* and *Stena Precision* were returned to Seatruck Ferries by Stena Line. Their place on the Heysham and Belfast route was taken by *Stena Scotia* and *Stena Forerunner*. *Stena Nordica* returned to the Irish Sea shortly afterwards to act as relief. In July, Seatruck sold the *Clipper Ranger* to Canadian owners for use in the St Lawrence.

Irish Ferries finally took delivery of the long-delayed cruise ferry from her German builders Flensburger Schiffbau-Gesselschaft; the new ship, named *W B Yeats*, arrived in Dublin for the first time on 20 December 2018. *W B Yeats* took her maiden commercial voyage to Holyhead on 20 January 2019. She made her first sailing from Dublin to Cherbourg on 14 March 2019. *W B Yeats* replaced *Oscar Wilde* which left Dublin on 2 May 2019 having been sold to MSC Mediterranean Shipping Company SA.

A second larger ferry had been ordered by Irish Ferries from the same builders for use on the Holyhead and Dublin route. This vessel

The 'cruise ferry' **W B Yeats** *(2018) was delivered six months late causing cancellation of advertised sailings.*

(Irish Ferries)

*Stena Estrid (2019) displaced **Stena Superfast X** from the Holyhead and Dublin service in January 2020. She is seen at Dublin with the Dublin Port Company tug **Shackleton** in attendance.*

(Stena Line)

was designed to have over 5000 lane metres of vehicle capacity. However, the order was later cancelled as reported in a statement by Irish Continental Group issued in June 2020:

> ICG has terminated its contract with the German shipbuilder FSG, who were contracted to build a new vessel for Irish Ferries. This follows the yard making an application through the German courts system to be placed in 'debtor in possession management' under the oversight of an Insolvency Monitor. As part of the original contract with the yard, ICG paid a deposit on this vessel for 20% (€33 million) of the purchase price with the remaining 80% due on delivery of the ship. This deposit was protected by third party guarantees and has now been returned to ICG.

Irish Continental Group will look elsewhere to build the new ship.

The **European Endeavour** left the Irish Sea in May 2019. She had worked on the P&O Liverpool and Dublin service since 2009 but was an increasingly expensive unit to maintain. She was sold to the Eckerö Group and renamed **Finbo Cargo**.

In 2019, the old lady of the Irish Sea, **Stena Europe**, which was completed back in 1989, was given an extensive 'life extending' refit. The work was carried out by a Turkish shipyard between March and September. In the meantime, the Fishguard and Rosslare service was maintained by **Stena Nordica**, commencing on 10 March.

Stena Estrid took her maiden commercial voyage on the Holyhead and Dublin route on 13 January 2020. This allowed **Stena Superfast X** to act as relief elsewhere. **Stena Lagan** finished service in the Irish Sea on 8 March 2020 and was replaced by the new **Stena Edda** the next day. The third ship in the series, **Stena Embla** arrived at Belfast at Christmas ready to replace **Stena Mersey** in the New Year, January 2021. The trio, part of the so-called E-Flexer class of vessel, each have an overall length of 215 metres and offer 3100 lane metres of freight vehicle stowage plus a low headroom deck for a further 120 cars. They can carry 1000 passengers and crew and have 175 passenger cabins.

The year 2020 and the Covid-19 pandemic was devastating for the ferry industry across the globe. Those companies that relied on tourist traffic for a large part of their business such as, for example, Irish Ferries, were especially hard hit, but freight traffic also declined as the world slipped into recession, but that is a story still to be told.

31 December 2000 was the date set for the end the Transition Period for the negotiation of a trade agreement after the UK had left the European Union eleven months earlier. Two shipping companies established new sea routes to carry freight vehicles directly from Holland, Belgium and Northern France to Ireland in order to avoid the existing 'landbridge' via UK ports and customs, and effectively remain within the European Union. The first was CLdN, trading as Cobelfret, who established a Cork and Zeebrugge service for unaccompanied trailers with the freight vessel **Mazarine** in May 2020, following the successful inauguration of Rotterdam and Dublin as well as Zeebrugge and Dublin routes. The second was DFDS who inaugurated a Dunkirk and Cork service in January 2021 also for unaccompanied trailers, both services with a 24 hour voyage time. These new routes will have a negative impact on traffic across the Irish Sea, despite Britain gaining a 'no tariff' trade agreement with the European Union just before Christmas 2020.

In December 2020 the Irish Sea operators and their routes had evolved as follows:

Stena Line
    Cairnryan and Larne: **Stena Superfast VII** and **Stena Superfast VIII**
    Birkenhead and Belfast: **Stena Edda**, **Stena Mersey** and **Seatruck Panorama** (chartered)
    Holyhead and Dublin: **Stena Adventurer** and **Stena Estrid**
    Fishguard and Rosslare: **Stena Europe**
    Cherbourg and Rosslare: **Stena Horizon**

P&O Ferries
    Cairnryan and Larne: **European Causeway** and **European Highlander**
    Liverpool and Dublin: **Norbank**, **Norbay**, **Clipper Pennant** (chartered) and **Stena Forecaster** (chartered)

Irish Ferries
    Dublin and Holyhead: **Ulysses** and **W B Yeats**

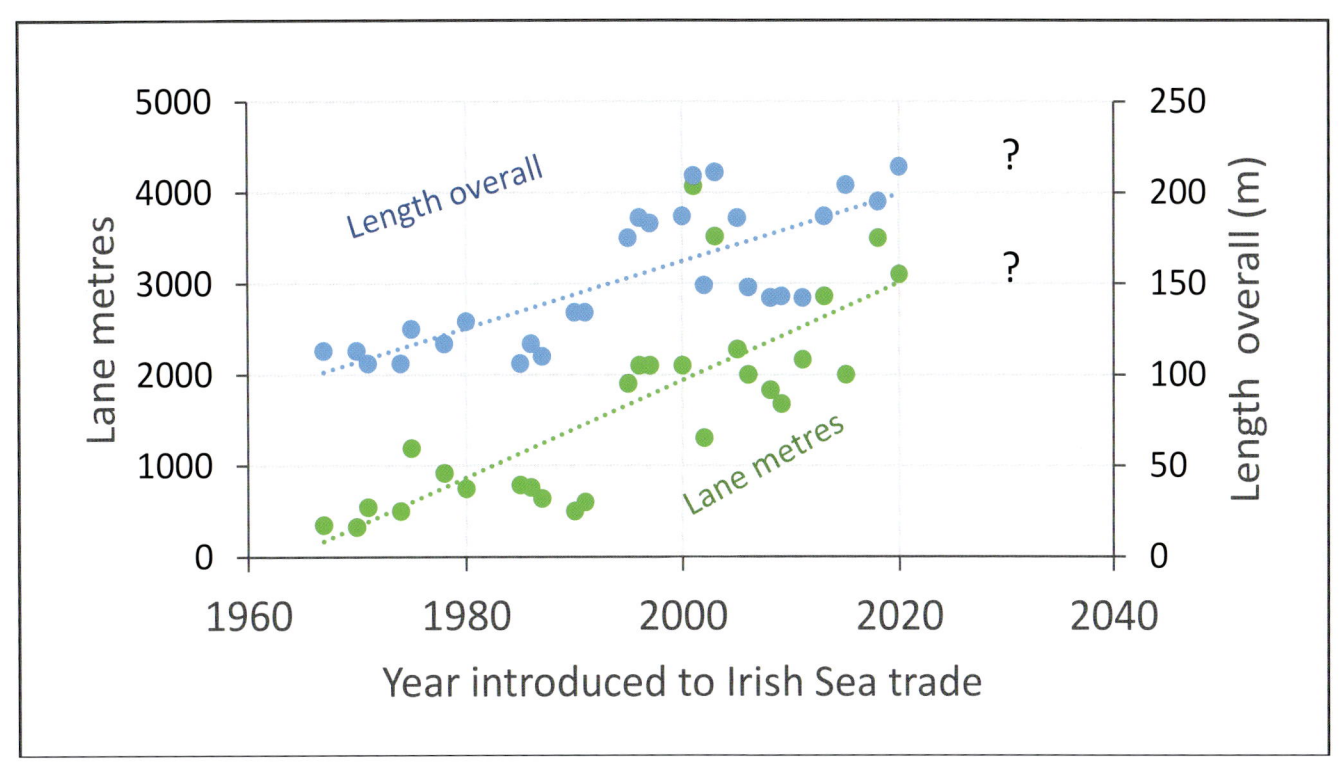

*Growth in overall length and in lane metres capacity of ships on Irish Sea routes between 1967 (**Antrim Princess**) and 2020 (**Stena Estrid**) showing actual data and linear trend lines.*

Rosslare and Pembroke Dock: **Isle of Inishmore**
Dublin and Cherbourg: **W B Yeats**

Seatruck Ferries
Liverpool and Dublin: **Clipper Point**, **Seatruck Power** and **Seatruck Progress**
Heysham and Warrenpoint: **Seatruck Precision** and **Seatruck Performance**
Heysham and Dublin: **Seatruck Pace**

Isle of Man Steam Packet Company (Isle of Man Government)
Douglas and Heysham: **Ben-my-Chree**
Douglas and Liverpool/Dublin/Belfast: **Manannan**

The huge success story was the relative newcomer to the Irish Sea, Seatruck Ferries. The company was highly adaptable and flexible, having at most times a surplus of ships that could be put to use on the charter market. The rewards for operational flexibility were substantial, for example, the growth on the Dublin routes rose from 3000 units shipped from Dublin in October 2007 to 21 000 units in October 2018. Between October 2015 and October 2016, the company enjoyed an increase of 25% in accompanied trailers on its 66 weekly departures between Heysham and Warrenpoint, Heysham and Dublin and Liverpool and Dublin. It also ran a weekly Avonmouth and Dublin service over the weekend to collect trade cars newly imported to Avonmouth, using a ship that would otherwise have been idle in port until the Monday morning.

The significance of short routes to maximise assets and provide hauliers with least times at sea was underlined by Graham McCullough, General Manager of the P&O services to Northern Ireland. He reported at the 30th anniversary of Cairnryan port on 10 July 2003:

> Our Larne – Cairnryan service is renowned for the short sea crossings, the frequency of sailings and most importantly, the reliability of our vessels which combine to make this route the first choice for both freight, and tourist customers. We are market leader with freight customers and are significantly growing our tourist market year on year.

The success of our service is dependent on the infrastructure to and from our ports. The A8, the Larne Belfast link, is currently undergoing major works which will vastly improve access to our port of Larne. While some plans have been announced for work on the A75 and A77 [in Scotland], more needs to be done.

The size and vehicle stowage since the introduction of the second-generation vehicle ferries has grown consistently up to the present. The landmarks are the **Ulysses**, with a length overall of 209 metres and 4070 lane metres of stowage space followed by the **Stena Adventurer** with a length of 211 metres and offering 3517 lane metres. The new **W B Yeats** follows closely with a length of 195 metres and stowage of 3500 lane metres.

The linear trends shown in Figure 4 suggest that by the year 2040 ships of 230 metres length with a capacity of 4000 lane metres would become the standard dimensions for ferries on the Irish Sea. However, statistics tell us that this would only be the case if there were no constraints or changes imposed on the growth of the dimensions of new ships as time progressed. Indeed, there are two significant constraints: the first is the capability of harbour facilities to take ever larger ships and the second is the Heysham-max length constraint of 143 m. It is likely, therefore, that the new ship for Irish Ferries Holyhead and Dublin service ordered originally from Flensburger Schiffbau-Gesselschaft, but later cancelled, will be the largest ferry to be built for the Irish Sea trades once the order is reinstated with another yard. Seatruck Ferries, however, with its emphasis on Heysham, will likely be constrained to ships of no more than 143 metres length overall.

Post-SOLAS 90 all new ferries tended to have a slightly smaller length to breadth ratio in order to enhance stability. They were also designed with a higher metacentric height after 1990, and this made for a stiffer ship with a more uncomfortable movement in a cross sea. However, this motion tended to be moderated by stabilizers or transverse flumes. In addition, the freeboard to the main vehicle deck increased with the larger ships from 1.5 or 2 metres to 2.5 metres and this created issues with some linkspans which could not be used during particularly high tides. From 1990 onwards all new ferries had to incorporate longitudinal bulkheads beneath the main vehicle deck. The available volume beneath the main deck had increased as engines become more compact, but it was a space that was no longer allowed to contain passenger accommodation, and instead is used for additional lower hold deck space for the carriage of cars and other low elevation vehicles.

SOLAS amendments are issued at regular intervals. The latest are targeted at fire hazard safety aboard roll-on roll-off ships. Nowadays there are numerous systems available to help mitigate damage situations, and most new ferries have bespoke software to assist in decision making towards best courses of action for maintaining ship stability.

There is another dimension to the construction of new ships for short sea duties. As costs of new ships increase, significant savings can be made by building to standard designs with each ship fitted out to its owner's specifications and equipped to suit the owner's needs. Stena Line has done just this over the years, and is now introducing the E-Flexer class, with **Stena Estrid** and sisters based at Belfast being the first of this type of vessel. It is likely that shipbuilding for the ferry industry will follow the style adopted by the aeroplane industry; a selection of standard ships might be offered by internationally collaborative groups of shipbuilders from which the ferry operators can choose and then oversee completion to best suit their own patterns of trade and shore facilities.

It will be interesting to see what the future holds for the industry. The post-Covid depression coupled with the withdrawal of the United Kingdom from the European Union will adversely impact the ferry companies for some time. But the ferry industry will bounce back once trade recovers and future operations will again return to a sound commercial footing. Success for each company depends on experience from the past: short sea crossings, reliability of service, frequency of sailings, good vehicle access to ports and attractive on board public spaces and passenger facilities.

REFERENCES

Chappell, Connery 1980 *Island Lifeline*. T Stephenson & Sons Ltd, Prescot.

MacRonald Malcolm 2005 *The Irish Boats, Volume 1, Liverpool to Dublin*. Tempus Publishing Ltd, Stroud.

Robins, Nick 1995 *The Evolution of the British Ferry*. Ferry Publications, Kilgetty.

Robins, Nick 2019 *Coast Lines Limited 1913-1975*. Coastal Shipping Publications, Portishead.

Sahlsten, Rickard Söderberg, Bertil and Bång, Krister 1992 D *Stena Line's Ships 1962 – 1992*. Stena Line AB, Gothenburg.

Sinclair, Robert 1990 *Across the Irish Sea, Belfast–Liverpool Shipping since 1819*. Conway Maritime Press Ltd, London.

INDEX OF VESSELS

Aallottar (1976) 64
Ailsa Princess (1971) 29-31, 41, 53, 55
Anderida (1972) 39-41, 44
Anglia Seaways (2000) 123, 126, 127
Antrim Princess (1967)
21, 22, 25, 30, 41, 51, 55, 58-60, 63, 131
Antwerpen (1970) 33
Anu (1972) 47
Arcade Eagle (1981) 84
Armorique (1976) 69
Arrow (1998) 123, 124
ASD Meteor (1971) 31
Atlantic Freighter (1978) 84
Attacker (1945) 15
Aurella (1973) 51, 53
Avalon (1963) 33, 35, 37, 41, 44, 48

Baltic Ferry (1945) 22, 24, 26, 30
Baltic Ferry (1978) 111
Bardic Ferry (1957)
16-18, 22, 30, 32, 33, 39, 55
Bassro Star (1976) 73
Belard (1979)
59, 60, 77, 79, 80, 84, 89, 92, 96
Ben-my-Chree (1966)
18, 22, 34, 36, 55, 59, 60
Ben-my-Chree (1998)
99-101, 114, 116, 118, 131
Bison (1975) 33-35, 39, 40, 43, 46, 64, 69, 72, 74, 81, 84, 87, 95
Blue Aegean (1972) 112
Bolero (1985) 91, 92, 95
Brave Merchant (1998)
99, 101, 102, 106, 112, 113, 115, 116
Breizh Izel (1970) 55
Buffalo (1975) 33-35, 40, 43, 46, 64, 67, 69, 72, 74, 81, 83, 84, 91, 96, 101, 116

Caledonian Princess (1961)
12, 14, 17, 21, 30, 32, 33
Cambria (1948) 37
Cambridge Ferry (1963) 48, 67, 69, 70, 74, 77
Carmen B (1978) 118
Carrier (1858) 5
Cartour Beta (2006) 127
Cartour Epsilon (2011) 129
Cassiopeia (1972) 78
Celtic Horizon (2005) 126, 128, 129
Celtic Pride (1976) 64, 65, 69, 74, 78
Celtic Star (1998)
105, 106, 111, 118, 121, 126
Celtic Sun (1978) 118
Celtic Sun (1991) 106, 107, 111
Cerdic Ferry (1961) 17, 18, 22, 39, 41, 43, 51
Challenge (1998) 116, 120, 121
Channel Entente (1974) 69, 72
Charger (1945) 15
City of Cork (1973) 107
City of Dublin (1975) 75, 76
Claymore (1978) 83, 89, 99, 100, 103
Clipper Pace (2009) 121, 124, 129
Clipper Panorama (2008) 124, 128
Clipper Pennant (2009) 124, 130
Clipper Point (2008) 121-124, 130
Clipper Racer (1996) 121, 124

Clipper Ranger (1998)
120, 121, 123, 124, 129
Commodore Clipper (1971) 91
Condor 10 (1993) 91
Connacht (1978)
43, 44, 47, 48, 51, 53, 58, 61, 62, 67
Cruise Muhibah (1970) 71

Dalriada (1971) 29, 30, 33, 39, 41, 47, 56
Darnia (1977)
41, 43, 44, 52, 61, 64, 70, 73, 74
Dart 4 (1985) 99
Dawn Merchant (1998)
99, 101, 102, 112, 113, 116, 125
Diplomat (1978) 115, 116, 121, 124, 128
Djursland (1995) 89
Donautal (1970) 30, 31
Doric Ferry (1961)
17, 18, 22, 24, 30, 33, 39, 43, 48, 51
Dorset (1970) 31, 33
Dover (1965) 19, 21, 28, 33, 37, 40
Dragon (1967) 29, 30, 63, 64
Drottning Victoria (1909) 5
Dublin Seaways (1997) 127
Dublin Swift (2001) 118, 129
Dublin Viking (1997) 115, 116, 120, 121
Duchess Anne (1978) 68
Duke of Argyll (1956) 17, 26, 27, 33, 37
Duke of Lancaster (1956)
17, 26, 27, 33, 37, 40, 41, 44
Duke of Rothesay (1957) 17, 21, 23, 26
Dundalk (1974) 34, 46, 56

Earl Godwin (1966) 39, 51
Earl Granville (1973) 67, 68, 70
Earl Harold (1971) 53, 55, 64, 69, 72
Earl Leofric (1965) 37, 49, 50
Earl Siward (1965) 40
Earl William (1964) 67-70, 74
El Greco (2000) 121
Elite (1996) 101
Elk (1977) 45, 84
Emadala (1978) 72
Emeraude France (1990) 118
Empire Cedric (1945) 6, 7, 16
Empire Celtic (1945) 7
Empire Cymric (1945) 15, 16
Empire Doric (1945) 7, 16
Empire Gaelic (1945) 7, 16
Empire Nordic (1945) 15, 16, 22
Epsilon (2011) 129
Equine (1979) 121
Espresso Olbia (1966) 47
Estonia (1980) 12
Essex Ferry (1917) 5
European Ambassador (2001)
109-112, 114, 115
European Causeway (2000)
105-107, 109-112, 116, 123, 129, 130
European Clearway (1975) 81, 83, 84
European Diplomat (1978) 111, 114, 115
European Endeavour (1978)
83, 87, 88, 95, 110, 112
European Endeavour (2000)
119, 121, 123, 125, 130

European Enterprise (1978) 83
European Envoy (1979)
96, 106, 111, 114, 115
European Freighter (1967) 77-79
European Gateway (1975)
10, 12, 48, 50, 51, 54, 55, 56, 81
European Highlander (1977) 95, 110
European Highlander (2002)
109, 112, 115, 116, 123, 129, 130
European Leader (1975)
96, 101, 102, 114, 115
European Mariner (1977)
110-112, 114, 116, 127
European Navigator (1977) 96, 111, 112, 114
European Pathfinder (1975) 96, 110-112
European Pioneer (1975)
95, 98, 111, 114, 115
European Seafarer (1975)
96, 110, 111, 114, 115
European Seaway (1991) 128, 129
European Trader (1975)
88, 90, 95, 98, 106, 110
Europic Ferry (1967)
22, 54, 56, 58, 63-66, 72, 77, 78
Express (1998) 115, 118

Felicity (1980) 71, 73, 74
Fennia (1965) 58
Fichtelberg (1975) 74, 75
Finnforest (1978) 121, 124, 128
Free Enterprise I (1962) 32, 33, 39
Free Enterprise III (1966) 32, 33, 39, 59, 60
Free Enterprise IV (1969)
38, 39, 43, 48, 51, 54-56, 63, 64
Free Enterprise VI (1972) 77
Free Enterprise VII (1973) 77

Gaelic Ferry (1963) 54-56, 63
Galloway Princess (1979)
44, 45, 47-49, 51, 55, 61, 64, 65, 74
Gleichberg (1975) 75
Global Freighter (1977) 121

Hampton Ferry (1934) 5, 6, 8-10, 16, 17, 28
Hansa Link (1968) 75
Herald of Free Enterprise (1979)
10, 12, 65, 72, 73
Hibernia (1948) 37
Hibernia Seaways (1996) 126, 127
Holmia (1971) 31
Holyhead Ferry I (1965)
18, 19, 21, 33, 37, 49, 50
Horsa (1972) 70, 74, 77
Hoverspeed Great Britain (1990) 79, 81-83

Ibex (1979) 45, 46, 84, 91, 94, 96, 111
Ilkka (1972) 45, 47
Innisfallen (1969) 25, 26, 43, 46
Innisfallen ex-Leinster (1969)
47, 51, 58, 59, 61, 63, 72
Ionian Sun (1969) 72
Ionic Ferry (1958)
16-18, 22, 28, 32, 33, 39, 55
Ionic Ferry (1967) 63-65, 72, 77, 79
Irish Coast (1952) 21

Isartal (1970)	33	
Isle of Inishmore (1981)	78, 81, 87, 92, 94	
Isle of Inishmore (1996)	91, 92, 93, 95, 110, 114, 116, 131	
Isle of Inishturk (1981)	92, 94	
Isle of Innisfree (1986)	76, 78, 83, 84	
Isle of Innisfree (1995)	84, 86, 87, 92, 95, 110	
Jaguar (1977)	39, 40, 43, 44	
Jetliner (1995)	89, 90, 95, 106, 107	
John Napier (1851)	5	
Jolly Bruno (1977)	78	
Jolly Giallo (1978)	78	
Jonathan Swift (1998)	101, 103, 116, 118, 129	
Julia (1982)	124, 128	
King Orry (1974)	72, 79, 83, 84, 89, 92, 96, 99, 101	
Koningin Beatrix (1986)	92, 94, 95, 98, 101, 103, 111, 112	
Kronprins Carl Gustof (1966)	25	
Kronprins Harold (1987)	118	
Lady Of Mann (1976)	34, 57, 60, 63, 69, 70, 72, 79, 83, 84, 87, 89, 92, 95, 96, 99, 106, 113, 114, 116	
Lagan Bridge (1972)	47, 48	
Lagan Seaways (2005)	126	
Lagan Viking (1998)	94, 95, 101, 106, 109, 112, 114, 115	
Lagan Viking (2005)	116, 125, 126	
Lancashire Coast (1953)	22, 23	
Lebola (1996)	121	
Leili (1999)	115, 116, 121	
Leinster (1948)	26	
Leinster (1969)	25, 26, 37, 43, 47	
Leinster (1981)	49, 51, 53, 58, 59, 61, 62, 67, 69, 72, 74, 78, 81, 87, 92	
Lembitu (1998)	101, 113, 116, 120, 121	
Leonard (1914)	6	
Leopard (1968)	30	
Leopard (1977)	91, 94-96	
Leviathan (1850)	5	
Lindarosa (1996)	113, 115, 116	
Lion (1967)	20-22, 31, 34, 39	
Lion (1977)	84, 86, 95, 110	
Liverpool Seaways (1998)	127	
Liverpool Viking (1998)	115-117	
Lohengrin (1964)	21	
Lord Warden (1952)	10, 41, 43-45	
LST365 (1943)	7	
LST3041 (1945)	7	
LST3507 (1945)	7	
LST3512 (1945)	7	
LST3534 (1945)	6	
Lune Bridge (1972)	47, 48, 63	
Maersk Anglia (2000)	123, 126	
Maersk Exporter (1996)	123, 126	
Maersk Importer (1996)	123, 126	
Maid of Kent (1959)	31, 37, 38, 45	
Manannan (1998)	118, 131	
Mandeville (1968)	31	
Manx Maid (1962)	18, 22, 34, 55, 59	
Manx Viking (1976)	42, 44, 47, 51, 55, 57, 59, 60, 63	
Manxman (1955)	17, 18, 54, 55	
Marine Evangeline (1974)	67	
Mazarine (2009)	130	
Mercandian Carrier II (1979)	60	
Merchant Bravery (1978)	78, 79, 99, 101, 110, 113, 115, 116, 123	
Merchant Brilliant (1977)	78, 79, 82, 99, 101, 113, 115, 116, 121	
Merchant Isle (1978)	65	
Merchant Trader (1972)	63, 65, 66	
Merchant Valiant (1977)	73, 74, 78, 79, 84, 86, 110	
Merchant Venture (1978)	66, 67, 74, 75, 79, 99, 103, 113	
Merchant Victor (1978)	73, 74, 78, 79, 95	
Merle (1984)	92, 99, 101, 103	
Mersey Seaways (2005)	126	
Mersey Viking (1997)	94, 96, 101, 109, 112, 114, 115	
Mersey Viking (2005)	116, 117, 126	
Midnight Merchant (2000)	109, 112, 113, 119, 121	
Mona's Isle (1966)	57, 59-61, 89	
Mona's Queen (1972)	34, 36, 60, 63, 64, 69, 72, 83, 84	
Monica Rusotti (1973)	33	
Monte Castillo (1976)	41	
Moondance (1978)	95, 96, 101, 112, 115, 116, 121, 124	
Mowbray Road (1943)	7	
Munster (1968)	25, 26, 37, 43, 51, 53	
Munster (1970)	71, 74-76	
Nanomark (1972)	31	
Neckartal (1970)	33	
nf Jaguar (1971)	31, 47, 51, 55, 56	
Niekerk (1971)	63, 67	
Norbank (1993)	108, 111, 114, 116, 121, 123, 130	
Norbay (1994)	108, 111, 114-116, 121, 123, 130	
Norcape (1979)	126, 127	
Norman Voyager (2008)	124, 128	
Normandy (1982)	95, 97, 101, 103, 104, 106, 110, 112, 114-116, 182, 121	
Normannia (1952)	18, 19	
Norröna (1973)	69, 71, 74, 83, 84	
Norse Lagan (1968)	75, 84, 91	
Norse Mersey (1969)	75, 84	
Norse Mersey (1994)	84, 94, 95, 113	
Norsea (1979)	46	
Norsky (1979)	46, 84	
Northern Merchant (2000)	109, 112, 113	
Northern Star (1998)	118	
Norwave (1965)	21	
Olympia (1985)	81	
Oscar Wilde (1987)	118, 121, 127, 129	
Panther (1975)	84, 96	
Penda (1971)	31, 33, 39, 47, 55, 56	
Peveril (1971)	31, 55, 56, 59, 60, 63, 79, 89, 92, 101, 107	
Phocine (1984)	123	
Pima County (1945)	22, 23	
Pioneer (1974)	79, 82	
Pointer (1970)	40, 58, 60	
Preseli (1970)	33, 40, 56	
Pride of Ailsa (1972)	77, 78, 83, 87, 88, 89, 95	
Pride of Bilbao (1985)	81, 89, 110, 119, 121, 126	
Pride of Cherbourg (1995)	110	
Pride of Rathlin (1973)	77, 78, 83, 87, 88, 98, 102, 105, 107	
Pride of Sandwich (1972)	77	
Pride of Suffolk (1978)	107, 111	
Pride of Walmer (1973)	77	
Princess Margaret (1931)	9, 17	
Princess Maud (1934)	18	
Princess Victoria (1939)	5	
Princess Victoria (1946)	7-10, 12, 17	
Prins Hamlet (1973)	67	
Prins Oberon (1970)	71	
Prins Philippe (1973)	61	
Prinsessan Desiree (1971)	49	
Puma (1975)	46, 47, 69, 84, 91, 94, 96	
Puma (1979)	45	
Purbeck (1978)	92, 94	
Rapide (1996)	110, 113-115	
River Lune (1977)	79, 92, 99, 101, 113, 115, 116	
Riverdance (1970)	91, 95, 101, 112, 115, 116, 121	
Rogalin (1976)	64	
Roro Anglia (1972)	39, 40	
Roro Cimbria (1971)	31	
Roro Dania (1972)	31	
Roseanne (1981)	72, 74, 75	
Rosebay (1976)	101	
Royal Scotsman (1936)	21	
Royal Ulsterman (1936)	21	
RR Arrow (1998)	116, 121	
RR Challenge (1998)	121	
RR Shield (1999)	116	
RR Triumph (1996)	118, 121, 124	
St Anselm (1981)	48, 49, 51, 73, 74	
St Brendan (1974)	60, 61, 64, 69	
St Christopher (1981)	48, 49, 51, 73-75	
St Columba (1977)	14, 37, 40, 41, 43-45, 48-50, 53, 60-62, 64, 67, 70, 73, 74	
St Cybi (1974)	68, 70, 73, 74, 77	
St David (1947)	21, 22	
St David (1981)	48-50, 51, 53, 58, 61, 64, 68, 74	
St Edmund (1973)	63	
St Eloi (1974)	69, 83	
St Magnus (1970)	31, 60	
St Nicholas (1982)	95	
Saaletal (1970)	31, 33	
Saga Moon (1984)	63, 67, 75, 79, 87, 92, 99, 101, 113, 115-117, 124	
Sailormark (1972)	31	
Saint Colum I (1973)	52, 53, 58, 63, 67, 70, 73, 74	
Saint Killian (1973)	40, 53	
Saint Killian II (1973)	53, 64, 76, 78, 79, 81, 83, 84, 87, 89, 92, 94, 95, 101	
Saint Patrick (1973)	30, 40-42, 51, 53	
Saint Patrick II (1973)	52, 53, 58, 59, 63, 67-69, 76, 79, 81, 84, 86, 89, 92, 94, 95, 101, 107	
Salahala (1977)	72	
Sally Eurobridge (1970)	79, 91	
Schiaffino (1970)	75, 79, 91	
Scirocco (1973)	63	
Scotia Seaways (1996)	126, 127	
Scottish Coast (1958)	17, 21	
Sea Express I (1991)	115, 116, 118	
Seacat Danmark (1991)	95, 97, 99, 101, 106, 110	